I0236660

A Lifetime of Writing

An Anthology

by

Eugene P. Clemens

ISBN 978-0-9977956-1-5

Copyright 2016 by Yesteryear Publishing.

All rights reserved. No part of this publication may be reproduced or transmitted in any form or by any means electronic or mechanical, including photocopy, recording, or any information storage and retrieval system now known or to be invented, without permission in writing from the publisher, except by a reviewer who wishes to quote brief passages in connection with a review written for inclusion in a magazine, newspaper, or broadcast.

Published in the United States by Yesteryear Publishing.

Books are available at **www.amazon.com** as well as through the author or publisher:

Yesteryear Publishing
P.O. Box 311
Hummelstown, PA 17036

www.yesteryearpublishing.com
yesteryearpublishing@gmail.com
(717) 566-3907

☏

A grateful word I give to Judith T. Witmer and E. Nan Edmunds, who steadfastly guided my writing to publication. Their editorial skills merit respect and their cordiality remains as friendship. I hold them in warm regard.

Eugene Clemens

Cover photograph by Marty Thomas-Brummè, Director of Major Gifts, Elizabethtown College

About the Author

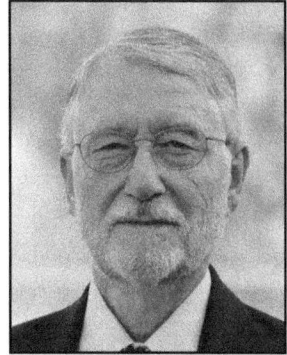

Though born a shy Hoosier boy, Eugene Clemens knew at an early age he was destined for the world. After earning a BA in history at Goshen College, a MA in philosophy and a PhD in religious thought, both from the University of Pennsylvania, Eugene and his family settled in Pennsylvania where he held an appointment as Professor of Religious Studies (1965-2000) at Elizabethtown College.

The book cover photograph was taken at the Peace Tree which Dr. Clemens and a student planted some thirty-five years ago on the college campus. The Clemens Peace Prize has been established in his honor as advisor to the student group, Advocates for Peace, and for his service to the Elizabethtown College Alumni Peace Fellowship; his being instrumental in establishing a peace studies minor; and his teaching Peace and Conflict Resolution. This prize is awarded to a student who applies the principles of peace-making to an area of his or her expertise.

Eugene Clemens describes himself as an eternal metaphor, sharing with several generations of students the mind's inquisitiveness. He notes that he is sustained by music, beauty, and a sense of the mystical, and these gifts became the basis for forty booklets of reflections which provide the core for this anthology shepherded by his son David. Through these words his soul's voice continues to influence thought and meditation.

He says that good fortune permitted him to travel to other lands; yet, the wanderlust was mainly for the inner journey into fuller humanity which he has shared with all who have known him personally and professionally. It should also be noted that for many seasons of soccer at the college, Dr. Clemens, or Geno as the team members have dubbed him, led a "Circle of Trust," by which the team members huddle and share inspiration. The scoreboard for this sport was established in his honor.

Eugene has been married to Vada Mae Hostetler for more than sixty years and they are the parents of three children—David, John, and Kristina—and grandparents to seven grandchildren.

Table of Contents

Table of Contents

PROLOGUE: *Pro-Word*

I do not recall exactly when it occurred to me that words are magical. It seems, though, I have ever been under their enchantment. I regard words as one of the nearest things to magical power left to the grown child. In childhood I played with toys. Now, my playthings are words, with no less wonder and fantasy. The miracle of words is that they are able to utter the reality of inner mystical awareness, giving wings to the imagination and voice to the deepest sentiments. Thus, I have chosen to write about words, in the hope my words encourage and reinforce the potential writer in others.

Just as I have revered words and their power, so have I witnessed the deadening infliction of empty words. The sterility and death of words occurs when they become cut off from the spirit and carry on a separate existence of their own, like some dreadful linguistic zombies. Without the freedom of imagination and the spontaneous flow of sentiment words are imposters, pretenders to the throne of the soul. Thus, my objective in writing this booklet is to incarnate words with the spirit. The precise, appropriate use of words relies as much upon intuitive awareness, as logical and grammatical rules.

I cannot say enough about my appreciation of words, for I would run out of words in the attempt. Think of it, the divine gift of words. We can get "lost in words," be "at loss for words," even "stumble over words." But, what would we be without words? Half our joy in life is in the very immersion; the other half derives from the utterance, however halting or confused. Our words are extraordinary because our experiences are sacred. Words can serve as sacraments of our holy emotions, the resonance of intimate encounter in our soul. Therefore, my writing is in highest tribute to the presence of The Word in my life.

I simply adore words, for what they do for and to me. They are my beloved friends.

A Handbook for an Errant Writer (2000)

The Genesis of an Anthology

First of all, this opening has to do with the origins of the anthology. But that simultaneously opens the question of why I have spent a long life in such ceaseless writing. I will use as my rationale, "I think; therefore, I write." I have come to regard writing as a birthright.

I estimate that over the years I have written several million words. Starting with class notes and assigned papers, my literary efforts grew to include a flood of letters and copious journals, one the inspiration for the other. My dedication to writing was sustained by the conviction that what passes through the mind and emotions is sacred and must somehow be preserved. A thought not embodied in word is lost to time. Of equal worth is the element of self-affirmation. We become what we express through our words; our words bear the mark of our being. Authentic writing is profoundly autobiographical. That is its genius.

For quite some years I desired to share my self-shaped words through official publication. After several unsuccessful submissions I revised the means of sharing. Undeterred, I turned to putting out a series of limited edition booklets to share with friends. Over the last thirty years I have written more than forty booklets, of varied scope and quirky title. I estimate these represent 1,400 pages of text. The inception of the idea for an anthology came with my son David's encouragement to reprint some of the out-of-print copies, in new format and in greater circulation. However, a perplexity presented itself: "Which booklets should be chosen from so many?" Thus sprang forth the possibility of a collection of pieces from each of the booklets, the best of what should endure. The better part of practicality, thereby, turned to an anthology. I am grateful to David, for both the encouragement and his assistance in preparing copy for printing.

As to organization of the pieces, initially I had considered clustering them under thematic headings, believing in that way they would represent my multifaceted personality. Upon better judgment, I have arranged the

selections under the title of the particular booklet, chronologically ordered. This format has the benefit of seeing progression in my writing, as well as constancy of theme. Persistency to my thinking there certainly is. From beginning to end I have sought wisdom in merging my intellect with my spirituality. A mysticism has pervaded my entire life. I trust this is evident in my selected writings.

I am fully aware an anthology generally involves an assortment of authors. It is not that I want to dominate the stage of thought, only that in my decline of life I consider it best to gather, yes, as a gift bouquet, what I most wish to be remembered for. It goes without saying, yet I will: This gift of my thought is an invitation to an inward dialogue. I trust your words dance as nimbly in your thoughts as they have in mine. Initiate some steps of your own in reply, adding to the total without diminishing the lively rhythm. My faith allows me to believe I will know this and will celebrate the friendship the meeting of words represents.

Words are flowers of a different kind; thought represents the blossoming of the mind. Just as the beauty of a flower is for mutual appreciation, so are words for the sharing. Years ago high on the side of a Colorado mountain I came upon a delicate alpine flower. Hesitating to pick such a rare blossom I mused, "What good is such exquisiteness, if I have no one to give it to? I shall save it for the sharing." In like manner I offer you my words. If words are sacred, the offering of one's own words must be an intimate act of communion. When the words meet with receptivity a marriage of minds and hearts is enacted. Writing has the potential of being a lasting bond. So may it be!

A Day Late in Autumn — A Lifetime
(1986)

A narration of an old man's last day of life. It draws upon the parallelism between the cycles of nature and that of life. Each day is a lifetime in miniature, four seasons in one. Loosely autobiographic, in that I envision a peaceful consummation to life.

The Lens Between Two Infinities

In beholding the beauty of the autumn woods, the old man's thoughts returned to a piece he had written in mid-life and he carried those words with him as he resumed his walk. On a wondrous spring day it had occurred to him that the Spiritual Eye is, in a higher respect, the lens between two infinities, the Universe and the Soul. The expression of this insight through the medium of words had given him great fulfillment then and he found a satisfaction, bordering on joy, in hearing the words in his mind once again.

The essential gist of the perception lies in these few sentences. "The universe and the soul are two corresponding worlds, one no larger than the other. The purpose of earthly existence is to enlarge the two worlds to their infinities. The two grow together, concomitantly and to union. The universe enlarges the soul and the soul's consciousness makes larger the universe. In the soul is mirrored the universe and the self is aware of only that in the universe to which it gives place. Being spiritual means to open the lens and to sensitize the plates of imprint upon the soul. In glorious moments of worship, the two merge into ONE."

Upon rehearing what he had written so many years before, his disposition became even more worshipful. He heard a final line returning, "There can be no greater depth to the night sky than the depth of the soul. The more worshipful the soul, the vaster the firmament." He then applied the words to the luminescence of an autumn day.

Noon: Respite

In the distance of the path he could hear the sound of water splashing. The forest was thinning and out ahead lay the widening of a stream and a sunlit meadow. It was a familiar stopping point, with the mountain more fully in view and water for drink. There, some seasons ago he had built in the bed of the stream a small waterfall with trailing cascade. In emerging from the woods he observed that the sun had nearly reached its zenith. Reaching down, he touched the fingers of his one hand upon the edge of a rock several times his own size, a resting spot, and felt it was well warmed by the sun's rays. He greeted the rock with a nod, smiling as he did, for this landmark sentinel reminded him a little of himself. There it sat, for the time immovable, in the very presence of flowing change. But first, before sitting in repose upon the old friend, he lowered himself to the current beneath the waterfall, cupped a hand, and drew several swallows of the clear, cold water. For him, this gesture was an instinctual act of communion, a way of making one with the place, and the upper reaches of its terrain. As sure as the wine made the communicant symbolically one with the Cosmic Christ, so did the in-drawing of a stream's water bring union with the locale's spirits. Upon his many mountain wanderings in America and Europe, he frequently paused to drink from the downward gushing streams. Not so much out of bodily thirst, as out of desire for oneness did he take from every brook and rivulet he crossed. The hesitancy before each draught was filled with the excitement of anticipated union with nature. In the aftermath of such communion was a brimming exhilaration, a sensation of being as much a part of the mountain as inseparable from the rocks, the snow, the mosses, the lovely alpine flowers. Each tread upon the path thereafter was not foreign imprint, rather a touch of familiarity. The heart was free of any intent at defilement and every step was as much a conscious act of merger as was a restful recline upon the grass of a high meadow. Eagerness and elation attended at all the rocky tables of communion throughout the upper regions of the world he had visited. But it was with great trembling that he drew the first handful of water up from the powerful glacial stream beneath the towering peaks of Mount Blanc. The enormity of the moment seemed more than he could bear. For hours afterward he would not speak, not even to the wind or to himself, for he was solitary. Nay, not alone, one with a mountain before heaven. He sometimes wondered, as he walked with erect bearing through a crowded thoroughfare, "Do these people know that this traveler in their midst is at one with mountains? Will I know when I meet another who is also at one?" The waterfall he had built so that he could listen to the splashing of the water and watch the sunlight glisten off the myriad of droplets, in remembrance of all the streams he had known as lovers, in the western Rockies, in the Alps, in Scottish Highlands, in Appalachian forests, in Bohemian meadows. His romantic heart heard in the melody of streams the song of water sprites and nixies. They revived the youthfulness of his spirit and prepared his life for movement.

Carefully bringing his body to rest upon the awaiting rock, this unorthodox priest took from one pocket of his coat an apple and from the other a hardened piece of bread. Placing them side-by-side upon this natural altar, he breathed an unspoken prayer of consecration and gratefully offered them as substance for his body's nourishment and emblems of his spirit's gratitude. When a child he had learned to travel to distant lands through the magic transport of select foods. An orange was a visit to a balmy, tropical place; an olive took him to Italy or Greece and put before his eyes scenes of classical days, cypress trees and togas. The sweetness of a date was tinged with an exotic flavor, mingling the air with a faint aroma of spice and bringing forward the mirage of a caravan crossing desert sands before a palm adorned oasis. But with the passage of time the partaking of special tokens became more than merely an imaginary venture, an alluring fantasy. These conscious, intentional acts of in-taking increasingly took on the character of sacraments joining the soul with the earth. Just as the drawing of the water from a spring created oneness with the mountain spirits, the Father Spirit Before Heaven, the ingestion of fruits from the moist, fertile soil spiritually reconnected the umbilical tie with nature, Fecund Mother Earth. An apple was the distilling blending of spring rain and summer sun, the succulent ripening of a blossom's seed. In each bite was a portion of the earth. A morsel of bread took him instantly to the Great Plains. As he meditatively chewed the mature grain turned meal, his mind was watching the wind send waves across the open fields of wheat. Nourishment became conjugation, and yet another integration of body and spirit took place. That was sacrament; that was bringing back of the Sacred to the physical, an incarnation. He portioned the apple and the bread, as an officiant would the Host. In an expanded state of awareness, approaching purest of worship, encompassing both his being and the earth's energy, he thankfully partook of the gifts. He thought upon the paradox: "In the breaking of My Body, you shall find wholeness." Then came the esoteric truth: In bringing spirit to the body, the soul is less bound to the physical. He knew he was spirit bound and bodily animated.

Evening: Fading Light

The sun was setting on his day. It reached the tips of the trees on the ridge to the west and then dropped below view. The lower sky glowed as an ember, red-orange at the horizon blending into pale and darker blue above. No clouds stood in the sky, only the thin crescent of a new moon. How greatly throughout his many years he had been transfixed by sun rises and settings and how entirely he had been enchanted by the mysterious powers of his Mistress Moon. The moon in all her phases, though each differently, was alluring, captivating, while not possessing. In giving himself to his mistress, she had opened up to him the secret depths of his own intuition. As he sang to her, he heard an even sweeter song in his own soul.

The sun ruled by day, giving its energy for light and growth. In assuming or relinquishing its reign, the monarch of the sky filled its realm with a splendor befitting its majesty. From such a spectacle one should not then turn aside. From all mundane occupations in that moment one is compelled to draw. It was a sacred act he always reverently beheld. The rising of the sun is creation and beginning, the embarking upon journey, the reaching out of God through soul into the particularity of matter. The setting of the sun is completion and ending, the return of the soul to its divine source, the absorbing of the self into perfect peace. Into him, as a voice of homecoming, came an overwhelming sense of well-being.

The light had nearly disappeared from inside the cottage. No longer was the air effused with gold, but was colorless in its duskiness. The old man's eyes are perceptibly closed, his head bowed. His thoughts withdraw entirely from his surroundings and reside beyond, in the realm of truth, beauty, and love. His awareness surges to one last thought: the satisfaction of having lived life well and gratitude of having been given the gift of life. The offering of gratitude, a prayer of parting, is transposed into an ineffable peacefulness. The glow of a last ember in the fireplace flickers out. Finally all is cast in darkness. In the night sky a bright star appears.

Intimations, Visitations, Glimmers and Glints: The Mystic Passageway

(1986)

Barrows heavily upon life confirming travels in Europe, with earlier poems added. The leading motif is the thinness of separation between the visible world and the longing of the soul for transcendence into a fairer realm.

They do not ill perceive, who deem each moment brushing the edge of eternity. Beyond the indistinct limits of our everyday activity lies a realm of exceeding grandeur. It beckons to us, invites our entrance. Through it we are born into our spiritual being.

This ever springtime land, fair with radiance, speaks to us in soft, subtle voice, calling, entreating. It comes to us in intimations and glimmers, each visit to us a Theophany. In responding, following its luring, we are taken into its limitlessness, a Transcendence. Though in the first encountering this other world seems far removed from reality and strikingly different in kind from the ordinary, over time a union takes place between the two, an Integration. In alternation the something more comes to us and we are taken to the something other, until at last, the two become one, inseparable in a Holy Marriage. The something beyond comes to place haloes around all the ordinary forms. The physical world, which was merely placed before us at our birth, is now transformed into glory and we walk a hallowed path toward paradise. This translation has been my salvation, my rescue from the terror that I should go back into the darkness of endless time, without having experienced anything more than waves of physical impressions. And, thus, in joyous, grateful acknowledgement, through this writing I seek to pay tribute to

> ... a sense of something more,
>
> ... an intimation of a reality beyond,
>
> ... a mysterious, random visitation,

... the greater meaning than what appears to be,

... the instance of depth and height, quality and value,

... the breaking through the surface of a transforming vision,

... exceptional moments through which a higher light shines
on the details of our existence.

The Mystic Passage is of two worlds merging, uniting: the physical and the spiritual, the surface and the depth. The two realms do not divide between oneself and the non-self, but between all that merely appears and the illuminating light from beyond. Often, it is not until the spiritual core of the universe is beheld that the self is made aware of its own spirituality. Then, the self is even more endowed with the Eye of the Spirit. The ever heightening, unifying cycle accelerates, intensifying the growth of spirituality. The great deliverance is in breaking loose from the mirage of the only physical.

Our consciousness is initially framed by the obvious, the external façade which we call physical reality. Yet, along the way we are sent messages from the inner world. At first, the apparition is ever so brief, a mere glint from out the periphery of the mind, a faint hint of a breaking through, a sheer fine thread of connectedness. It would seem these starry flashes are here for but a second and then are gone for a lifetime. We sigh, "If only I could follow." But gloriously we can follow, and in the following bring paradise to earth. Such momentary intimations prepare the way for the opening of the portal, the conduit by which the evidential is flooded by the extraordinary. That the moments are instantaneously fleeting does not make them any less real, only elusive to reason's reality.

At a length of preparation, in an overwhelming experience of standing in the gateway—the spiritual event of penetration—the flat surface of ordinariness is shattered and our re-created eyes see into the depth of all before, surrounding, and within us. It is no longer simply and plainly a world of forms and properties, but an endless array of indescribable splendor. The beauty of the something more radiates from everywhere and emits from everything. As William Blake testified, "The eye altering, alters all."

Human Encounter Transforms the Countenance

The person we see before human encounter is not the same person we see after.
What we see before is the form, possibly attractive and certainly recognizable as a human presence. Bodily chemistry may be in attendance, or we may be relatively unaffected by the person. In all cases, the person deserves our civility and generosity.

Then, with some kindred spirits comes the experience of drawing together at the deeper level of selfhood. In the opening up and sharing of the inner self a new dimension of relatedness is revealed and what we perceive thereafter is so much more than what we saw before. What seemed lovely before now possesses for us a beauty of greater depth. Beyond the beauty of the apparent emerges the beauty of disclosure. To beauty is added the transfiguring spiritual dimension. A new bonding is created and it touches us deeply, far more than that of the body. More lasting than the physical, an enduring attraction draws us to the other.

Once there has been encounter of the spirit, that person shall forever appear different to us. We will relate more sensitively to that person. If we then choose to be hostile, in order to free our self from the bond, we destroy something precious in our self in so doing. We may be hurt by that person, still they remain more than just another human form.

The wise and fortunate person passes along life's way bonding through encounter and extending the unitive process to the entire world. Eventually all takes on a more glorious countenance, a radiance. More than just an object, it is connected to our soul.

Is a thing merely a thing, or but the physical face of something more?

Are some things just a face and nothing more?

An empty thing, a face and nothing more,

lies spiritually unborn.

A spirit born

sees in a face

something eternally more.

A Heretic's Loving Thoughts After God:
Contemplation Unceasing
(1986)

An assortment of short pieces on religion, introduced by a longer essay narrating my movement away from conventionality. The story is bittersweet, for the loss of tradition never brings an end of longing.

Introduction: A Journey from Tradition

It has been a long journey, taking me over terrain I had not anticipated and redefining expectations I had too narrowly focused upon. At times the search has left me weary, discouraged, a long way from the goal of my dreams and the desire of my heart. But I have never doubted the rightness of the departure or the worthiness of the destination. I was being faithful to a calling within, a voice I could not name but toward which I have always felt a profound reverence and drawing.

Though it was not my predetermined intention, I found myself challenging a goodly amount of well-established tradition and leaving behind much time-honored thought. Because of a strong dedication to truth, my initial steps were not as respectful to inherited belief as my elders may have wished. In consequence of this undeniable calling to intellectual honesty, my search transgressed upon many thought-to-be sacred grounds of tradition. But youthful zealousness eventually modulated into a thoughtfulness, and impatience with thoughtless obedience slowly gave way to a modicum of charity. I did not return to the stolidly established tradition of my beginnings. Still, I learned to see more deeply into its heart and to deal more kindly with its shortcomings.

I was baptized as an infant in the Lutheran tradition, therewith entering the gates to the Kingdom through the remission of original sin. So I was told some years later. For quite some more years I was steeped in the dusky doctrinal waters of its teachings, Sunday school and liturgy without end. At the age of fourteen, having for a year and a half undergone the moral tincture of catechetical class, I was confirmed in the Faith.

Although the questions and answers of the Catechism left great gaps in my youthful curiosity—they were not my questions and no other answers were permitted—this infusion of the Faith left little doubt as to the sinfulness of man or the absolute necessity of the crucifixion, at least if there was to be any chance of salvation. The absolute sufficiency of the Faith did not go to waste. Accepting its veracity with unwavering certainty, the faithful argued its validity with a confidence bordering on arrogance and held to its superiority with an attitude approaching smugness.

In spite of this thorough indoctrination and almost entire disregard for my own intellectual integrity, in retrospect I bear no resentment at being led by defenders of the tradition, for they were sincere, though sickly, in their concern for my soul. Neither do I regret the heavy exposure to parochial teaching. Ever after I was to take religion seriously and to quest after matters of the spirit. While Baptists may be "hard-shelled," I was, without a doubt, a "hard-core" Lutheran, stalwart and upright.

During my college years I underwent an intense period of religious awakening, what might be called a birth of self-awareness and spiritual consciousness. Accompanied by a blend of earnestness and induced guilt, an unfortunate inheritance from both my Lutheran and Anabaptist backgrounds, my religious convictions took expression in the form of a moral rigor coupled with strong personal dedication, what the Anabaptists termed Nachfolge, "following after Christ." It was propelled by an anxiety over salvation and eternal life, yet in the finest respect the motivation was a desire to be faithful to the noble calling of my spirit. I was being true to a deeper self, now emerging. This self was still heavily colored and bound by unwholesome feelings, yet I was conscientiously responding to the leading of an inner light.

The journey was continuing and was a necessary stage to further growth. I am no longer that person, but I lovingly smile upon the severity of those years and extend charity to those who are now passing through the anguish of spiritual birth. Better to be flawed but earnest, than indifferent; more preferable imperfectly to seek awareness, than to be unconcerned.

In consequence of the spiritual intensification, following three years of teaching I entered seminary for exploratory study. Promptly I felt a sharp difference between myself and the other students, both as to self-perception and life expectations. The uniqueness of my journey became all the more apparent. I remained a second year, but with the clear realization that I would not go into the pastoral ministry.

I discovered that I was a thinker and a teacher of the mind, not a confident expositor of scripture from the elevated status of a pulpit. It bothered me to think I should have to aver some dubious article of belief from that ordained position, to reinforce the simple, uncomplicated needs of a congregation. To that which did not authentically reflect my innermost experiencing and most rigorous thinking my intellectual honesty would be required to say, "No!" Already it was evident I was destined for a journey whose course would take me far from the conventional path. I sensed serious potential differences and I neither wanted to trouble others nor, more importantly, violate the conditions of my spiritual development. Thus, I left to teach two more years, prior to entering graduate school. I was to be a teacher of philosophy.

Sorting Things Out: On Becoming a Heretic

I must confess, the journey was not made easier by the certainty of religious persons. Quite the contrary, their complacent, fixed positions more often than not represented hindrances to my journey instead of reinforcement for my convictions. They were obstacles and stumbling blocks. I have had about as many problems with religious persons as with so-called heathens and unbelievers. Discovering far more vital life force in some religious derelicts than their reputations would allow and dismayed by the low level of spiritual sensitivity in many self-proclaimed believers, I decided it was necessary to sort out a few things for myself. The lines between belief and unfaithfulness, spirituality and irreligion were not as clean or clear as my catechetical lessons had led me to assume. In result of a new sorting out, I found a few very significant beliefs left out. Every now and then a cleaning out of one's personal temple and an inventory of what honestly can be kept for veneration must be made to prevent stagnation and encourage revelation. This self-officiated rite of purification graciously, gloriously just might prepare for the next stage of growth, eventuating in a more profound spirituality. I now joyously confess, that was precisely my experience.

Ah, yes, there you have the first of my observations on what obstructs spirituality: the intolerable domination belief has over the full range of human experience. Religious persons are often more aware of what they ought to believe, than what they are actually experiencing. To believe we block off reality. God's existence is based upon belief more than upon the actual awareness of a sacred presence. What they take for "God" is only their belief. Rather than experiencing an existing God, they are experiencing their belief that God exists. And what, might you ask, produces this tyranny of belief over experience? An interlocking aggregation of components combine in this conspiracy against and suppression of what we would be aware, if only we allowed primacy of experience. To be sure, the accumulation of revered, but unexamined, artifices and innate, but inane, loyalty to tradition contribute greatly to the misinterpretation of experience. However, the key, and underlying, element is the stultifying effect of feelings of inadequacy and low self-worth, both reinforced by the doctrine of human sinfulness. More than anything else, this is what locks believers into a self-perpetuating spiritual sickness. The pathos of it all is this, the crime has been perpetrated by a religion brought into being by the very illness. The irony is that the medicine is what prolongs the malady. Those who elevate the illness of depravity are experiencing their own lack of acceptance, projected into a cosmic plan of salvation, rather than the essential spiritual nature of life, the Divine Presence.

To be a heretic is not to be an unbeliever. Rather, to be a heretic is to believe in an unorthodox manner. After too many abuses by belief, agnosticism becomes the better course of intellectual honesty.

Rejoinder With Myself: Tradition Revisited

Once the world had been revealed anew through the opening of my spiritual eye, I found myself going back to old terminology in reconsideration. In the way of a Great Life Dialectic I had gone through the credulous acceptance of the tradition (thesis), to the abandoning of it all in a critical search for pure ground (antithesis), arriving dialectically at an appropriation of selected traditional symbols by which to express heightened spiritual awareness (synthesis). Without the sensitizing of my spirit, the tradition would have forever remained offensive to me. Alone, the tradition became an empty form, all the more loathed because of its destitution. Then I realized, it was because of the spiritual sensitizing that the tradition had come to be odious. Additionally, once the altar was cleared of meaningless content, I was prepared to give old forms new potency. With the spiritual eye the tradition can be brought back to life. While not returning to the meaning it earlier contained, the symbols can be brought to a consummation of meaning. Through the working out of the dialectic process higher religion is born.

Each individual consciousness must pass through the cycle during its life journey on the way to spiritual realization. Experience is the fountain into which the spirit must be dipped on the course to perfection. After a period of time in the wilderness, away from the religious establishment, I found my anger subsiding. I had found much in the primal immersion in life to satisfy my spirituality and did not need to go back for traditional sustenance. Still, it seemed as though I was destined to return, to revisit the tradition and to make further peace with a part of myself. It was both a rejoinder and a reintegration.

In returning, one of the first misgivings I had to work through was that of vocabulary. Could I use such terms as God, prayer, faith, and spirit, without being accused of insincerity? If others had any idea of how differently I understood some of the conventional religious nomenclature, would they be disturbed by my presence in worship, for even worship had altered in meaning? I had withdrawn, in part, to leave the tradition in peace, not wanting to trouble or be troubled.

For a while I was acutely self-conscious, aware of how drastically incongruous were our respective understandings of what we were saying and doing. "If ever they had any idea," I often thought to myself. But, then, at a deeper level of human recognition, I felt less and less uneasy, more and more assured that I had no reason for apology. I genuinely felt a kinship, even in heterodoxy, empathetically identifying with many of my traditional students, for I had once been there myself. Their sincerity and good will have become bonds of genuine regard. I sense a higher purpose in sharing my experience with those who will have to travel a path similar to mine, from tradition to doubt, to authentic claiming of what is real in the self. I found myself using the traditional religious vocabulary more frequently, turning the words over in my thoughts, to taste them in new reference, in the thick, savory stew of what I had experienced.

Across the Earth, Through the Seasons, To a Fuller Self

(1988)

A paean in tribute to life's cyclical rhythms within the orb of nature. As the self opens to nature and its seasonal changes it enlarges to fulfillment. All driven by a powerful wanderlust coupled to an affirmative life urge.

The earth stretches out beyond our ken, summoning the free spirit to explore and to partake. With each discovery understanding is enlarged, of the world and of the self. For the searching self, life is an alternation disclosure of the outer and, then, the inner. To take up a new portion of the outer is to lift up from the depth a yet-to-be-integrated aspect of the potential self. Simultaneously, we can expand what we know and what we are. Only to know of the world is to leave the self incomplete, humanly undeveloped. Understanding is for wholeness, to become. In each place we visit we are offered an additional part of our self. We respond to the call of life in order to fulfill the urge of our being. Life is movement toward completion, a journey to fullness.

Life also journeys through seasons as it crosses the earth. We go from the season of birth, spring, to the season of repose, winter, having passed through a season of ardent work, summer, to bask in a golden period of repose, autumn. Within a whole life journey are many pilgrimages. Each turn of the year's cycle, nature's annual birth and death, is a journey in miniature. The season, entire life and yearly, are perennial motifs for self-understanding. Just as we learn of our potential self from the places of the earth, each season opens for detection yet another dimension of our multiple personality. They, too, are guides to our growth.

From deep within the self comes the call of its members, toward movement and growth. Many the miles to go, e'er I sleep.

Autumn ~ Life is Fruitful

A season of growth is followed by a season of fruition, fruition by harvest. The gathering is accompanied by a song of gladness, for the plentitude of life and the trustworthiness of nature. The process of sowing and reaping, work and product, hope and return nears completion. Provision in accumulation is the assurance for the body; golden wisdom in witnessing the lesson of the seasons is wealth for the soul. So, too, is there recognition without and within. The diligence of the season of work deservedly receives the admiration of community, especially if it is an achievement for the whole. But far more to be treasured is the acknowledgement known only to the soul. The soul can speak and hear for the universe. Quite so, that is one of its principal priestly roles and the true nature of worship. Its canticle of praise is: "See what time and hand hath wrought." However, the soul knows that sharing the rich harvest of the field is a truer expression than psalm and that the reputation of honest labor is to be preferred over gold. The Hand of the Harvest is none other than the Common Soul in our midst.

Autumn is a phase of transition, just as is spring. Summer and winter are like unto life and death; spring and autumn, birth and completion. As transitions the seasons of the equinoxes serve to prepare and to process. The energy saturating their dominion is unlike the growth impulse horizontally circulating in the earth of summer. More quixotic and restless are the winds of spring and fall, for these two seasons are vortexes of heavenly and earthly, eternal and temporal energies. Spring plants the seed of the soul in the ground of earthly experience and summer endows the soul with the substance of growth. Autumn calls the soul back once again to the mystery of its origin, having granted it a union with earth and a fulfillment of its desire. In this stage of its transit, the soul is mellow unto an aching sentimentalism, yet serene from out the wholeness of completion. It has become one with the earth and intuitively perceives the subtle currents of nature's energies. However, it is in this golden, radiant time the soul must also give its goodbye, the song of the swan before the end. In fact, the soul may be revived for one more, or many more, rebirths of spring. But each autumn is a dying, prefiguring the ultimate absorption into the Universal Soul, along with the termination of a cycle of seasons. The earth, with which summer had brought union, is dying; thus, the soul is compelled to let go of a lover. The voices of summer and winter, life and death, are in duet, one becoming fainter, the other stronger. In a day of perfect balance between the two the soul finds its supreme resolution. This is the apex of its ascent into spiritual consciousness, the seal of its consummation.

The Making of a Social Ethic

(1996)

For over thirty years I taught a course in Social Ethics, longer than any else. This writing is a compellation of the concepts and paradigms most stringent in analyzing social dysfunction. These take morality beyond individual behavior to the ethical import of structures.

Social justice is not an easy road, not intended for the faint of heart or the readily discouraged. It is a life of commitment, involving the conscience as well as the mind. What it involves is speaking truth to power and risking much in the encounter with injustice. Social justice requires the dangerous work of confronting the power underlying the structure of injustice and presenting to it a consequence. Put otherwise, social justice is the everywhere and always work of making power and its structures socially accountable. This task is to go on forever, before the revolution and after. Here is the hardest truth of all: The power of injustice must be met with countervailing power. The question of the nature of the opposing power is itself a moral quandary, likely more on the basis of the situation than on pure principle. But the fact of power is unavoidable for the person who takes up the cause of social justice.

The inescapable reason why injustice must nearly always be confronted with power is that no person gives up power voluntarily. Privilege is undergirded and endowed by power. Power must be used to abolish the privilege representing injustice. The hypocrisy of privileged classes blinds their conscience to the injustice, the rightness of it already morally rationalized. Good will, education, and moral enlightenment alone are rarely effective in dissuading the holders of privilege. That is because, in the course of acquiring the privilege, the possessors modified their moral values so as to justify their circumstances. They will oppose you, not only with self-interest, but also in the righteous name of their morality, countering all calls for structural change with patriotic jargon. Their morality functions as justification, not clarification. The charge of injustice is to them both a personal affront and a moral offense. You will be countercharged with undermining decency and the social order. Following the cause of social justice, you are caught between the horns of a dilemma: On the one side is conscience and on the other tranquility. The good self always wills peace, yet conscience must speak truth to injustice in behalf of the powerless victims. True peace is not silence, not mere absence of conflict, but is to be found in justice.

To Be a Self— To Become the World: Writing an Ethic from Inside Out

(1997)

The initial booklet used in Social Ethics, *in revision. Based upon the assumption that a positive self-image is essential to social actualization. Acceptance of the self and affirmative social policy are indivisible.*

A Dedication to the Reflective Life

Some persons use their minds merely as a means of getting through the unending series of circumstances they take to be life. "One has to use their wits," they say, "deal with reality, learn to cope, solve problems." In the worst of situations the mind, for them, is an emergency tool with which to extricate the self from disaster. In the best of times the intellect serves as a clever device by which to avoid boredom. Others, rarer in number, reflect upon life, ponder its meaning, and extract wisdom. They perceive that life is for learning and that authentic learning comes from reflecting upon what one is experiencing.

Life is ever so much grander than simply surviving. We were put here for growth, the perfecting of the remarkable creatures we are. As we grow toward that more perfected being, we discover it is not just knowledge in the mind we have accumulated, but power of choice and wider options for fulfillment. Though some would dispute that we can achieve heightened awareness and that such awareness empowers us to be liberated from some of life's narrow confinements, this has been my experience. I know what it is to be freed from self-imposed prisons of obliviousness and limited visions of reality. *I have experienced what it is to be integrated and to become whole.* And, I am firmly persuaded the reflective life has assisted to make this possible. I believe in the way of enlarging consciousness on the road to becoming. That is what I have given myself to; that is what I share through this writing.

Most important of all, I offer what I have learned about the healing of the self. It is to this way toward wholeness that I dedicate the reflective life.

The reflective life is not all there is to life, but it enhances life ever so greatly. Through it love, beauty and worship become immeasurably more. This leads me to believe awareness and spirit are inextricably associated. As one rises, the presence of the other is more fully realized. Consciousness and conscience, awareness and valuation may be the most we shall know of the divine principle of the universe. In the reflective life I unite my mind, my spirit, and my soul. Only in this wholeness can there be healing of the severed self and the restoration of the social order—may we say, *a whole self for a whole world?*

The common notion that we think in order to know is only partially correct. There is much we can know from a life of conceptualized thought. But that is not its highest purpose. Contrary to what rationalists may assert, thought is not in itself an intrinsic value. The purpose of thought is to become more fully human, to cultivate and nurture those qualities which make possible tolerance, love, and community. Although thought is to be rigorous in its acuity, it should not participate in the dissecting of community, for then it would betray its humane purpose. Reason, as with religion, when loosed from our common humanity, can wantonly destroy. Thought and a fuller self are inseparable, only if reason be the instrument of love. May our affirmation be: *Tough-minded and tender-hearted.*

A Lifetime of Learning:
A Hoosier Schoolboy Unmastered
(1997)

A somewhat light hearted expose of my life within the educational establishment. The emphasis is upon the intuitive perception of meaning. A little at odds with traditional methods, I develop a more spiritual relationship between the teacher and the learner, an empathetic mode of pedagogy.

Substituting Method for Meaning, Syllabi for Magic —Or, Slow Death by Methodological Strangulation

Generally speaking, method has been the attempt to structure an imposition from without, not a setting free of a power from within, all pedagogical euphemisms to the contrary. While the ideals may glow with dedication to the learner, in practice, method works for the interest of authority— ranging from remote market needs to the ever-present didactic whim or the instructor's predilection. Teachers, because they are in charge, assume they are to be in control. However, the genuine arrangements for learning are the outcome of witnessing the miracle of meaning in the mind of the learner. Method has a mind of its own, often entirely independent of the actual learning process. Think of how very in control course objectives are, knowing the outcome before the divine spirit has even visited!

In contrast, the best teacher is the one who has learned (with stubborn refusal not to forget) the process by which meaning emerged and strives to provide the most effective setting for its reoccurrence in the lives of others. The master must never cease to be the learner. Meaning is not in the memorization of procedures, though they can be the means unto. Rather, it is to be found in the spontaneous recognition of new intricacies in the interplay with the experience of life. This is not to say the true teacher does not need to be well organized. Indeed, the preparation for the magical moment is most arduous. But these skills are more in the nature of a "bag of tricks," than a priori lesson plans. Tricks ignite; plans steal glowing embers, only to extinguish them. Confidence in the craft is ready for the "moment," and control rolls out the perfect syllabus, the magnificent lecture, the bright and shinning course objectives.

A Guard at the Gate; An Angel Beckoning: Reason and Intuition

In our ordinary use of the mind we post a guard at the gate of thought. Armed with the sharp sword of discernment we permit entrance only to those bearers of meaning that meet with our conceptual and logical approval. The light and purity of reason, fearful of what the darker depths of consciousness would bring, admits only to that which it can control, blocking off the way to the Sacred. Rationality is largely a security officer, tragically cutting itself off from cosmic ground in its fear of chaos.

But the self, which would "know" God, must throw caution to the winds and tear down the wall of protection erected by the limits of reason. In its building of a fortress against unreason, the mind is separated from the source of its ultimate security. While the unconsciousness—may we also call it the cradle of the spirit—is chaotic, it is the terrain of transit toward an encounter with Primal Being. What the insecure self, locked in its isolated consciousness, fears is the death of its presumed self, the ego. The mind is confused by the deeper self. But the mind will, in time, die, and if it is union with eternity that is sought, the security the shell of consciousness seems to provide must be abandoned. The wall must be breached, the gate-keeper dismissed.

Once the guardian of rationality is taken from its post the passage may be in the reverse direction. In the remote recesses of the unconsciousness is an angel beckoning. This divine appearance will grant to us the very wings of intuition and the halo of spiritual sight. Awareness now courageously enters the chamber of mystique, the corridor to infinity. Nothing of meaning is denied to the inquiring spirit. Through the Angel of the Oversoul all of spiritual reality is available. Each venture is revelation. The journey is not a physical one, but possible upon the wisps of the spirit's desire. Spiritual longing supplants the courage guarding the body.

My Will and Testimony: Last Thoughts

I have always felt as an outsider to the educational establishment, both as a student and, more so over the years, as a teacher. It is not as though I am a natural born rebel, for I really do desire to belong. The matter is more based upon the awareness that my nature and that of conventionalized learning are at odds. Something about the whole operation seems contrived and artificial, in comparison to what I know to be the transforming experience of being open to the experience of Life. The assumptions coming down from a hierarchal scheme of things have been difficult to swallow. I must not, however, be too severe in criticism of educators, for their intentions have been decent enough and the dedication of most colleagues deserves some commendation. Still, at times they have appeared to me as functionaries and their "profession" has too much resembled a business.

My petition to education is: Redress the imbalance of mind over heart, method over meaning. With persistence and regularity, bring yourself back to the electrifying magical moment. Think less of your paraphernalia and more of the sacred fire within each student. Neither reason nor knowledge is an end in itself. When an end, learning becomes forbidding, cold and detached, cruel and deformed. Reason does not touch the pulse of life; rather, separated, it negotiates with its own products, largely remote from the experience of being human. Without intuition, the direct and most intimate connection with Life, reason's touch is dehumanizing. But together, with reason as the counselor to the finer perception of intuition, awareness can be enhanced and living enriched. Reflection upon experience does raise our capacity to care.

I have regarded my work as a sacred art, a witnessing to the holiness of Life. It is with blessing I leave teaching—one received and one given. A deep gratification fills me, to know I have "served them all my days." I think of future generations and pray there will be true teachers to serve them all their days. Who will, above all, listen to their hearts, the whispers of their spirits? In closing, I most of all thank my many, many students for their generous response. They have made it all worthwhile. Adieu, but only from the classroom. I will continue to converse in spirit through my writing.

Cultivating the Spiritual Eye

(1998)

A second edition of a booklet distributed in the class, Forms of Religious Experience. Intended to shift the focus from the beliefs and practices of religion to the characteristic religious moment. In result, traditional terminology is set into a new context. How the Eye sees is as important as the what.

Introduction: Religion versus Spirituality

In making the distinction between religion and spirituality, I do not wish to denigrate one beneath the other, but to make clearer the role of each in the further evolution of the spirit. The essential difference between the two is a matter of refined consciousness. The legitimacy of either is not in question.

Religion may be considered the avenue leading to spirituality, not as an end in itself. Religious corruption comes principally from its being treated as the destination, instead of skills for journeying. Religion is the disciple stage to the higher destiny of spiritual awareness. Without the accoutrements religion provides, it is difficult to sustain the spiritual life, but "without the spirit, the letter is dead." The very exercise of religion may become the chains imprisoning spirituality. What is given to the spirit as an aid often becomes its tomb. The protection against this travesty is in granting to the spirit supremacy, ultimate authority. Religion is the support and spirit the guide to the higher evolution of our cosmic membership.

In each of us, in every successive generation, the spirit seeks to be born anew. Providentially, the birth is prepared for by the very traditional establishment that would control the life of the spirit. Yes, the self-same practitioner of religious conventionality participates through parenting in the greatest challenge to its complacency. The tradition is the cradle in which is regenerated the purpose for its existence. So, you see, though in perennial tension, religion and the spirit are not enemies. The Eternal Spirit of the Ages, born anew in each receptive individual soul, is none other than the indirect author of that tradition held to so fervently by the preceding generation. The clear distinction to maintain is: The tradition is the product of the age and is culturally conditioned, while the visitation of the spirit is eternal. Together, tradition and spirit prosper; separate, tradition dies.

A Handbook for an Errant Writer

(2000)

Written in conjunction with the teaching of a Freshman Seminar, which included a writing component. Subtitled, "What I Did Not Learn in English Class," the booklet stressed the expressive role of language over the informative, with a touch of wit.

My Here Forthwith: To Live is to Write

I shall refrain from presuming to speak for all persons. Nevertheless, for me to live is to write. Nor shall I maintain a great writer lies awaiting within the life impulse of each person. Human souls have far too varied a life calling and the psyche is amazingly diverse in gifts. However, I do claim for myself the inescapable need to write. My writer's syllogism goes like this: **To live is to give; to give is to write; therefore, I live to write.** Timid and uncertain as a writer in youth, I did not just stumble into being a writer. I was born to be a writer; writing is an essential part of my nature. In one way or another, this nature would will out. Retrospectively, what stands out are not the details to my evolution as a writer. It is that I had no alternative. I am a writer.

I revere my thoughts as currents of divine energy. I know not what the Holy Spirit is, other than the endless stream of intimations of life. Sometimes the current is alternating, yet ever direct and trustworthy. If not from out the silence of eternity, certainly these flashes of epiphany are from the depth of soul consciousness. *Writing is the arduous and faithful discipline of translating the emanating sentiment into the vocabulary of symbolic representation,* that the gift of life be given. Our inheritance of words is wealth abounding and ever is the spirit of impression speaking. So, diligent must be the writer to keep the commitment, to remain responsive to life. Writing is not just an avocation. *Through writing I realize what it means to exist,* my act of transforming experience into awareness. Writing is my record of valued thoughts, a profound form of worship.

To write is not only to share the golden grains of existence, but to live. The heightened state of awareness in appreciation of life, necessary to writing, is what it is to live abundantly! Both are true: I live to write, and, I write to live. Even if no one were to read my writing, my writing has enabled me to live more perceptively. 8/21/86

How to Court a Muse

Now, as to muses, I can no more say they do exist, than that "the higher angels of our nature" do. Still, I believe in them both. The ancient Greeks had nine named muses, including Calliope and Clio, goddesses who presided over literature, the arts, and the sciences. The Greeks did believe muses whispered to the poets through the wind in the trees. With that I can agree, for I have heard their sweet voices myself, murmuring in the stillness of the night. They have been my spirits of inspiration. As for me, my Muse's name is Ecstasy, as superbly depicted by Maxfield Parrish in his calendar illustration. She graces the bedroom wall of my writer's river cottage, arms thrown back behind her uplifted head, her tip-toes making the slightest touch with the peak of a mountain promontory. *She symbolizes the uninhibited, free spirit within me, reaching to the limits of passion, the necessary state of being for writing.*

Having recognized that you have a muse, how do you go about the courting? The muse is a beloved, to be responded to, at the deep reverent and sensitive level of the soul. *To the muse the writer must entrust the soul.* The writer of the Sacred Art hearkens to each murmur of the muse, willing to pursue the quest to realms far beyond. This devotion to your divine muse may appear to another as an amorous affair. Marriage between two, self and muse, may very well represent a higher form of soul companionship. When I speak of my muse, I am actually referring to an aspect of our higher nature. Thus, *to have a muse is to be in a harmonious relationship with your capacity for passion and inspiration.* The power of writing comes from within and a muse represents that power. Why should writers not esteem the source of inspiration within? Even so far as to offer laud and honor?

With this internalization of the muse, we reconsider what the ceremony of honoring entails. The practice consists mainly in regularizing time and space for aloneness. Writing requires inspiration and inspiration comes in an altered state of mind. My "rules" to achieve this precondition:

♦ Shedding of extraneous preoccupations.

♦ Establishing a place of undisturbed separateness.

♦ Concentrating on the urge to express.

Our muse cannot speak to us, if our immediate concern is with practical tasks—office work, home maintenance, child care, on and on. Worry and anxiety are colossal nemeses for the writer. Along with the inclination to avoid the exhausting intensity of inspiration, the tempters of the writer are temporizing through "a thousand things to do." Secondly, to write is to separate. It is not surprising to me, many of the renowned composers/writers had a "space apart." Mine is a cottage above the Susquehanna River. On a good day of writing, trees surrounding me, the river flowing ceaselessly, I can see forever. Whether spatial or psychological, *writing calls us to sanctuary of union with the inner muse.*

Once sequestered and attuned to the voice, the state of expanded awareness begins to author and guide the words. It is a true love affair, creating progeny. The writing is born in passion and becomes beloved. Vitalizing and exhilarating, the affair confirms the selfhood of the writer. No one else is needed to "authorize" the legitimacy of the offspring. It is born of the soul, thus, self-authenticating. Simply, the key to writing is: *Fill yourself full of life; stir up the passion; raise the temperature of the enthusiasm; soar with the energy burst, pouring out its abundance; give beauteous form to thought.* In this simplicity is to be found much intricacy and complexity.

Finally, The Rendezvous with the Muse is a dreamlike Ever-Ever-Land, as near as we ever get to that mysterious orb of creativity, the Divine Center. To enter this realm we undergo mystical transformation. We might think of it as an **Intuitive Trance**, ever so restorative and fecund. After a time in this state, the writer in me comes forth pregnant with new life. The practice of "stepping back" and "entering in" (from the task to the trance) accounts for some of my best writing, that which is born from my deep life desire. My muse is my Beloved.

Addresses on Religion: Not to Its Uncultured Demisers

Further subtitled, "A Spiritual Autobiography," this booklet is the most extensive account of my religious progression, emphasizing the influence of graduate study. More theoretical than other religious writing, the attempt is to conceptualize what in traditional religion I have found objectionable. A main theme is the distinction between what is believed and how religion functions.

An Opening into a Very Long Story: A Lover's Quarrel

In all my years I do not recall a time I did not love God. Always of a serious bent and ready to question everything, nevertheless, I have ever possessed a deep reverence for what I now call the Sacred. Disposed to challenge absolutistic claims about God's will and admittedly suspicious of arbitrary enactment of rules, revival preachers' talk of human sinfulness has ever left me cold. Yet, never have I felt in rebellion against God. Revivalism's core tenet just never reached to where I was.

In spite of heavy dosages in my Lutheran upbringing of "falling short of the Glory of God" and the necessary redemptive intercession of Christ, this dark theology never took hold. True, I did go through a "dark night of the soul" in my early twenties, in which I suffered under the effects of this negativity, somewhat like a suffocating soul gasping for breath. But I can honestly say the breakthrough came when I was able to throw off the unbearable weight of its hideous presumption of being "God damned." Rather than giving in to its sick construction of a controlling "guilt-trap," little by little I removed myself from under its influence, until I have repudiated it. If there was a rebellion, it was a revulsion against the moral repugnance of "salvation theology." The Sacred and I have always been on good terms, and I bear no small measure of resentment toward those guilt-ridden missionaries of "human worthlessness." They nearly snuffed out the "spark of the Divine" in me. In trying to save my soul, they revealed how very wretched were their own souls. I may be a wayward child of tradition, but not of God's.

No, the lover's quarrel is not with the sacred; it is with religion. The love affair has been a lifetime of mixed fascination and contention. I can be one of religion's severest critics or one of its most reverent defenders. The difference is all a matter of "for whose purpose?" Religion is a microscope of the soul. In no other area of study do we delve deeper into the human psyche (soul), than when we ask the religious question. When the inquiry is begun aright, I am positively intrigued by the venture; when posed negatively, the course of affairs is absolutely abhorrent. The outcome is either bliss or torment, Heaven or Hell.

Religion positively pursued harvests authenticity and meaning. If the business is given into the hands of negativity, the product will be an artificially constructed self, alien to its own being. The bliss of this tortured soul is contrived, like a restrictive garment concealing inner turmoil. The spiritual schism is transparent in the harsh judgment against "non-believers," always framed in terms of God's righteousness. Once the worth of the self is abrogated, the self becomes victim to the control of whoever can exercise authority over it. Thus, my regard for religion has become quite ambivalent. When healthy, religion shines bright and beautiful; if lost in negativity and self-loathing, religion is hellishly grotesque. Yes, from birth I have been extremely religious. But that does not gainsay I have not also been repelled by the cruder religious aberrations. Call it snobbery, if you will. But I do have a sense of good taste.

Formerly it was a question of what is truth and whether revelation validates the truth claim. Yet, the longer I persisted in the search for understanding, the less important was the question of truth. As this interest faded, a new set of questions emerged. The central question then became, "How do belief systems function, what are the consequences?" Soon after came the quizzical "Hmm, even if it were true, what kind of person would want to believe it?" In that instant, like a flash of clarity, theology transformed into psychology. Truth had very little to do with the search—one can find in canonical scripture whatever truth one desires. It is a matter of how the religious scheme serves personal needs, entirely subjective. As I pressed the question further toward comprehension, I grew more and more dissatisfied with orthodox religion.

Thresholds on My Spiritual Path

Event, Catalyst, year, and age when each occurred

Event	Catalyst	Year and Age
Religious Awakening	awe and curiosity	1947 (circa 14)
Concern with Sin and Death	brooding somberness	1951 (circa 18)
Seeking a Loving God	warming of the heart	1958 (circa 25)
Seeking Truth Through Knowledge	scholastic birth	1962 (circa 29)
Absence of a Personal God	turbulence of the age	1968 (circa 35)
Passion for Life in the World	Knight of the Rose	1970 (circa 37)
Rejection of Salvation Theology	revulsion against piety	1973 (circa 40)
Acceptance of Mortality	death of a mother	1978 (circa 45)
Loss of a Personal God —Mysticism	sustained deepening	1983 (circa 50)
Leaving an Impression of Love	becoming a grandfather	1995 (circa 62)

How I have changed:

- ♦ Demons of guilt and darkness are no longer a terror.
- ♦ A personal anthropomorphic God is no longer needed.
- ♦ Schemes of salvation based upon worthlessness no longer touch me.
- ♦ I oppose moral distinctions between this world and the Divine.

Coming Clean at the Last of Life—A Soul Confession

Odd as it may sound, I feel "cleaner" toward the end of my life, than I did toward the beginning. What we ordinarily mean by the expression, "coming clean," is to "'fess up" and be honest. Thus, I begin my unreserved confession. I believe in what I shall write, yet do not insist for others to think the same outside their own experience. I prefer the word "song," the free expression of inward spirituality, a joyful praise of life. Before I emote the core of my being, I offer **Ten Admonitions for Living,** golden rules of wisdom born of union with Life.

Before I emote the core of my being I offer eight golden rules of wisdom, born of my union with life.

Admonitions for Living

1. *Live Fully, Heal Repeatedly, Live Gratefully.*

2. *Regard Life and Others as Sacred.*

3. *Take the Full Measure of Life's Cup.*

4. *Do Not Fear Being the Fool; Float on Life's Current.*

5. *Allow Nothing Which is Human to Be Alien to You.*

6. *Intimately Share Your Soul with Others.*

7. *Live On in Those You Touch with Your Soul.*

8. *Above All, Love the Sacred in Your Self.*

In the mythologizing of my life experience I am convinced that some good things abide. Every touching of life in tenderness leaves the world forever changed, just as every cruelty momentarily dulls the beauty of the soul. I believe that love creates new entities. In me are contained the sum total of what I have opened my heart to. What is the Gift of Life, if not willingly received by the soul? Moralism built upon guilt and fear would judge the merits of life experience, shutting out much of the human quest. My morality is authored by an inclusive respect for life and a strong sense of what elevates the human personality, not by what is forbidden. *I believe that one single sensitive soul can contain the entire world and that within the World Soul is the sweet harmony of all that is.* I believe the core of life is sacred, durable beyond the darkness in any single heart. I believe that a soul whose wings have been crushed by disappointment can with a new spring fly again. None of this is believed because it is said to be so, but from the actual experience of it. I need no external truth, for the Divine is in me.

As we come to an end, we come toward death. Death is still an uninvited guest, though not an enemy. Death is the ultimate, heavy symbol of Life's natural process, growth and dissolution. One cannot curse death without diminishing life. Lusting after eternal life has, for too long, subtracted from sincerity toward life, almost as though a misallocation of attention missed the experience of living. I know not where or when death shall take me. I do know I have been attentive and reverent toward Life, cherishing its every sensate gift and rejoicing in all its pulsation. I know that death cannot entirely destroy all that I have taken from Life and have given to others. Life has taught me that even the faintest whisper of hope reverberates throughout the far reaches of the eons. Not all is lost to the maw of oblivion.

Ah, but what instruction for life has the thought, "What is it that survives the dissolving of the body?" Each of us has the momentous choice as to what legacy shall be left, our most enduring gift. Some give form to the craft of their hands. Others find lasting fulfillment in the nurturing of the young. I choose to give form to what I have prized the most, awareness, so that it may live on. Thus, I write these very words you read. I have made a profession out of transforming experience into meaning, wisdom. With many students I have shared the finest of my thoughts. Yet, because I am "academically unpublished," my thoughts will live on for only a relatively brief time. That my awareness shall go on with the caretaking of friends gives consolation to my spirit. My thoughts shall live on, beyond my death. *I bequeath my writing to all who would travel with my soul.*

Aphorisms, Pithy Regards, and Other Snapshots of Life

(2001)

Having been told on occasion that my writing is too prolix and convoluted, I thought best to practice succinctness. The art of brevity is to put as much thought as possible in the least amount of space. This booklet is the first of such exercises.

While I do not believe any shortcut to wisdom is available, I will allow that a few well-chosen words can set new angles on what we experience and provide excursions into broader awareness. Wisdom worth having is the residue of a sincere affair with life and comes, if at all, slowly and with great patience.

My intention in putting together this collection of thoughts from years of observation and writing is to cut though the blur of leaving things the way they are, unpondered. My life has been primarily an incessant query, reflecting on the meaning beneath the surface appearance. May this booklet of pithy reflections assist you in your pondering.

Though I have sought to avoid borrowing directly from the quotations of others, undoubtedly I have been influenced, inspired, and challenged by thoughts, insights, and wording from the reading of many years. I firmly hold, once one mind has passed a thought through its loom of meaning, it becomes communal property in that Great International Guild of Meaning Weavers.

I send you off on your browsing with this caution in mind. Do not grasp any one line or word too tightly, for in that you will turn off the light of inspiration. These aphorisms are not proposals for truth or articles of belief. Rather, the ruminations I have put to words, in clusters of themes, are to be considered lenses by which to focus attention, "cracks" on the surface through which to see beyond. Just as poetry is congealed-emotion-come-to-consciousness, so are my "bits and pieces" economy of thought. My weakness is in being prolix. Here, I have striven for compactness and instantaneous brilliance of coherence. Like that of a haiku, I wish for my words to break through to greater enlightenment.

OF SELF

Aphorisms of Self

- *The road to the true self is fraught with doubt.*

- *The inner voice articulated is a soul affirmed.*

- *In telling stories of what may be, we draw out the self's hidden possibilities.*

- *The guarded self lives in a self-imposed cell, its jailer assigned to keep others away.*

- *The more we sell ourselves, the less we know of the self.*

- *Stiff certitude is a compensatory cover for suppressed inadequacy.*

- *To be known is to be vulnerable.*

- *Guard the entrance to the soul with angels.*

- *We seek others' light for guidance. Yet, in doing so, we may close the door of self-knowledge.*

- *The more attentively we listen to the self, the more fully we hear the voice of others.*

⟋ OF ULTIMACY ⟍

Aphorisms of Ultimacy

♦ *Time is but the meadow above which the blue sky of eternity appears.*

♦ *Those who do not know the largeness of life busy themselves in a lifetime of small particulars.*

♦ *It is within the imperfection of the mundane that we act out an awareness of the extraordinary.*

♦ *One single sensitive soul can contain the universe.*

♦ *Even the faintest whisper of hope can reverberate throughout the far reaches of the eons.*

♦ *Unless we attach the self to one, love will lead us to all.*

♦ *The heart can be trusted, for it is bound to divine longing.*

♦ *In witnessing to the light shining through, we become angels to one another.*

♦ *The burning desire of the heart for God is none other than the need of the soul for total union.*

♦ *Love extends blessing to those who shall live on.*

♦ *The sun of one's wakeful dream must set, so that the guiding star of the Universe be seen.*

A Primer for Peace: Of Personality and Perspective, Personal and Political

A Personal Postscript to Perspective

As I look back over the years of my commitment to peace, I see how eventful it has been. I see what a remarkable journey I have undertaken.

It began in the period of the Korean War, with its intense antipathy toward all things "communistic." Then, during my college years, principally out of a deepening religious conviction, I took a decisive position against war and declared to the Selective Service (at that time in charge of military conscription) to be a conscientious objector. The basis of the conviction was not prudential, nor based upon pragmatic consideration. After a sincere examination of the Gospels, I simply did not see a compatibility between discipleship to Christ and military service. Thus, I began my journey with a near uncompromising statement of pure ideal.

The subsequent years have a dialectic process of combining the ideal with the hard, sobering realities of physical existence. Unless my ideal was to remain "other-worldly," I needed to give viable answers to troubling contextual realities most humans are forced to live within. I was haunted by the gnawing question, "Of what earthly good is a heavenly vision?" The ideal may be good enough to get me "saved" and transported to heaven, but of what relevance was it for thousands of millions of other humans? The more I became involved in the affairs of this world, the less I was willing to rest my personal integrity upon purist grounds. In no way do I regret my affair with the ideal. Indeed, I strongly affirm that this responsiveness is the essence of my integrity and the definition of being human. I now see more clearly the primary force at work throughout my life of peace. *It has been the unremitting demand for relevance.* To know is to understand; to understand is to love. I was learning about humanity and did not want an affectation of "cheap love."

The laboratory of testing the ideal was the Vietnam War and the Reagan foreign policy toward Central America. The Sixties politicized me; the Eighties brought sophistication. During the Fifties my religious orientation was quite apolitical. But the intellectual rigor of graduate school studies, 1962-65, intersected with conscience-searing developments in Southeast Asia, pummeled the luxury of a heaven isolated from the human condition. The more I opened myself to the history and plight of the Vietnamese people, the more I found myself conflicted by what I heard from my own people. Empathy and American ideology were offering opposing views, the disconnect exposing the delusions of the latter. It was, from a purest point of view, easy to be against the war, just as easy as being for the war. Religious objection to the war and patriotic support of the war were on similar ideological grounds, absolute.

However, from my perspective the ground was shifting. Out of more detached, prudentially relevant viewing, if there was to be war, one could plausibly argue the case for Vietnam independence. The whole debate seemed so morally arbitrary. My ideal was tried and found to be wanting. The Reagan years only impelled my movement further, reinforcing the conviction that American foreign policy had been driven by a myopic vision of reality, as seen through the paranoid prism of anti-Communism. In the ensuing years the concept of social justice had grown and found contextual meaning in the struggles of disenfranchised people of Latin America. If there was to be a "right" side in the conflict, it clearly was not the U. S. intervention on behalf of counter-revolutionary elites.

Sad to say, merely condemning the violence on both sides was irrelevant, no matter how religiously pure. Understanding was in the cauldron of reality and I was in a stew. Still, I have had faith that the "cookers" of life might just very well be the distillers of wisdom, as well as the perfecting of morality. *I had moved from an absolute objection of war to a prudential, selective critique of structures.*

Purists, whether religious or political, might reply, "See, look what happens, when you put yourself upon the slippery slope of expediency!" But therein do we have the declension of our two perspectives in the Great Divide. What has changed is not my heart; rather, my mind. Yes, largely from engaging life has my perspective altered. In consequence, so has my understanding of "peace" undergone revision. I am entirely convinced that it is not the mind that should remain fixed; rather, it is the loving heart. Here is the internal conflict, between the heart and the mind. Relevance requires mutation, change. If it is not the mind that alters, it is the heart that changes. May I render this frightening verdict: The heart, when ruled by an imperial, absolutistic mind, becomes hardened, unavailable for empathy. *There is no choice. Where love reigns, the mind must change.* Otherwise the heart cannot keep up with the changing times. For what use is the mind, if it cannot read the ever altering circumstances of life?

So, trusting that my heart of compassion has remained constant, in what ways has my mind changed? Remember, the modifications are predicated, somewhat premised, upon the historical developments of my lifetime, making the adopted strategies thereby relative, something the moral absolutist would never confess to. There you have a major change. I have a strong aversion to moral absolutism. Almost magically, this opens up the door to a myriad of revelations.

First, having discovered a meaningful distinction between prevailing perspectives, I now see that the issue of "Who is for war and who is against?" is far less significant than what had been previously thought. Far more crucial is perspective. We have had our categories ill defined. And it is imperative to have them beneficially identified.

Secondly, I find decreasing benefit in conversations with absolutists opposed to war and increasing purpose in working with affirmative attitudes, even though these persons may be involved in the execution of war. It is out of such dialogue that workable programs for peace can be forged. All too often, the Adversarial Perspective, beyond being irrelevant, serves to foment the very spirit of estrangement, even when it professes to be nonviolent. The real intractable conflicts are those in which the opposing parties both assume the Adversarial Perspective, what is referred to in mediation as "hard bargaining." I am, more than ever, willing to join with all persons of an open perspective in the task of peace, no matter their position on war.

Thirdly, the challenge for the future in this dialogue is to construct places between the inspiration of idealism and the prevailing reality of conflict. It is here that tenable agreements can be reached. Previously I had conceived of this as the work of "peacemakers." Now I perceive that many are already involved, in ways that defy old categories and labels. All are welcomed, in this coalescing of multiplicity into commonality for a world at peace.

Along with these major changes were lesser, yet nonetheless necessary, mental adjustments. Re-visions, if you will. Being of tender disposition, I once thought of conflict as "bad," something to be avoided. I am now willing to make a qualitative distinction between conflict and war, disagreement and violence. I recognize that within conflict is the potential seed of war, depending upon how the conflict is interpreted. Conflict is in the nature of human interaction, given diversity and need, subjectivity and assertion. The "evil" is not in conflict, but in how it is viewed and managed.

The adversarial personality manages conflict very poorly and is greatly in need of perspective modification. Corollary to conflict as morally neutral is the postulate that peace is not compliant or submissive. Having witnessed too many situations in which power functioned to defend inequality and injustice, I hold that peace involves the courage of confrontation. I understand the meaning of the old prophetic proclamation, "Peace, peace, when there is no peace!" Again, the difference is one of perspective. Adversarial posturing confronts to destroy the adversary, whether physically or in character; *peace confronts, deftly, perceptively, in order to correct the relationship.*

I know that other times and different circumstances would have led me down a different path of peace. Thus, my story is more of a testimony than a conclusion. But I am convicted of this: Lasting peace requires the diminishing of the adversarial personality in us all, and the flourishing of a new relationship, based upon a more inclusive consciousness. The affirmative personality is conducive to peace, possibly the very nature of the peace process, not just a favorable personal quality. We have come so far, not to press further. I am encouraged by the awareness that I have been a contributor to the path. Having largely finished my part, I can only say, in the words of the folk ballad, which became a classic of the Civil Rights Movement, "Carry it on!"

An Introduction in Explanation of a Perspective

A combination of curiosity and concern has led me to this writing. Tracing as far back as a college psychology class, I have long been intrigued by the great differences in human personality. Limitless have seemed the possibilities. With further attempts at making sense out of the puzzle, I found certain patterns clearly emerging. Here is the point at which concern entered in. With an equally long commitment to peace, I asked, "Cannot a deeper understanding of human personality be used to promote peace?"

My interest was not only in establishing what is the case. I sought an explanation to empower the altering of the human condition. Merely passively to know is not worthy of us. I was motivated by a more affirmative, pragmatic concern: How can we resolve diversity into harmonious community? I was convinced the problem is not in the diversity. Rather, the problem is in the manner of viewing it. If there be a flaw, it must not be imbedded in human nature, for that is much too pessimistic. My incorrigible optimism insists, "For every ailment, there is a cure."

After a lifetime of observing the "frailties" of humanity, I am persuaded a more adequate means of repair does exist. In no way suggesting a social panacea, I do believe a more effective approach to laying out the problem is possible. To a large extent this reformulation requires a redefinition of the problem, the application of an alternative paradigm. The predicament is not due either to difference or conflict of interest. The "rub" traces to how those differences are regarded. *All differences are an interpretation of reality, each interpretation predetermining the course of the subsequent relationship.* Some interpretations are counterproductive, some redemptive. Peace, therefore, is dependent not so much upon agreement, as on how we view our disagreements. Certain perceptions cancel out agreement. These I shall call "adversarial." In contrast, a more affirmative perception allows for the enduring relationships upon which agreement is based. Out of affirmative perception agreement grows; adversarial perception cannot long sustain agreement, having a more contentious notion of agreement to begin with. Peace relies upon moving perception from the adversarial to the affirmative.

Conflict in human association is the given; the outcome is dependent upon the interpretation chosen to manage the friction. The adequacy of our models of interpretation can be measured by the costs, both material and spiritual. We must pay for their use. We might choose more carefully the piper for whom we dance, if we were more aware of the costs. Interpretations can be delusions in the custody of charlatans, as well as Stars of Bethlehem. Are there not angels of light, in preference to the demons of destruction?

My concern has frequently intensified to consternation, consternation to dismay. As I study disputes, from the personal to the political, I am simply perplexed by the extent of animosity. The longing for the good is so easily taken captive by the blindness of malice. Under this impulse, grievances are exaggerated and accusations rise to a flood of rhetorical hate. So many times have I observed disagreement degenerate into a tragic impasse. *In the tragedy of the part is revealed the malady of the whole.* Reflexively, what we see as dysfunctional in the larger political order discloses the distortion at the personal level. The personal and the political are no more separated than abuse is from war. The adversarial relationship carries through in both. The principle stands: As go personal relations, so goes the political.

This booklet is dedicated to "a way out." Neither necessary nor inevitable is the adversarial, in which two sides are diametrically opposed to each other. In reality, the two competing adversaries are not functionally that different. In their worlds of good and evil, each is committed to the abolition of the other. Taking sides in adversity is actually a "no choice." Neither gains as much as it loses, in spite of compensatory rationalizations. The real choice is between ideological entrapment and a holistic perspective of humanity. These are qualitatively different moral perspectives, the traditional dualistic one and the one I propose. We are not required to be enslaved to each other's hostile perceptions, but reconciliation necessitates a breaking free. For this were the Gospels written.

A Guidebook to Retirement: Landscapes Unforeseen, Changes Not Planned

(2002)

Based upon the notion of life as a series of distinct stages, this writing is a first-hand reflection upon the experience of letting go and being reborn. Each stage has its unique purpose and orientation, one not to be confused with another.

Making Way for a Larger Self

Change bears many metaphors. When a cyclical pattern of coming and going is implied, we speak of "the turning of the wheel." Taking and giving is imaged as the falling and rising of the tide. Both metaphors allow for loss, yet, in the case of retirement, the severance seems far cleaner cut. More apt for the consolation I am seeking in this loss of a longtime self is the notion of emergence. I have learned through the course of many losses to be assured that when something important is taken away the space is reserved for something awaiting. Often the replacement is of equal value. But at this time of retirement my sense is that a supreme phase of my life has been ushered in. The something has evolved; the sequence of changes is reaching culmination.

We are born into ordinariness. The work of the soul is to guide us toward ultimacy. Little-by-little, through the many gates of human experience, we receive intimations of life's grand import. Youth is impelled by a great zest for life, but only gradually, if ever, do we become acutely aware of how wonderful life is. Vocation channels the moral scruples of our conscience. Then comes retirement. From the standpoint of ordinariness, it would seem, all is over. To counteract this, many retirees fearful of where the road may lead continue a life of ordinariness, basking in the warm sun of leisure.

For those who would hear, however, retirement is the forethought to death, calling the self to ultimate consideration. Since a career is generally a major part of one's life span, retirement should naturally throw thought toward lifelong questions. If leisure is lackadaisical, my retirement is not for leisure. The only leisure I seek is freedom from ordinariness. In contrast to a comfortable notion of leisure, retirement is for the work of putting the pieces of life together, a mosaic in tribute to life. It is a time out of time, in which the smaller portions of life are fashioned into a holistic cloth of meaning. The story of my life, I vow, shall be the ever-expanding scope of consciousness into the heavens of transcendental appreciation.

Our mortality is not the enemy. Far more tragic than physical death is the denial that fear of death brings. Nothing seems a greater loss, than rejecting the perspective of ultimacy by pretending that death is merely a glitch in immortality. Worst of all is moralizing death for the purpose of dividing people into perdition and preservation, the extreme in power politics. When we embrace the inevitability of death, its reality becomes our enabler. Death forces us to take life seriously. In that seriousness we are drawn toward a Larger Self. Death tells us, "No time to lose!" Urgency is inseparable from finality. Oddly, we conjure up fanciful notions of an afterlife and therewith elude the lessons death would give us. It is significant to note, how very ordinary and self-indulgent are most of these afterlives envisioned. I do believe in a present day afterlife, the life allowed in the full awareness of ultimacy. In terms of disengagement, we can speak of this as retirement from the ordinary. For me, it is the profound meaning of Death and Transfiguration. Or, to appeal to the chapter title, retirement is provision for the emergence of a Larger Self. Unless Death is confronted and overcome, the ordinary self cannot be transfigured to make way for the Universal Self.

One of my great fears in growing old is the possibility of being trapped in the company of incessant talk about illness and decrepitude. Putting it kindly, these anxious ones are recoiling from the inevitability of death, inviting sympathy in the conversational exchange. But this is no more conducive to the emerging of the Larger Self, than feigning perpetual youth and pretending age is not attended by increasing frailty. To put it more severely, both dispositions abort the seed of the Larger Self and close the door to the soul's culmination. Neither is the culminating stage of life primarily for the purpose of cleaning up the clutter, like some final episode in the childhood training of putting your toys away before going to bed.

Due consideration for the survivors does include the drafting of a will and some jettisoning of meaningless accumulation of goods. But this compulsion for tidiness may very well be a diversion from the more serious work easily left undone, though I cannot wholly fault the virtue. It is a matter of priority, with which concern the self should be occupied during the years remaining in retirement. To my way of prioritizing, the seventh decade is preparatory school for the role as elder to the succeeding generation, as well as a graduate level course in understanding life's meaning. Some never make it through the entrance exams, not having paid attention to life's lesson. Others are distracted by lesser preoccupations in avoidance of grief at Death's door. Graduation is not guaranteed by age alone.

Ordinary existence is conducive to a self of small dimensions. A self of small dimensions will hold to a religion of ordinariness. Could there be any greater ordinariness than the preservation of the earthly ego? Conversely, out from the Larger Self will flow revelations of a higher religion, all-embracing and life-affirming, the realization of transforming wisdom. A career requires engagement; retirement permits circumspection. Though a rhythm back-and-forth, from ordinary involvement to detached transcendence, should provide a cadence throughout life, in retirement the shift is in favor of detachment. Detachment, however, does not represent disinterest. Giving does continue, yet from a more encompassing vision of life. Given the presence of a Larger Self, volunteer work is a sacrament of blessing. Political regards are from the position of "senior statesman," rather than in the fervor of street demonstration. While some of the old forms remain, a new and fuller motivation fills the deeds of the day.

The reclaiming of life by the Larger Self inaugurates a more advanced purpose in being, that of blessing the ordinary with the grace of the extraordinary. This is the traditional function of the Sage, the Wise One, to lift up all of life in the light of a more circumspect frame of meaning. For myself, I call it the "Grandfather Clause." In this role I shall pass on my Larger Self, down through all of progeny. Not just to my blood lineage, but to all whom I touch. It is a giving back and a blessing to Life. Only in gratitude and reverence can this be successfully done. The blessing of the Larger Self is of the soul and universal. The Divine Voice, ever longed for and always sought, at last, speaks through my thoughts.

Quite so, my body is falling apart. I have been achingly aware of the fact for some years. A progressive weariness has set in. However, while my physical form is breaking down, the pieces of a lifetime are coming together. The notes of life's melody have already been played, but the greater composition has yet to be completed. To bring all into tune, I expand to the limits of my Larger Self. For this, I welcome the Self-of-Me-in-Retirement. The sum can only be added by the whole of the Self. In the culmination of life, I undergo completion.

A Consolation for Others

Casting aside all concern over redundancy and repetition, allow me to collect together what I have discovered about the transition called retirement. All I proffer is in a gesture of consolation.

Retirement may really not be as bad as it sounds to the good fortune of a fulfilling profession. While, on the other hand, those who welcome retirement as an escape from a career may find post-employment not as good as hoped for. The result can be either empty idleness or tiring busyness. What is anticipated as "good as it gets" needs to be received as "no better than you make it." The "switching of the gears" involved in the transition has to do with quality, not speed. Speak to yourself in these terms: Deepening, Enriching, and Heightening. A new level of self-importance is availability, for those of undaunted spirit, who would willfully respond to the call for a final step upward.

The best advice I can extend to others is to "lighten up." Do not overburden retirement with ordinary affairs, for this is the time to celebrate the extraordinary, the Supreme Love Affair with Life. More than ever, the self is to experience an "incredible lightness of being." Live reflectively and reverently, for these are the openings through which the beauty and goodness of life shine into the soul. To the extent the power lies within you—and great powers reside within the assurance of love—cast out anxiety, fear and negativity. These are dark dungeons of torment, not fitting residences for the Soul-Bound-for-Glory. Light of the spirit is a beacon for the lightness of the soul.

Do not dim the golden light of retirement with needless chatter or hidden agendas. The time for coyness has passed. A transparent self releases the soul from the unwanted confinement in social propriety. Concern over what others may think and say is too great a weight for the failing nerves of age. Live luxuriously and lavishly, not laboriously. Unwarranted dependency upon the labor of others is never commendable, yet retirement is a time for release from labor. Live simply in want of physical needs, but extravagantly in need of the spirit, for of such is made the wealth of old age.

Though I like beginnings better than endings, a book is not complete without the last chapters. Beginnings are electric with anticipation, but a long life empties the vial of scintillation. When life is full, repose is more sought after than excitement. Rhythms, which once awakened the body, are better exchanged for musical strains bringing serenity to the spirit. With all the verve available and to the honor of life, compose the finest chapter of all for the finale, well written and resplendent in good will.

In Tribute to True Romanticism
(2002)

Born and ever remaining a romanticist, I draw out the full picture of loving sentiment, going beyond a lover to the complete romanticizing of life.

A Task Most Daunting

I undertake a task most daunting. From the onset I am beset by the awareness that my endeavors will fall short of my desires, a built-in disappointment. My desire is to write transparently of that which is purely subjective, knowing I will be able to do no more than to be suggestive. Though it is in the nature of inchoate experience to be ineffable, I proceed undeterred. Of what do I speak, if not of that fairer world opened up by the imaginative power of mystical romanticism? I have been visitor to realms richer in exquisite beauty than the heavens described by earlier visionaries. The two, mine and theirs, are incomparable, at least in the vividness of inner experience. *We are speaking of the nearest thing to the sacred I have ever actually encountered in my lifetime.*

For many years I did attempt to bring the God of traditional religion to my experience. But I can say, quite honestly, the effort was more of an exercise in pretended simulation than an experience from within. I was striving to duplicate what others had claimed about the sacred, what could be called "rumors of the fluttering of angelic wings." If that is their reality, I can only be happy for them. Still, I remain dubious about the authenticity. Based upon my own experience, there seems to be something fraudulent about the extent of the claims. In my most questioning moments, I wonder whether orthodoxy is no more than a hoax, foisted upon needy souls by those who could not bear to face the honesty of their own experience. Do they fool themselves by their too much believing? While I hold the person of Jesus in reverence, I cannot truthfully say I have ever genuinely felt his presence, as diligently as I have tried, any more than what is mystically available with all of life. Almost all of conventional religion has, for me, receded into an abstraction, so reified as to be beyond experiential recognition. Yet, *my experience with life has been vast, wonderful, and magnificent.*

67

Thus, I came to romantic sentimentalism by virtue of default. The rumors of a personal deity having failed, I was left with what I experienced directly. If I am not permitted to embrace this, I will have been robbed of a sacred relationship, left with nothing. But I have experienced so much of the extraordinary. *In an instant, at the appearance of an evocative sight or with the invitation of a seductive melody, I can be transported to a realm of grandeur, transformed into a state of ecstatic awareness.* This is the most I have experienced of the sacred, and … it is enough! With these experiences of the sacred the life impulse leaps; without, I sink into despair. While others may confess that without the presence of the Lord they are lost, my salvation is in regular visitations into the romance of sentimentalism. I regard these visitations as sacred. Why should I not sing poetically?

The Heart and Soul of a True Romanticist

The adjective "true" is very relative to the romanticist, and the noun "romanticist" is more of a self-ascribed honor than an exact designation. Admitting to the subjective relativity of both, it is all the more incumbent upon me to give the terms meaning. I ask the reader to withhold preconceptions and conventional connotations. "True Romanticism" is merely a comfortable designation for what has been my life of intense sentimentality. What you read may or may not have correspondence to what other self-proclaimed romanticists have articulated. I only plead; listen to my story of an unending love affair with life. Judge of its value for yourself and some others. But, above all, open your heart.

What we ordinarily think of when we hear the word "romance" are lovers and belles lettres, Valentine's Day and ardor. To be sure, my romanticism embraces lovers and delights in tête-à-tête intimacies. Yet, lovers are but the initiation and final consolation of what is infinitely larger, confidants in the tryst with the Greatest of Lovers: LIFE. Just as with the specific lover, companion of our soul, we seek to draw in and unite with the entirety of Life, so with our Greatest Lover do we desire to taste, feel, and absorb all, in the fullest measure and magnitude. Thus, *the lifeblood and heartthrob of my romanticism is sweet sentiment and passionate yearning.* I thank Life for so well endowing me, from birth, with desire, longing, and aspiration. Though discouragement and weariness have sometimes made the life impulse faint, romanticism has been a faithful mistress, my true abiding love.

I confess to carrying on a love affair with romanticism; even the word itself stirs deep urges.

Life as Reverie: A Trilogy

(2002)

Always intrigued by interaction and dynamics in motion, in this intuitive writing
& describe the mystical process occurring within. The image of three aspects
dancing in my mind to provide the primal disposition of my life pleases me.

A Foreword in Three Words

Life as reverie! The thought captures more than my fancy. The words are an apt description of how I have lived my life. Movement toward reverie is the gravitational pull of my heart's desire. I understand this to be more than pure pleasantry. Reverie is the natural state of harmony between the body's magnificent senses and the unbounded reach of the spirit. Through reverie our world is enhanced. Reverie is the magic carpet of enchantment. In the absence of reverie I think I should go spiritually blind. The power of which I speak bears other names—*fanciful musing, dreamy reflection, imaginative rumination*. But the name I have given to this exceptional inner disposition is *reverie*. It is my preferred state of awareness. To know me is to know reverie. To its celebration this work is dedicated.

Trilogies are not born full-formed, like some literary triplets. Their members meet upon the course of life's musing. In this case, my writing instincts were developing simultaneously along several seemingly independent lines. The more they whispered to me, in those vague initial intimations, the clearer it became that three of them were drawing together, as if to say, "We are siblings of one creative parent." They spent much time together in playfulness, eventually announcing their intentions of being billed together in a play of their own making. Their case was really quite irrefutable, though I had originally envisioned separate appearances, on three different stages. Thus is the genesis of this trilogy. Like some children they will just have their own way! If three of my booklets choose to hang together, who am I to deny them? Their voices in trio may be stronger than in solo. Let there be a family portrait.

71

As I observe, the triangle is the most stable of architectural designs. In regards to conceptual configurations, the triad, when properly balanced, offers both integral unity of the part and interaction of the whole. Each of the three booklets can be read in its own right, strong as each is, in its own voice. Yet, taken in company, a trilogy offers the conversation by which the picture enlarges and the significance of each part grows by compound interest. We might even say *trilogies are the realization of language's social nature.* While I caution against the imposing of a dialectical sequence, the succeeding part emerging out of the preceding, I do intend for a progression of thought to be at work. Throughout the progression the implications deriving from the interrelationship of the three parts will be drawn out. The order of reading is somewhat left to the reader's interest and choice.

True to its literal meaning, this trilogy has three words. They are SENTIMENT, SENSATION, and MEMORY. The ordering is not inferential, that is, logical. The relationship is more circular. On a purely experiential basis, sensation would seem to be prior to sentiment, with memory the outcome of sentiment's interpretation. But I choose to begin with sentiment, in that it is the essential element in the achieving of reverie. Without sentiment's guiding influence, its predetermination, sensation would remain merely impressionistic. Sentiment applied to sensation can become memory of a higher order, reverie. Subtract sentiment from sensation and memory consists mainly of a vault for automatic sensate deposit, not a palace of creative wonder. Let this preceding chain of thought be a forewarning to the reader. I shall take you on an intellectual ride, as well as articulate the deepest stirring of intuition. And this, for the purpose of conscious appreciation, is an act of reverence.

In introducing the three main dramatis personae, may I say something of each unique inception. *SENTIMENT: The Magic of Meaning* is the irrepressible outgrowth of reflection upon the reality of my nature. A sentimentalism of this first booklet's authorship discloses the secret story of my life, the what and why of my existence. My greatest endowment has been passion, sentiment the staying quality of my will. As a romantic immersed in the delicacies of sensuality I have discovered richer meaning than provided by the sterile confines of denotative linguistics. I speak of this as *SENSATION: The Art of Living,* defying the limits of conventional grammar and syntax.

One can parse a verb or decline a noun. But what structure can be imposed upon the meaning of leaves burning in autumn, crystal snowflakes falling in the stillness of night, or sweet rain splashing upon spring puddles? To be an esthete is to dive completely into the creative pool of sheer subjectivity. From out waters of sensible being come droplets of poetic utterance. Just as with sentiment, sensation can be grasped only autobiographically. Of these pleasures I wish to pour forth. In this language I endeavor to write.

Life well lived discovers entrance into a magical land of memory, wherein sentimental sensation can review all times and spaces, from here to eternity. This movie house of transmuting images and sensations I have long indulged, in and out of dreaming. Then came the urge of these spectacles to spin. Thus was conceived the literary child, *MEMORY: The Mirror of Life*. Soon it became clear that this offspring did not want to stand alone. This work belonged to a family and could flourish only in community with its older members, in recognition of common genetics. For, in the truth of the matter, what have my films of memory been, other than a sentimental production of life's most sensual encounters? In memory I have found like treasures in an attic of accumulated artistic creativity, the substance of human existence. The third booklet is a confession of the wealth time has stored in me. Alas, the account shall be closed in death. But while I live, I shall draw upon it, in reminder to others of the riches memory bears within.

These sheaves of Foreword and Postscript give binding to the three booklets. Read each in the stream of your own reverie. If it seems conducive, read under the influence of lovely, flowing music, for under such spell were they written. Go leisurely, reflectively on, pausing in due time, for inward meditation, to join in the end the larger encompassing circle.

In the Embrace of Nature: A Natural Love Affair

(2003)

Written in tribute to my father, Leonard Arthur Clemens, & simultaneously pour out my lifelong dependency on nature for peace and wellbeing. Through its pages emerge the belief that nature is the screen upon which the Divine is read.

A WALK IN THE WOODS: A Shrine to My Father

While catechetical lessons instilled in me doctrines of the Church, another education, less orthodox, was going on beneath the surface. Quite naturally, my father, like most fathers, wanted to pass on to me his own thrill of innocent childhood. One day late in winter he brought forth a book, *Two Little Savages,* from the time of his youth. I took it to be in preparation for the invitations of spring and summer lying ahead. The story told of two little savages who found recourse and solace in Nature's fields and forests. The book was published in a period of American history which idealized and emulated the naturalness of the Indian. In adulation of my father I received the entreaty enthusiastically. As an adult I understand the role this gift of reading had in cultivating in me a love of Nature. I wonder whether he was aware of how pantheistic the results could be. Like a folk religion beneath the purview of the official, a nascent nature religion flowed in my veins. The great pagan traditions of Beltane and Samhain may have been conquered by Easter and Hallowed Eve, but a love of Nature kept them in close association in my thoughts.

Though my father would deny their "heathen" (dweller of the heath) significance, his woodland walks were nothing less than in reverence and worship. If hard pressed, he would have explained them in doctrinally sound language, or would have turned the question aside as preposterous. I never recall him saying, "I love Nature." But the affection was unmistakable and its transmission to me irresistible. Catholics have their Stations of the Cross. We had Shrines of the Woodland. Without a doubt, the woods were a shrine, for my father and still for me. The difference between the two of us is that his rituals were without conscious liturgy, mine fully intentional. However conventional his mindset, a priest could not have known more of the Host than my father knew about the gifts of the forest. He taught me how to distinguish the trees by their bark and leaves, what wood was good for what. The wild flowers of the woodland floor, exquisitely delicate and elaborately designed, he would point out with an admiration approaching solemnity. These were not merely plants of random occurrence. As an artist in his own right, my father saw in the find of a single flower a trace of Nature's endless beauty. In specially designated plants—wintergreen, sassafras, teaberry, and digitalis—I became aware of Nature's medicinal benefits. If you lie close to Nature, you will be cared for.

Parts of the summers of my father's youth were spent in the woodland naturalness of west-central Michigan. His grandparents on both sides resided there, an extended family more numerous than that of his later home in northern Indiana. His parents grew to maturity in Michigan and he was born there, the nuclear family moving south when he was four. Although he developed an attachment to his new home, I sensed in my father a mystic calling northward. During his lifetime he traveled through most of the United States, expanding his appreciation of how vast the wealth of Nature is. He spoke more of natural scenic beauty than of cities and crowded streets and certainly left an affected depth in himself wherever a oneness with Nature was experienced. He was quite a self-taught historian, but nothing pulled upon his sentiments so strongly as the lure of the woods. He was a Wolverine! If Robert Burns' heart was in the Highlands, by virtue of youthful affection my father's heart was in the North Woods.

Admittedly, the North Woods is a mythological realm, but it is constructed of lived legend, told and experienced. This mythic land is rich in lakes, streams, meadows, glades, and primeval forests. Creatures, large and small, whose presence goes back to time immemorial, inhabit it. Important to the myth is the sense of frontier. Rather than in the sense of "wild and uninhabitable," the frontier designates an edge between human cultivation and Nature's own maintenance. In the days of my father's youth, and even my own youthful visits, ancestral Michigan mixed the two, with only a short walk in between.

At about the age of nine I walked right into the myth, creating a legend of my own. It was during the Second World War and my father planned a week's fishing vacation with a friend at work, to be spent at a lake in Michigan some 130 miles north from where we lived. I was allowed to accompany the two into the mystique of the woods, mainly, I presume, to relieve my mother of one additional child to care for. My sister and toddling brother remained at home. The trip could have been regarded as a rite of initiation into the mysteries of malehood, except that I was apparently adjudged not quite old enough. I was to stay with my grandmother, who at the time resided in a shack as we called it, next to her mother, on barren, sandy land my great-grandfather had carved into a farm of meager existence from piney woods.

I was permitted to go with my father and his fishing buddy as they set up camp. The small lake was accessed by a two-track, sandy off-road, leading through woods from what could scarcely be called a country road. At that time, the roads were shifty sand, so loose that one drove with the anxiety of becoming stuck. Before gravel came to these roadways, horse and wagon, then Model-Ts were the most reliable means of transportation. We made the venture in my father's 1936 Terraplane. As we passed through the last thicket, there appeared the most pristine lake I had yet seen. Unlike the lakes I was acquainted with in Indiana, no cottages ringed the shore of this sequestered pond of a few acres, only reeds and sandy banks. On a grassy slope, under a cluster of hardwood trees, these two fishing buddies, co-workers at our town's newspaper, pitched a canvas umbrella tent and, like pioneers of old, settled in. I thought my rite of manhood was before me, but crushingly it was not to be.

I was sent back to the women of the tribe. There, for a day or two, I sulked, bitterly lamenting my fate. Finally, I could bear the disgrace no longer. So, I defiantly announced to my grandmother that I was going to walk to where my father was. Given that the lake was three or four miles distant and I had been there only once, I do not think my grandmother quite took me seriously, construing my words for grumbling. Yet, off I embarked into the wilds. Not only did I follow a naturally endowed keen sense of direction, I even cut across the diagonals to save distance and time. The day was warm and the sun shone down unrelentingly, making the sand rather scorching to the feet. But I pressed on, undeterred. Finally, I arrived at the "unpromised" land, the idyll of a lake. My father and friend were somewhat taken aback to see me. While my father's words were in stern rebuke, I choose to believe a glint of admiration shone in his eyes. I had created my own rite of passage and had passed the test. Still, back I was taken, to a troubled grandmother, who probably never forgave me for the fright. She must have had some vision of bears and a lost grandchild. As self-confident persons are wont to proclaim, "I was not lost. I knew all the time where I was!" Blessed with a strong sense of direction from the beginning, I have pressed forward with my way throughout life and with this learned that dearer than the destination is the enduring emotional bond. Wherever I access the myth of the North Woods, I am in the heart of my father, he in mine.

Each myth has its empowering rite; every venture onto sacred ground has its finely prescribed ritual. My people of the North Woods retained a vestige of what might be regarded as a Rite of Redemption, a ceremony in which the totem is sacrificed and a feast of communion is held. By it, season after season, dependency upon Nature was proclaimed and freedom from want was celebrated. A remnant of ancient nature worship continued to stir in their blood. The main prescribed rituals were hunting and fishing.

While the two cultic observances intermingled and were personality preference dependent, the further into the North Country one went, the stronger hunting's confessional call. My great-uncle and family lived furthest north and, in that remoteness, the Faith of the Hunt was well professed. His brother, my grandfather, had been brought up under the Hunter's Creed; one of his early photos bearing his manly figure was one of a hunter dressed in outfit and holding a gun. Each visit was an immersion into the myth. By an early age I had already tasted of deer, bear, porcupine, squirrel, and opossum meat. My ears tingled with delight over the tales and my curiosity thirsted for initiation.

One fall, my senior year in high school, after the end of the football season, I went north with my uncle to be initiated into the fraternity of deer hunting. It would not be full membership, for I was without the prerequisite gun and investiture of outfit. Yet, I would know of the experience vicariously, like some war correspondent. We, my cousin and I, arose before dawn and, following the customary breakfast of all hunters—scrapple, eggs, and fried potatoes, entered the forest. For what seemed an interminable suspension of time, we crouched in our blind, peering into the growing light of morning. After several shifts of location, the day pressing on toward noon with no sightings, we reluctantly prepared to leave the "unhappy" hunting grounds.

As we were walking stealthily and yet still a little hopeful, my cousin, with ears and eyes sharper than mine, heard a rustle down the rustic path and saw a movement in the undergrowth. By instinct honed from youth he swiftly raised his rifle and a loud report resounded throughout the woods. The deer, a young buck, fell with a crash to the ground, turning over several times as it did. We approached cautiously, for the stiletto sharpness of a wounded deer's hooves was legendary. It was soon discovered the "kill" was accomplished quickly, my cousin's skillful shot having struck near the heart above the front flank. The sacrificial deed was somewhat merciful, for the animal has some time earlier been shot through the rear flank, the 30-caliber bullet exiting with horrifying rending of flesh. My cousin muttered something about how unqualified hunters from the city should be kept out of the forest. I took that to mean a faithless unbeliever in the myth. But, we had our meat for the tribal meal and I gained personal knowledge of the ritual. I never went hunting again. Still, ever after I understood my people, those of the North Land.

My father was never to become the hunter. That may be due to a more genteel, quiet disposition or because he chose to become the consummate angler. As far as I could tell, he had no difficulty in eating red meat. It seemed more a matter of preference and style. The skill and savvy with which my father fished still leaves me in awe. His sense of what fish were "thinking" was uncanny. When I first remember tagging along behind him, it was "fish worms and bobbers" with pan fish mainly in mind. That was eventually elevated to the casting rod and the trout, in its multiplicity of species and streams. It was very like my father to perfect whatever he undertook and understood, and trout fishing was invented for the aristocracy of anglers. No sloppy-minded, bumbling dullard need apply. In contrast, the artistic streak in my father came through, whether in the poise of his cast or the incredible intricacy of the flies he tied. My elder was an accomplished fisherman, in all the various ways one can fish. Although he tried deep sea fishing several times, it never became an attraction. Maybe it was partially because of accessibility, but I suspect it was more a lack of proximity to his beloved woods.

Memories of fishing with my father center on three vivid vignettes. When I was about ten, on a last cast in a nearby lake he caught a 32-inch Northern Pike, a lanky creature with a terrifyingly sharp set of teeth, not too far removed from the age of the dinosaurs. A picture was taken of me holding this monstrous catch, the fish extending from my face to the floor. Next, I remember my father and fishing from the one-week vacations we took in the nineteen-forties at a rented Stone Lake cottage. Usually he worked during the days, but out onto the lake we would go evenings, thrilled at the thought of "seeing whether the fish were biting." We dabbled in such arcane science as why, and why not—whether the phases of the moon influenced the habits of underwater life or how much does the overcast of the sun dispose the fish not to bite?

I learned the highly developed etiquette of inquiring as to the number of fish caught by the boat we passed, without jealousy or gloating. Through it all was the absolute edict: "Don't bang on the boat and always speak in a soft voice so you don't scare the fish!" All the more did this constrained behavior add to the solemnity, in due respect of the momentous undertaking. I was in admiration of my father's prowess in conducting the ritual. A reverence befitting an officiating priest prevailed. I may indulge in the hyperbolic, but I write through the revering eyes of boyhood.

The third indelible impression left by my father's dedication to the art of fishing came in July of 1965, when he, my brother Fritz and I took a pilgrimage to the crystal clear streams of the Colorado Rockies, there privileged to fly-fish in the fabled East River of the Gunnison. Though we did not remove our necessary waders, we were on high holy ground. I do not recall the exact number of fish drawn from these icy mountain streams, or by whom, but we did have ample number in our creels for the awaiting skillet. The week glistens in memory as sparkling as the streams themselves, this time when the three Clemens men visited fishing heaven. If anyone deserved entrance, it was our father, for his endless devotion and unblemished sincerity in carrying out the enactment of the totemic rite.

I never really picked up the habit of the fisherman myself. That was left to my brother, who, in his own "rite," became as accomplished and adept a fisherman as our father. Over time I have caught my fill of fish, but always in the company of someone else. I never go fishing by myself. My fishing is more for thoughts in the stream of consciousness. I do, however, feel some obligation to take willing grandchildren fishing upon the river at my cottage, so that I may tell them the legendary tales told to and coming down through me. And I would eagerly jump at the drop of a fly hat, were my father here beckoning me to take up the lure again. I know that our father is with my brother whenever he ventures forth to re-enact the holy rite. The holiness comes not in the success, or failure, of the catch itself, but in the awareness of union. When my father fished, he was at one with the natural world, connected to a source of solace and revitalization.

My esteemed father taught me to love the woods and all things in it. He would accept almost any good excuse to stroll through the woods. Being of a provider mind, nothing delighted him more than to hunt and gather nuts and mushrooms. He would go to great lengths to locate the best yielding trees, to remove the husks after gathering and to crack the shells in order to extract meticulously the meat of the nut. These extractions usually ended up in the sweet batter of cookies. But nothing raised his learned sophistication higher than his dedication to identifying and preparing mushrooms for the communal meal. He became a self-taught aficionado of fungi, to the extent of learning their Latin names and consulting with well-known experts. We knew them by their common names—Sponge, Cauliflower, Chicken-of-the-Woods, Ink-Caps—and devoured the delicious morsels with relish, that is, floured and fried in butter, overseen by the attentive eye of our mother.

Our eager ingestion relied upon our father's expertise in knowing what was not to be eaten. Of all the mushrooms of the woods, none was so life threatening as the amanita muscaria, or any so intriguing. This was the "Death Angel," beautiful to behold and deadly to consume, except in very small quantities. Native Americans would ceremoniously use its carefully prepared substance so as to produce a hallucinogenic effect. The first time we discovered one such species my father's voice took on a rather somber tone. As he pointed out the veils beneath the cap and over the bulb, I felt a mild dread. I drew back, thinking the very breathing of it would put me into a swoon. To this day, I believe I would have no difficulty in spotting this deadly white member of the mushroom family.

My father's system of general identification included gill, bulb, and spoor examination, the latter to be conducted overnight, the cap being placed upon a sheet of paper. Never was it "pure" science for my father. Only the beauty of nature is pure. His devotion to the mushroom was merely one of several foci to his appreciation of God's magnificent creation. Without being philosophical about it, he somehow communicated to me that beauty is in the detail and the grandest of beauties is the culmination of reverent meditation upon the smallest wonder.

Possibly nothing better illustrates this than his adoration of wood and the trees from which the wood came. How he doted over wood! The grain, the touch, the utility, all were therapeutic rapture for him. He made things out of wood, but it was in the touch of the making that the heart of the matter was entered. He especially found a high calling and great joy in the art of turning and carving. No wood gave him greater joy than that of the aristocratic walnut tree, its warm brown, tight grain a nobility to behold. No log or branch of walnut would go orphan. There would always be a spot in the basement for it. It was as though in working with this totem an intimate relationship was established. His artist's eye gave to the wood its form; the wood then became the substance of his own nature. Over such there should be blessing!

Ah, trees, if spirits did not dwell in them, certainly they could be spoken to and protected. In trees is also companionship. I believe it must have been from my father I wordlessly gained the principle: Everything has a right to exist, unless you can find a pretty darn good reason otherwise. This clearly applied to trees. When he built his house in the woods, he even altered the location of the foundation to accommodate an old dogwood tree. He just could not cut down that tree. I think a whole lot of his great love of trees was to be found in that one gesture. It would have killed something in him, to kill it. Further, the grand old dogwood was an unspoken gift to my mother, who was especially fond of its spring beauty. When it did die a natural death, I detected real remorse in his heart.

Nature has always been a haven and a sanctuary for me. In earlier years the technological accomplishments of civilization had a powerful grasp on my admiration. I was irresistibly drawn to those hubs of energy, those hubbubs of activity represented by urbanization, whether our own "downtown" or the city of Chicago where my grandfather lived. In this metropolis were the great achievements of culture, on display in captivating museums, with the epitome of modernity in evidence throughout the life of the city. And I was a willing recipient of my culture and its ebullient spirit of progress. This was my external, outgoing self, the child who wished to partake as fully as possible in the larger human experience. Nothing human was alien to me. I thirsted after it all.

With the passage of time, however, a degree of disillusionment and a weariness with social engagement has set in, an increased aversion to the noise and congestion of the city. More and more, I repair to the sanctuary of Nature. This is my introspective, introverted self calling. Always a bit shy and ever a little self-conscious, when the focus of attention is upon me in a public gathering, I await the moment of withdrawal. It is not as though I feel rejected or unaccepted. But it is not from large social encounters that I derive my sense of belonging. My spiritual home is in Nature. What was supposedly my spiritual home, the church sanctuary, always left me feeling rather unacceptable. In contrast, all of my Walks in the Woods have bestowed upon me a perfect peace of acceptance. I do not need to apologize or explain, seek forgiveness or make sacrifice. I am quite all right, just as I am. This produces a great surge of confidence. A rejoicing raises my spirits, in the gladness of being in friendly territory, no questions asked. I have never felt a fear of Nature. In spite of grizzly stories of bears and a ready aversion to snakes, I can honestly say, I have always felt at home in Nature. The wonton destructiveness of humans detached from Nature frightens me far more than thunder or tornadoes. Nature has been good to me. Respect requires that I be good to Nature.

I know where from my love of Nature comes. It is from my father. Whenever I take a walk in the woods, I am in the shrine of my father. There I am in communion with him. This is written in tribute to his gift to me. I have given the legacy an amplified version, but I know its source. My father's endowment to me is an affinity to Nature, for which I am deeply indebted.

Meeting Death in Every Vein, at Every Turn

(2003)

Aging brings thoughts of death and a revised perspective of life. Neither to be denied nor fixated upon, the inescapable reality of death can draw a clearer picture of life.

A Preface Before All Ending

Not to be reluctant in going directly to the point, allow me to make an introduction to an ending. Grimly put, *life is the play and death is the finale.* All else must be arranged in those terms.

I do not mean to say life is no more than death. On the contrary, life is abundant and death is sparse. And the sum total of what one life represents is far greater than what death can abrogate. In speaking of the twin motifs, I will strive for accuracy and balance. The two must not distract from one another. Life can descend into morbidity, just as frivolity will deny death. I seek alternatives to the extremes. Life must not fear death and a vain love of life will not lead to contentment. Thanatos is surpassed in the seed Eros plants, and in that act the urge is toward life. The arousal of life's passion dispels the shrouds of death. But the body, in time, will dissipate into dust, regardless of love's undeniable dream. For its own edification, Life must converse with Death.

If one lives long enough, there will be a lot of thought about death. Youth has heard about death, maybe even has witnessed death at first hand. But it is not until the larger part of life has passed, that the thought of death becomes a constant companion. Some days the contemplation of death numbs the passion for life, like some Novocain injected into the emotional stream. Most days are, however, served simply by thoughts of one's mortality, a wake-up call to an appreciation of life, down to the finest details. Once fear is taken from the meeting of the formidable specter, Death can be a wise counsel and dying a supreme act of worship. Death is the enemy only if we make it so.

As to the "in every vein, at every turn," I mean to stress the physical and psychological effects of aging. Aging does not begin as a mere concept. Senescence is something which happens to you, in muscle and bone, slowly rising up to take hold upon how life is viewed. Only messages from the body give content to the concept. And the concept is not separable from natural death, unless premature death is but the terminus of aging. The process can result in a glorification or a damnation, a hymn or a curse. My intention is to praise life, not diminish it. For all the murmuring, I trust you will hear a higher, clearer voice, reaching upwards into the highest vaulting of the spirit's cathedral. While the body is engaged in a downward pull, the angels of our ascending enable us to bear the suffering of our aging. The spirit is as a kite. If in our youth we devote the energy of our body to lifting the spirit, legs swiftly running, arms ardently pulling, in old age the spirit flying high in splendor will uphold the failing body. The furthest thing from my intentions is to add to the dark tones of cynicism and the crushing weight of pessimism. Life is real, life is earnest. And, while there may be a grave, we are not destined for spiritual perdition. Life is a talent and must not be squandered, especially in the face of death.

This writing is far from an instruction booklet on how to die, though it does make personal resolution on how to preserve dignity to the end. In that we alone live our unique life, no one can die our death, nor we theirs. Some will choose the standard package, rites administered by others. The rare and few, more possessed by the one-time, unprecedented gift of their life, feel compelled to compose the program of their own memorial. So, this booklet. These pages are a testimonial to my own confronting of aging and death, not advice irrespective of others. The self-indulgence of the reflections has opened my humanity, however, to the condition we all hold in common. For all shall die. The only question is, how! My choice is in full awareness and unreserved appreciation of life.

At this stage of my life, the essence of my existence can be described with these words: Never has the taste of sentimental memory been so sweet; never have I had less time to live.

THE RAPPING, TAPPING OF TIME

Each nightfall,
> every New Year's Eve,
>> the death of a parent,
>>> the birth of a grandchild
>>>> is a somber note struck on an ominous bell.

Each toll is a number
> on the clock of existence.

The hand sweeps onward
> past number after number.
>> The sand is sucked with dreadful force
>>> through the gaping opening of Life's hourglass.

If only we can catch
> a few moments of eternity
>> before all is through.

The experience of life is a stream; aging is the staccato of losses. Back and forth, between the exuberance of life and the awareness of death, swings the pendulum. Youth accents the upbeat, age pauses a bit longer on the down. Whether the reminder of mortality be from a Raven or the messages the body regularly emits, the ticking of the clock goes steadily on. In the silent chambers of meditation the rhythmic sound is clearly heard. When detached from life's merry song, the measure of time will reduce to a funereal cadence. And, if the golden grains of Life's hourglass are not grasped with ecstasy, the meaning of our days flattens unto shallowness. In the absorbing of losses and the greater embrace of life is discovered meaning unto death sufficiency.

Youth is on the outward bound, taking in with little attentive to loss. Yet, death made early claim upon my marveling at life. Ever has there been eeriness within the somberness of death. That strangeness always produced the deepest thoughts about life's miracle. Every immersion into the strangeness was followed by expanded awareness. Even more than by the fascination of geography did my world grow larger through the ultimacy death forced upon me. Out of these excursions into the mystery of life and death arose an unlimited transcendental realm, wherein all that I was to gather from life, the entire human experience, was in perpetuity deposited. What the loss of time and death were to take away was more than compensated for by what transfigured in consciousness. I did not need to be given the scriptural admonition, "Lay up your treasures in Heaven." I was already practicing the principle.

Learning to Say Goodbye

No sooner than we truly learn to live,
we must honestly learn to die.

Anxiously in youth & made my beginnings; joyously I made my journey's way. Along the path many greetings were given and many goodbyes made. The goodbyes were softened by the confidence that, with each goodbye life brings a new greeting. Life empties, in order to be filled. After the grief of loss comes the solace of life's next gift. But at the end of the road, all beginnings will be behind me. Then, one must face the goodbyes of all goodbyes. Just how does one go about doing that? No matter how long you live, you have no precedent for your own death, no practice in goodbye. You have only others' deaths to draw upon. Some persons speak of "near-death" experience, but that is not even a good dress rehearsal, only a good reminder of how precious life is. Parents give life and later may give an example of how to die. Still, in the end we are on our own. It is ours to work on, life's greatest project. As with all of my life, I want it to be a work of art. In my death, may I teach my children how to die, just as in life I have demonstrated how to live.

Many times I have contemplated what my last moments of life might be like and how I will try to receive them. Not gladly, I suppose, yet gracefully. Though I would like for my ending to be as memorable for others as the final scene in a movie's idealized version, most likely it will have the urgency of an emergency room, offering little opportunity for eloquent soliloquies. Any memorized "famous last words" would, in all probability, be garbled or mumbled. With these odds against me, I have resolved to formulate in writing my goodbye and to imagine a fitting scenario. It disturbs me only a little—well, quite a lot, to be honest—that my actual last breaths shall be lacking in grace and the desired exchange with loved ones. For I have enshrined my goodbyes in this booklet, as well as in other writings, and I have already filmed the majesty of my demise in my imagination. For the past ten to twenty years I have said goodbye with each beautiful sunset, a sigh of awe and a whisper of reverence. I have tried to stay in good practice. The point being, I am not waiting until the last moment.

As a high standard for the imaginary filming of my end, I have in mind two actual movies, both idealized renditions. The brilliant Swedish film director, Ingmar Bergman, after all his black and white classics, produced a color film about the early Scandinavian settlement of Wisconsin, *The Immigrants*. In it, an adventurous brother goes off to the gold fields, only to return mortally poisoned by toxic waters consumed. The homecoming passes into autumn and on the day he knows he will die, into the depths of the woods he takes his weakening body and lies down, next to a flowing stream. There, he gives himself over into the arms of death, as golden leaves flutter down in the dimming light of day. That is true euthanasia. The second scene of life's passing—I choose to believe closer to my own—is from a movie on the life and death of Frederick Delius. This lyric nature composer in his music transports me more readily to fairer worlds that any other. Nature is in its fullest, sweetest blossoming and Delius lies dying. His spirit passes peacefully from him, as he lies on a couch in his dwelling. The windows and French doors are open to a verdant English garden. Into it goes his lover, returning with a bouquet of freshly picked flowers. Gently she lays this symbol of beauty upon his stilled bosom, in perfect eulogy. Delius died in his seventy-seventh year, an age I am nearing, his life span overlapping my birth by one year. This is especially meaningful to me, for he is possibly my favorite composer. I need not worry about how the actual final act of my life turns out, for I have already played the part, in the idyllic world of imagination.

That one must die at all is a very strange thought. This comes not from egocentricity. It is in the very nature of consciousness. Consciousness, once in existence, cannot conceive of its nonexistence. So, what are we saying goodbye to? I refuse to close the door, through some nihilistic conclusion. But, what happens to the soul, when it is required by death to say goodbye?

I can well understand the persistent belief in the survival of consciousness trans-death, whether it is called the immortality of the soul or eternal life. It is nearly incomprehensible, that all which represents consciousness, after a long life of experiencing, should be extinguished in the flash of a moment. Consciousness, as we experience it, seems more of the spirit than of mere synapses and neurons. How can these delicate intimations of "something more" be entirely obliterated, be subject to the limitations of time and space? Do I have the right to hope for a wakening after death, in a bright and shining world of love? While I know how this belief has served as a denial of death, I shall not deny it. For, I, too, have that hope born in me.

Irrespective of what survives death, if anything, the more pertinent question is: *How does the quality of our living affect the terms of accepting death?* One would think it easier to accept death, if life is meager and paltry. However, I do believe there is an inverse relation between following your bliss and not being able to say goodbye. If we have been faithful to life and to that which bestows bliss, at death we are strong enough to prepare for death with the poise saints are said to possess. Death denial is both a resistance to annihilation and the disappointment of not having lived as one ought to have. To achieve bliss, you must break from the restraints which deny you and live true to the wisdom life will give. If you do not acknowledge death, you cannot say goodbye. Denial does not have the power, or courage, to say goodbye. The two, living and saying goodbye, are intimately related, one not divisible from the other.

The belief that as you live, so shall you die, is a pure act of faith, a hope springing from the soul. I have nothing reliable to go upon. I have not heard from the dead, so as to verify or falsify the belief. For all I know, the bargain may be in reverse: Until the soul curses life, it is not ready to be turned over to death. However, I will not believe that for a minute, for my soul reviles against it, as the vilest of profanities, the greatest of apostasies, the ultimate offense against the gift of life. I must believe the most peaceful death comes by blessing life—that which has been and which shall remain. I will live this, 'til death does take away all manner of belief. This I do know, my belief enhances the quality of my living.

Death can take care of itself. Of this I am convinced. The most peaceful death is to bless life. To bless each day has become my principal form of daily devotion, along with reverence toward all life therein. As in life, so do I hope it to be in death. More than a quarter of a century ago, I wrote, *"To My Children, My Loved Ones When I Die."*

> *I must now say goodbye to you and to life.*
>
> *I am sad to go, but not with regret. I have lived life well, with kindness and a worship of life's goodness. There are many things I would like to have done, many deeds undone, desires unfulfilled, journeys not undertaken. Yet, I have tried to live fully, to prize the worth of each day, the smile of friendship, the hand of tenderness.*
>
> *My great consolation is that life—vibrantly pulsating and powerfully desiring—shall go on. I am not a selfish person, and though I have rejoiced in the possession of these great gifts of life, I do not begrudge your possession of them. This shall be my joy, that you go on beholding the beauty of each day and feeling the completeness of love, the pleasure of being alive. So, I pass on to you this life.*
>
> *Look upon the world with the same keenness and appreciation as I have. Meet and embrace one another with the same generosity and compassion of heart as I have desired. And love it all, glory in it. Do not fear or resist the great rhapsody of life which comes from living fully, enormously.*
>
> *In this, you shall fulfill my wish for your life, my blessing upon you. In your living I shall live. And when it comes time for you also to pass from life, give what I have given you. By this means we shall all live forever.*   *—1/13/78*

The goodbye, however, is not only to loved ones. In the end, at death, the blessing is to Life and the Self, the primal lovers. We die alone, in solitude, but replete with life! So shall be my Swan Song.

> *The important thing is to be able*
>   *to write and to sing one's song to life.*
> *Before one dies,*
>   *to sing lustily from the soul!*

Even more important than the lover
becomes the song.
Once it was for the lover
that the song was sung,
the passionate embrace
the longing of the song.
But, then, with the fleeting, stealing away of life,
the song is to life itself.
For, is it not in the end,
life which we love supremely?
It was life that gave us the divine breath
to sing to the Universal.

11/27/78

When I die they will bury a very large heart. In life, many dear souls became inseparable from my soul. I will leave the spirit of me, my great love of life, with those who still live. But I shall take those in my heart with me, as I go into that mysterious realm beyond. You will not need to mourn my death for long. Throughout life I grieved it sufficiently; little more is left to be done.

The soul sown among the flowers
will resurrect with each Spring.

The Impossibilities of Relationship: Love and Its Opposite

(2003)

Having discovered in the course of living that not everything called "love" is love, in this booklet I delineate the abuse coming from its misrepresentation. The object is not to lessen the importance of love in our relationships; rather, it is to free its power to transform. After reviewing the impossibilities of love in relationship, I conclude with a tribute to love.

A HYMN OF BENEDICTION: I Still Believe in Love

The word, benediction, comes from the Latin, meaning a well-spoken word. That is a blessing. My blessing comes from the heart of love.

I know that love is possible, for I have abundantly experienced love. I have received love; I have given love; I have been fulfilled by love. Therefore, I believe in love. I am secure in the faith that love will abide as long as I shall live, and beyond. Love has been the sustaining power of my being.

Scarcity of love has not been the problem. I have more love than I know what to do with. The "rub" comes in the giving to love the limitations of relationship. The incompletion of our lives is that the completion we seek in relationship is never full. We are given one another to love, yet the love remains greater than all the relationships of our lives. I have needed an entire world to accommodate all the love I feel.

Love arises from the fullness of the soul. When the soul is full of Life, love overflows. It is the most natural occurrence in creation. Love may not be all you need, but without love all else remains empty of its meaning. Love is from the fountain of the soul's contentment. When love is flowing from me, I know my soul is well.

I still believe in love. It is my hymn to life.

A Provisional Philosophy of Knowing and Being

(2004)

Being the mild skeptic that I am, I have been extremely cautious of excessive claims of certainty. Thus the "provisional." One of my longer writings, sixty pages, the booklet is a revision of my philosophical studies based upon a life of reflection.

A Prolegomenon to Whatever Follows

From the start, a warning. Beware all fixed world defenders. I am an iconoclast. Not because I like to break things up; rather, because I like to seek for new points of view. I highly suspect there is a blindness in seeing life through only one template. Thus, I believe in multiple models of seeing. That is to say, I am constitutionally opposed to "one-wayism."

This explains much about my philosophical and religious history. Nothing more annoys me than arbitrary absolutism and all absolutism appears to me to be highly arbitrary. Absolutism begs multiple questions and overlooks alternate possibilities. Thus, I have been very faithful in challenging conventional ideas.

As certain as it is that pigs cannot fly, what it means to me to be "pig-headed" is to see a question from only one point-of-view. This includes most conventional thinking. No more than not wanting to break things do I wish to be oppositional—at least with persons. What I oppose is the demand that I see life in only one way.

I do not understand people who do hold "one-way solutions," though I have psychoanalyzed them. I mean, I understand them in terms of my own experience. In almost a dread, I hold them in contempt of life. What conservatives have in common is what I constitutionally revile against, a fixed way of seeing life. At times, they seem incorrigibly intractable, even distorted examples of what humans are to be.

My style is much freer, playful in curiosity and humble in making claims. Absolutists make for good bullies, willing to punish you "for your own good." I am the one to open the exit to closed-in-thought, through troublesome questions and alternate modes of viewing. That is why I love and exalt metaphor, for its power of new perception. Give me one ounce of metaphor and I will give you all the truth tradition has preached to me. Spare me the artful dodge of the indubitable and the smug certainty of true believers.

I put forward a "provisional" philosophy. Not that I cannot make up my mind. The reasons are philosophical, derived from an ethical principle: No philosophy is to be rendered useless through deification. Life is to be in the nature of a conversation, consisting of much reflection and endless exchange. To finalize thought is tantamount to cutting off the conversation and playing God. If a person wishes to make absolutistic claims about truth, he should have the decency to up and die promptly after the pronouncement. Such truth ought be buried in memorial and sent along with its maker. Why obstruct the work of philosophy with dead gods lying around? Adamant and staunch adherence to set views obscures the horizon opening up before a responsive self.

A pragmatism adheres to my pursuit of philosophy. Just as a long journey calls for "provisions," so does life go better with reflection. However, "provisional" does not mean timidity or temporizing. The probing, questioning, deliberating disposition involved in philosophizing "provides" for relevant living. Those are the best of provisions, in order to avoid the pitfalls of mental rigidity. For good reason is the power of discernment in search for novelty of understanding. By continual revision is the mind in engagement with endless modification in the world. I agree with the noted American pragmatist, John Dewey, "Every thinker puts an apparently stable world in peril." Thought is subversive of the existing order, so that life can again be rendered new. Thought which does not turn in on itself (reflection) ossifies into inactivity (truth claim). Like a body without circulation, ideas without direct reference to experience undergo entropy, until, at last, they bear only dead weight. Ideas are tools for thought, not concrete blocks for system building. I hold to an instrumental interpretation of thought. That brings us to THE ROLE OF PHILOSOPHY: To keep us from becoming too comfortable with our ideas. An idea held too long ascends to a throne of unquestioned tyranny. To prevent thought from becoming despotism we must eternally question.

I know that I deliberately avoid categorical statement and final answers, for fear of being walled-in by my own mental construction. To set up the edifice of Truth, we cap the well of thought. But, the road of honest thought goes ever on. If life is a journey, thought and writing should be no more than reflections, musing, recording of awareness. When the traveler stops to erect a temple of proclaimed revelation, the mind is no longer on the path. Attention is taken away from what is coming into each day and preoccupied with a fetish. Life must go on. A temple to truth has no more life than a tomb. I see a definite tie between certitude and its demons: doubt, arrogance, and insecurity. The price for certainty is pretense and artificiality. "Truth" may be no more than a façade for protecting a sense of vulnerability. Honest thought combines courage with cogency.

Before entering into the main text of this provisional philosophy, it would be a mark of fairness to lay out my Core Axioms, REOCCURRING THEMES by which my thinking is directed. They are *philosophical biases*, not provable but valuable.

1. All contents of the mind are human constructs.
Ideas should be regarded respectfully, but only instrumentally.

2. There is no way out of the subjective predicament.
All truth and knowing is relative to the consciousness of the perceiver.

3. Ultimately, experience is the source of all understanding.
If merely borrowed, understanding is artificial, likely the product of unexamined assumptions.

4. All relational knowing comes intuitionally.
Only the mystical is metaphysical, the Sacred is not known by reason.

5. "Truth" is a function of words upon the quality of life.
Fixed thought has an encumbering effect upon life.

6. Empathy is morally superior to principle.
Care for life (nurture) is more important than "being right" (moral).

7. Dichotomies are only proper for comparison and contrast.

They become vicious when used by a moral absolutism.

8. Morality without aesthetics is puritanical.

Without appreciation for beauty, the goodness of life is held captive.

I am a philosopher of the old school, what has been referred to in more benign philosophical circles as the "Perennial Philosophy." Though my forte is not rote memorization, I have a keen mind and follow the line of inference quite readily. If Anne of Green Gables would choose to be smart over being beautiful, my choice is quickness of thought over mere retention. I have seen too many beautiful actors, whose heads are filled with lines, but whose replies to insightful observations are *non sequiturs*. For my part, I am an incorrigible ponderer, deliberating over this and then over that. Sometimes the thought process is leisurely, musing and reflective. But being also a mechanic of the mind, I often end up tinkering with ideas. Not so much to construct a system into a fortress, as to see how parts fit together. I have a strong sense of how this might be related to that. So, from contemplating to cogitating, from analyzing to synthesizing, without a doubt I am a philosopher. Unabashedly, I proclaim my inalienable right to think, rigorously and insistently. To ponder is my birthright and critical thinking is my wand of magic. Not being a social joiner, I do not seek membership in the Philosophical Academy. But my life has been a philosophical undertaking, no matter what credentials I bear.

To put it quite simply, the booklet is written *in testimony to my philosophical bent,* to show my friends what goes on in my mind when I think critically and conceptually. This will be one of my more "heady" writings, filled with discerning distinctions and abstruse features of relationships. By contrast, I do also have a very mystical side and have produced many writings out of pure intuitive awareness. In this booklet you will see more of my cognitive side, though I will move progressively back toward my "right brain." This philosophical discourse could be regarded as a rational justification of my intuitionism, an apologia. However, it remains important to me, to be articulate in the communication of how this intuition interacts with my reason, to create a particular and unique consciousness.

Humble Skepticism Engages the Fair Maiden of Intuition: A Marriage

Herein shall you find a culmination, presuming upon all stated previously, in order to draw together a philosophical position. Though I would like to believe each chapter is a piece in itself, able to be read with a sense of unity, this concluding chapter will not be intelligibly received without an appreciation of the preceding. Into one basket I toss the pieces, seeking tentative resolution. In that respect, we are engaged in a synthetic integration. While I have attempted to avoid repetition, it would do well to keep all the content in mind.

Ah, yes, a marriage. What do I mean by that? Well, "Let us not to the marriage of true minds be an impediment," if what is meant by that implies the obstacle of incompatibility. But the marriage of which I speak is really the harmonic integration of my own mind. Not until that joining occurs can there be found a comparable companion mind. Good philosophical company rests upon the obligation we have to ourselves. Without a faithful and honest relationship to our own minds, we cannot keep faith with the minds of others. Thus, let us approach with gladness the holy altar of philosophical matrimony. The marriage broker may well have been both paradox and conundrum. At a logical level, paradox is contradictory and conundrum a brain-knotting puzzle. The purpose of it all is to anesthetize the cognitive powers, so as to open up a deeper level of awareness. Do I hear a bridal procession? Kant limited reason to make room for faith. I laid aside stiff cognition, to receive the bride of intuition.

I intend no specific gender assignment, in spite of my analogue of marriage. Though I associate reason with my masculine side and intuition with my feminine, the point is in the unity, not the gender. The tale has been told of a youthful bout with the Archangel of Rationality. As best I recall, the humbling was not a defeat, but rather a chastisement. Arrogance was scoured, absolutism eschewed, and a fair-minded skepticism taken to heart.

Reason without limits is immature, essentially dishonest with itself, like a callow schoolboy. Waiting in betrothal was a lovelier sprite of my higher nature, a troth I could not deny, without betrayal of myself. Brother Reason was destined to meet and be absorbed into Sister Intuition, in order to form a more perfect union. I know from out a holy center within, into which only the purest impulses of the heart can enter, any other marriage would be infidelity. I vowed devotion to my inner guiding light, believing that the more my cognitive nature learned of its spouse, the greater it would understand its role in life. In union, reason and intuition, life reflections in the revealing light of a magical mirror, would come to "know" each other better than they knew themselves alone, thereby becoming helpmeets of one another. With this engagement I was prepared to rest confidently in anticipation of a philosophical state of bliss. Oh, I could have stood on other grounds, before another altar, adopted by one of the many historic philosophical schools. But I knew the children of the conjugal union would not be authentically my own. Only by marriage to myself could I stand upon my own two philosophical feet.

So, would the real Eugene Phillip Clemens, Ph.D., now please stand up! What philosophical stance, after all these years, does he assume? By what acquired title shall he be known? I shyly demure, "What is there in a name? How misleading and pretentious are titles." Yet, rising to the occasion, as humbly as my skepticism will permit, I shall announce my philosophical nomenclature. I am, provisionally, a Prudential Pragmatist, practicing an *Agnostic Analytic.* Yes, a Prudential Pragmatist! My *pragmatism* is made up of three ingredients: Empiricism, Deliberation, and Relevance. This, then, is qualified by *prudence,* meaning "being judicious" in matters of application. From this it follows, whether in deliberation or conclusion, all is to be regarded tentatively. I will analyze everything, piece by piece, yet with a certain agnostic reserve, never freezing thought in permanency.

Agnosticism is not lack of clarity and suspended final judgment is not the absence of decision. My agnosticism is a disposition, proactively open to listening to life and retroactively not absolutizing conclusions. Skepticism is the condition of thought's freedom, a declaration of independence. Paradoxically, it is thought finalized that stymies thinking. We think, only to think again. This agnosticism is not of the common garden variety. Possessed by all the rigor the analytical power of the mind is capable of, my agnosticism yields nothing in the way of unexamined assumptions. Thought, by nature, is fluid, and, though it can be congealed into paradigm snapshots of life, must not be ossified into certainty. When a stone, thought deadens itself. The vitality of thought has too often been entombed in the crypt of doctrinaire infallibility.

The greatest intellectual sin is asserting the indubitable. So exists an inherent tension between intellectualism and piety. My agnosticism does not deny a sense of the Sacred, but will not tolerate human thought "playing God," that is to say, making particular thought sacrosanct. As a matter of conviction, with a strong measure of mysticism mixed in, I regard such arrogance as an obstacle to an awareness of the Sacred. Above all intellectual virtues, I take my philosophical stand out of a sense of decency and self-esteem.

Put into practice, my philosophical operation takes the form of a Balancing Scale. Much of reflective thought consists in bumping into a question, for which there is more wonder than an answer. It is in this encounter that the thinking kicks into another gear, the counterpoising of possible considerations, factual and logical. To the balance of deliberation reason brings the weight of "evidence" (witnesses of empirical reality and testimonials of logical implication), pro and con. Witnesses are neither automatically denied seating by virtue of disagreement nor is testimonial excluded because of party affiliation. All is judged according to veracity and consistency. That necessarily involves the unveiling of ulterior motive and assessment of vested self-interest. Even tentative decisions should come after the exhaustion of inquiry and extensive deliberation. Rarely have I found prolonged deliberation concluding in irresolvable equilibrium, intellectual ambivalence, logical impasse. Progressively, the scale tips, toward one side or the other. The exigency of life often demands action, in lieu of protracted deliberation. But the human condition should ever be under its purview. Actions of impending moments must not become immovable precedents, forever binding. On the other hand, no decision of deliberation should be taken as other than prudential and tentative. Like thought, judging is a matter of a never-ending, ever-repeating obligation.

What is to be avoided is the dishonesty of "putting a thumb on one side of the scale," through preferential bias or constitutional prejudice. Here is where the true believer comes marching in, adamant in defense of Truth and God. "True belief" is inimical to my doing philosophy. I am astonished at the ease with which this type of personality offers up indubitable answers for questions of which they have little comprehension. Neither have they agonized through the emergence in thought of the question nor have they engaged in an honest, fair deliberation represented by the balancing scale.

Fundamentally, "true believers" are intellectual cheats. Just because they can state emphatically their absolute answers does not exonerate them. Their intellectual "game" is to "rig" the deliberative process to their ideological advantage, by introducing what they claim are indisputable truths, God's own. It is as though a player enters a game and audaciously claims to have a trump card not dealt. The presumption to prerogative is more than perplexing. It is downright preposterous. Morally or politically the true believer's leading perennial trick is to fixate upon one particular to distract from consideration of obvious pertinent knowledge, a tactic of diversion. Screening reality through a tightly controlled set of preconceptions, true belief resorts to generalities, vague references, and unqualified rhetoric, in pretense of actual thought.

Reason disinterestedly deals the deck of evidence, adjudging the weight of each datum and placing all in its respective place on the continuum of deliberation. Intuition watchfully attends to the teetering of the scale, continuously revising the question and its import. As with all venues of deliberative dialogue, the gain is as much in the process as in the product. To declare the product as Truth, is to sacrifice the benefits of the process. Truth is cheap, especially when declared by a "true believer" without regard to rigorous deliberation. It is no more than a frozen creation of the mind, missing the touch of finesse for life. In contrast, the benefit of the process is wisdom, a disposition, not a conclusion. Not only is it possible, but likely, that proclaimers of Truth lack the perspicacity of wisdom. Wisdom is the after-effect of careful and persistent deliberation, internalized as empathetic identification. The blessing of philosophical inquiry is not in what you know. Rather, it is in the way you understand your knowing. And that is wisdom. This brings us back to the title of this booklet, all made possible by the integration of the intellect's power to know and intuition's fine sensitivity to being. We reason, but we are wise, if and only if, we do our deliberative work well.

Thought is of reason, but wisdom is a personal grace. So were the creative seeds of the mind and quality of the soul joined in oneness. The wedding recessional was a hymn to Sophia, beloved fair maiden. I believe I would not be truly wise, had I not wed my feminine intuition in holy philosophical matrimony.

To Live Philosophically Happy Ever After: A Postlegomenon

As I conclude, a mild bemusement comes over me. It is not, "Vanity, vanity, all is vanity," though I smile at how vain (futile) all this may be. My good humor is in the darting thought that all I have been engaged in over all these pages is a re-writing of my master's thesis in philosophy. I have no intention of re-submitting it to the University of Pennsylvania for credit. The writing serves a far higher purpose, to put into the place of time a lifetime of philosophical musing. The road does not end here, yet I do not foresee another edition. I am content in the place to which I have come, knowing that each day will mix and mutate thought further. I would characterize this philosophical writing as a collection of bits and pieces, in residue of much thinking. In no way have I sought comprehensiveness. I have left much behind. These chapters are filled with what have been, for me, persuasive considerations, what I value and hold to, when it comes to philosophy. I would be reluctant to offer more.

Another thought captures my mind, "Everything we say is autobiographical." In looking back over the text, I am struck by how much the writing reveals the personal me. If the booklet serves no other purpose than to be a personal revelation, then I have accomplished the greatest goal of any thinker, self-awareness. In completing this writing I see more clearly the contours and movement of lifetime thought. By my example I fervently trust others will be encouraged to engage in the same exercise of self-reflection. In speaking about the world, we learn about the self.

In what lies before, I have made no attempts at objectivity or professional philosophical equivalency. The style has been ever so casual, with ready parenthetical inserts. Freely I admit to subjectivity, with little restraint of personal perspective. Consistent use of the first person was deliberate. This writing arose unapologetically out of me. It is my provisional philosophy! And, in that, I feel an accomplishment. I have not provided a neatly organized system of philosophy, to resemble the many ambitious tomes throughout the history of philosophical publication. Quite otherwise, efforts were taken to avoid the appearance of fixity or finality. Hopefully, tentativeness and reflection have carried thought throughout the booklet, curiosity refusing to land on the square of final conclusion. A subtitle could well have been, "Ruminations Without Certain Destination."

The text is loose and the thought sometimes rambling. Still, I trust the vagaries of the writing did not obscure what I believe to be an insistent following of a thought's inhering implication. I rather pride myself on being able to follow the leading of an idea, no matter how subtle it may be. I disavow discourse for abstruse sake, no matter how abstract my ruminations might be. Words are valuable for the power of their many possibilities and so I have used many words in a unique turn of the phrase. A word is not powerful because of its size or infrequency of use. Yet, erudition consists in a wealth of sophisticated words to expand thought. I may have sometimes stumbled in my use of words. But, thought reaching for expression will go to great length in finding the appropriate word, even if conventional use is stepped on. Choice is for expression, not impression. I think I must have been born for the reflective life and my writings surely reflect that nature. I possess a most serious bent of mind, but in fear of my words being nailed to a cross of literalism, I move slyly, laterally, ever on the protective edge of wittiness. That, too, accounts for my looseness and elusiveness. I do want my Being to evolve out of my modest claims to Knowing. I am a being in the process of knowing. Articulation is inseparable from the effort to understand, but the knowing must always remain tentative. Otherwise, I intellectually die.

Upon my retirement from teaching, a valued colleague, as young as my own children, bestowed upon me what I consider to be a supreme complement. "Without hyperbole, I can say that Gene is the most reflective person I have ever met." Though I would prefer to be thought of as a metaphorical poet, I believe she had it quite right, hyperbole aside, as I was born to wander and to wonder, to plod and ponder. Conundrums arise upon the way, but I have made them my friends, in the form of elucidating paradoxes. Thinking brings uncertainty, yet its perplexity is still capable of human resolution. I am privileged to be philosophically gifted and happy to cast my reflection upon each good day given me. Never shall I fully retire. I shall practice my forte until I die.

Myth: To the Fountain of Religious Experience

(2004)

Long a proponent of assigning religious language to the metaphorical, it follows that I should articulate myth as the appropriate container for the spiritual. Myth becomes the frame for the subjective experience of life, to be understood as valuable when treated other than objective fact.

To Myth, or Not to Myth, That is the Option

Myth has come into disrepute in the modern world. If not dismissed as primitive superstition, many minds of the enlightenment regard myth as little more than a fabrication of irrationality. In today's common usage, the nobility of this poor orphaned word has been relegated to a synonym for untruth. As in the use, "Oh, that's just an old myth!" Fearing religious fanaticism, the modern mind considers the exercise of myth as dangerous and the exorcise of its influence as the recovery of rationality. From this abuse I intend to extract myth and to re-establish its awareness as a royal road to profound insight. Not only is this path an option; rather, *the embrace of myth is essential to the authentic religious disposition.* Long live myth!

While I do not wish for my plea to be construed as a legitimization for the bizarre, a license for irresponsible truth claims, I will risk the charge of "mystification" from linguistic analysts, in behalf of spiritual consciousness. Now, there is a word for you, mystic, often lumped together with the mythic. I embrace them both, but on my own terms. A mystic, in my book, is not necessarily a wooly-headed non-thinker. As any intellect-respecting mystic will affirm, rationality is not sacrificed on the altar of the mythic, on the way to the heavenly realms of blind belief. Rather, the mythic is an alternate mode of relationship, not incompatible with the most acute edge of reason, unless a cantankerous person chooses to make it so. Just to illustrate the compatibility, it is precisely the intellect which in this writing deciphers the difference between the mythic and a mystic, only to bring them into concord. Either may conceptually, or in practice, exist in isolation from the other. Yet, understood in combination, the mythic power of the mystic increases. I use the terms in this manner. Myth is the vehicle and the mystic is the passenger. And, this traveler needs a highly developed intellect. Thus, pressing the matter further, we discover the choice is not exclusive. The question is better framed, "Shall we both myth and retain a respect for reason?" May I hope the response is a resounding affirmation? Be assured, you do not need to leave your mind behind, to follow the path of myth.

Taking up the discerning lens of intellect, on the road to a fuller appreciation of myth, may I further point out some of the unhappier notions floating around in our thoroughly modern scientific minds. Myth is not what divides us from the ancients, as in Greek mythology versus objective reporting, or biblical narrative in differentiation to archeological data. A regrettable attitude attaching to this delineation is the presumption that objectivity should, and will, progressively relegate myth to the dustbin of history, where it rightfully belongs. Under this misguided framing of the question, myth and reason, as well as religion and science, are pitted against one another in a zero-sum, inverse proportion relationship. The more of one, the less of the other. What can be explained scientifically depletes what myth has to offer. According to this, as science probes the universe, the mythic, therewith the sacred, is evicted, until the world loses any claim to our reverence. If this is followed consistently, would not the Sacred eventually be reduced to a relic of the past? To be told that science will never be able to explain everything is of slight consolation and misses the main point. Mythic consciousness is not merely the product of lazy thinking. Superstition is neither the author of myth, nor is blindness its affliction. The truth of the matter is this, to myth is to be human. In this context I might be so bold as to say, *Humans are myth-creating beings.* Or, "I myth; therefore, I am."

If our humanity depends upon value assignment, then myth is indispensable, for mythologizing is the very act of valuing. We cannot live meaningfully without creating myth. The alternative is ahuman, if not inhuman. Again, there is no option. The real choice is between embracing myth, while being honest about it, and repudiating myth, while making equivalent dishonest value assertions. Yet again, there is no choice, not at least a desirable one. Without myth there is no value since science cannot create value because it is itself a "value." Far better for honesty's sake is opening up myth to the inspection of the intellect, than to closet our principal value presuppositions and to posture "enlightened." Reason becomes myth's benefactor in that it can serve to ascertain the nature of myth's origin—malicious (pathological) or benevolent (affirmative) and to examine myth's consequence—destructive or life sustaining. We may not always live comfortably with the inherited myths, but we cannot live well without myth.

I push forth upon my voyage with this stroke of introductory statement: *Myth is an uniquely subjective manner of relating to and perceiving of the world, inner and outer.* While this is neither a definition nor an adequate single description, nevertheless, I put forward this observation at the beginning, believing that it will provide the best initial focus and establish the most natural direction for an unfolding of appreciation. Little good is accomplished in a comparative study of mythologies, if you are unable to detect and testify to myth's operation in your own experiencing of the world. This undertaking is not based upon an academic question, reserved for detached observation. Without subjectivity and direct participatory immersion, you will not locate the living, breathing presence of myth. Let us be clear, subjectivity is the gate to the mythic; otherwise, you are an outsider.

Allow me to expand upon this subjective, experiential opening by speaking variously of how myth works, including its aspects/dimensions/functions. To my delight, and hopefully yours, I have intentionally been free with imagery. Intuition, or the spiritual eye, relies heavily upon imagination. Intuition is set into flight by the play of imagination upon potent images. Without intuition, there is no entrance into myth.

1. The GROUND METAPHOR, by which we understand our relationship to the world and meaning is created.

2. A SACRAMENT, by which the life of the spirit is cultivated.

3. An ICON, by which a particular activity is given larger significance.

4. An EMOTIONAL TREASURE CHEST, in which we repose our most cherished sentimental possessions, secure from the adversities and contradictions of life.

5. A DOOR OF ENTRANCE, through which the longing for an ideal state of being may pass, into a fairer world of dreams.

Out of the necessity for survival, humans are creatures of habit. But it is out of a need for meaning we myth. Meaning does not just jump out in some moment of epiphany. The template of meaning is imposed upon the world by a relational power of intuition, an entirely subjective enterprise. Over time and repeated experiences the sense of meaning is synthesized into a unifying myth. The meaning necessary for purposeful existence comes not from reason. Reason can do remarkably well in sorting out and assembling information, but the meaning provided by value assignment originates elsewhere. The meaning rendering life tolerable arises from the symbolic interplay between our image-making psyche and the conditions of existence. This act of myth-creation rescues the world from arbitrariness and anomaly. More properly myth spares consciousness from the insanity of chaos, for myth is attributed to the world, not derived from it. Neither a priori (innately a product of consciousness) nor a posteriori (drawn from experience in the world), myth is relational, arising out of an interplay. Meaning is not created in abstraction; myth is an embracing of a value in this world, or the next ("otherworldliness"). Myth is the container of value and the vehicle bearing existential meaning.

The myth-making involved in meaning—and value-attribution does not generally end in a conscious **Ground Metaphor**. That is only a figure of speech, by which I choose to illustrate the function of myth. Our value universes usually are, at best, a loose collection of like-minded dispositions and attitudes. However, to give some degree of unity and consistency to the mix, we are likely to utilize a hierarchical principle, what I term the Ground Metaphor. This is what functionally is known as God. For orthodoxy this unifying ground is "God's Will."

Stoicism somewhat depersonalized the point of unity, yet still conceived of it as a Divine Mind, the Logos. For the "new science" of the Enlightenment, the abiding principle is "the uniformity of nature." The possibilities may not be endless, as beneath our moral/religious discourses are quite a variety of unifying principles. Scarcely aware of the differences, we wonder why we disagree "in principle," all the way from sexual mores to public policy. Conservatives and Liberals do have different Ground Metaphors. When a swashbuckling, absolutistic God becomes aware of dissent, he declares a Holy War. (You can readily identify this God. The swatch of his swash reads, "Thou shalt have no other Ground Metaphor before me!") The Ground Metaphor for apocalypticism is eternal vigilance in the ongoing battle against ontological evil. By their offspring shall you know them: Love creates its own myth, as do paranoia and brutality. In this light, might we not say, "Choose well your myth, for thereby shall you see?" In our mythic seeing we create reality.

Once a Ground Metaphor is adopted, ways are arranged by which to cultivate an ongoing relationship with the indwelling "spirit," be it a demon or an angel. A **sacrament** is defined as a channel of power, "a visible (outward) form of an invisible (inward) grace." The metaphor is the identification of the Sacred, the ultimate reference point, but the sacrament is the aspect of myth providing for daily communion. Means to partake of the myth's spirit on a regular basis advances its effectiveness and heightens conviction, a self-validating devotion. By consuming the inhering "body and blood" of the myth, we are empowered to live life, of whatever quality that may be. The myth not only defines reality, it decides the manner of living. Depending upon its indwelling spirit, myth can either enhance life or sell it down the River Styx, affirming the goodness of the created order or cursing life with the guilt of "original sin."

In a slightly altered function, now for the purpose of speculative diagramming of reality, the metaphor becomes an **icon**. As we gaze into the mystery of the icon, our day-to-day activities fit more acceptably into a scheme of meaning. Call it a map, a mandala, or a theology, focusing upon the icon apparently renders an individual life hopeful. One small existence finds its way into a larger pattern of significance. The oppressive, paralyzing threat of nonentity is put at bay. The hell of existential meaninglessness, prefiguring an afterlife of perdition, is counteracted by the icon's power to set everything in place, be it God's Will or Karma. Meager as it may be, we feel better when we know where we are.

Over the course of a lifetime, purposefully guided by the Ground Metaphor, the especially valued Gifts of Life are collected and drawn inward. Myth absorbs these treasures as precious jewels in a safety box. As indicated, myth serves several worthwhile functions, not the least providing a framework for meaning. But if myth is a container, its contents are emotionally charged. A point is to be made: Myth does not begin in superstition, rather it is supersaturated with sentiment. Sentiment is the lifeblood of the spirit and a functioning myth takes on the people, places, and times, to which sentiment is attached. Myth is an emotional repository, growing fuller and richer by the years. Unless shattered by disillusionment or numbed into dysfunction by trauma, the acquired myth will become its own self-generating state of wellbeing. Even if demented, detached, and deluded, myth provides a reason for being. That is the reason for its staying power, a mighty fortress against all dissuasion.

To attack a person's myth is nearly tantamount to assaulting the security system upon which their sense of selfhood and worth is based. Though those who most need to cleanse their myth of pathology are the very ones least open to the positive life force, therein lies the cure. The accumulated wealth of natural affection is an antidote against so much ailing us, a tonic and a restorative. Our vitality and our myth's viability rely heavily upon the Emotional Treasure Chest buried within myth, held precious by the most affirmative of instincts. What more suitable place to invest our enduring affections than myth?

A final feature of myth's utility is directly related to the soul's need for depth. Metaphorically, I speak of a **Door of Entrance**. The entrance is not into another time—past or future—as into an alternate dimension of the present. Some myths do concentrate purpose in the extension of the present into a future time, an "eternal life." But equally conducive to spirituality is the availability of the Eternal Present. The healthy soul thirsts for quality (intensity) as much as quantity (time), completion (fulfillment) more than salvation (redemption). Salvation is in enlargement, through an opening into a fuller realization of spirituality. This dimension is not separated from the ordinary world in either time or space. The two are coincident, parallel to one another. The extraordinary is to be superimposed upon the ordinary, transforming and elevating it. The separation is in the eye of the beholder.

The switch is with the mythic mode of perception. In a twinkling of an eye, a "fairer world" can be revealed to the desire for idyllic awareness. Like some French doors opening to view of a spacious garden, our living room can be flooded by mythic realms of exquisite beauty. Through this passageway flows life's essential goodness. Revelation comes in the bathing. This immersion in the mythic is the wellspring of authentic religious experience, from which the other four functions are drawn.

A Myth is as Good as a Smile

The thematic unity of this chapter shall be the nature and effect of myth-creating, the *what* and the *why*. The following chapter concerns the means of entering the mythic, the *how*. The two are in tandem; thus, each somewhat presupposes the other. Unavoidably, the thoughts will run together, somewhat mixing, then, going off on their own, not fully knowing which chapter to bed down in. It shall be fun, keeping up with the scampering. Proceed with a free, fanciful spirit.

We start with the effect, "a smile." One of the most desirable benefits of creating a personal myth is the good feeling induced, a euphoria. At the birthing and in the process a felicity attends. A smile is the signature of that state of well-being, a seal of approval. A smile can be forced, but this one breaks forth spontaneously. This state of well-being is good for us, for it allows the parts of the self to relax into place. I have explained myth-creation as an investment of meaning. The achievement of meaning is, in itself, a source of contentment, bringing complacency ("a feeling of quiet pleasure," in the sense of being in the right place). But "mything" goes even beyond that need for sense-making to a purer state of being. Natural states of wholeness do occur and mything is one of them. We are back to our nature as myth-creating beings. Something deep is revealed and fulfilled in the very act. I know of no better way to be "true to yourself," than to myth.

A darting thought has entered my mind, compelling a consideration short of a qualification. The euphoric effect comes from testimony to my own experience. For me, being in the mythic mode is "the land of smiles." But, maybe, certain requirements pertain. The first consideration coming to mind is, from where does the disposition arise? So, may we tentatively lay down this proviso? When the mythologizing is drawn from an affirmative, positive well within the soul, the certifying feeling is one of felicity. Creativity does involve the travail of intensity, yet throughout streams the joy of fulfillment.

In contrast to a myth springing from a life-affirming expression of a healthy soul are myths born of urges for revenge and vindication. These are self-creating hells, ultimately cursing the creator along with the enemy assigned to that hell. The ensuing paranoia reaps its own punishment, encased in the myth of its own perversity. *A myth is no better than the consciousness giving it origin.* Myths of white/male/cultural superiority, and all the values pertaining thereto, are products of an accursed soul. To be born into and to live out life through the distorted vision of such myths is a damnation of its own kind. As to the emotional effect of creating diabolical, negative myths, since I have been spared the misfortune, I can only conjecture, as an outsider. I would surmise the "satisfaction" to be akin to the "joy" in masochism, sadism, and mass murder.

Having dismissed the negativity of traditional religion, it will likely seem strange that I should associate mything with **worship.** However, that is what I propose. Worship, as bowing down in servile submission to a sovereign, righteous God, prayerfully begging forgiveness, is not the worship I have in mind. Such behavior is the figment and warped value peculiar to a patriarchal myth of reality. That, however, does not exhaust all the possibilities for a worshipful relationship with life. In my spiritual journey, post-patriarchal worship took me further and further into reverence. And, well-refined reverence brings the serenity of stillness, as close as we might be able to get to Nirvana.

But we can take worship even a step further. Beyond cajoling and importuning a judgmental God, prayer is a connectedness, a placing of the self in ultimate relationship. In this respect, *mything is a cosmic prayer.* And, that is an act of worship. In the very process of assembling and connecting to what we have affectionately embraced, we are worshipping. From that worship emerges our moral universe. Worship can be the product of very narrow provincial needs, the basis of idolatry, or it can reach to the stars. The further out we myth, the larger our soul. The larger the soul, the greater the divine consciousness. Mything and worshipping can be quite one and the same, extending upward into the heavens.

To summarize the point to which we have arrived, we myth because it is our nature to. And in fulfilling that nature we undergo shivers of ecstasy. We myth because it brings us closer to a reverential and worshipful relationship with life, thereby connecting the soul to its primordial roots. In consequence of this all, we smile, the inscrutable smile of the Enlightened One, the Buddha. So accomplished, now may we turn to the what we are doing when we myth.

Myth is *a qualitatively different way of perceiving, intimately connecting us to life*. It does not represent a different world, so much as a different relationship. In order to connect with the ground of our existence, awareness must undergo a subjectivity. This alteration is the essence of myth, the subjective participation in the world. Objectivity bars this relationship, stripping the "object" of all subjectivity. Good for science and the manipulation of the phenomenal world, objectivity deprives us of connectedness, in that it invalidates the glue of relationship, emotion and affectation.

Objectivity can "know" an object; objectivity cannot form an emotional relationship. Relationship is a bond, nonexistent without the subjective qualities of personhood. Laws of motion and thermodynamics, the theory of relativity, or subatomic analysis may explain natural occurrences, but they cannot provide a reason why we should care. That can come only from the intimacy of subjectivity. That is precisely what we are doing when we enter into mythic perception. We perceive the "other" as worthy, possessing a value for our life and the human community. Without the mythic we are without soul. By mything, through the power of intuition and the bond of affection, we realize belonging and overcome alienation. Thereupon, the mind and creative imagination can become one with the universe. Again, the close nexus between the mythic and mysticism.

With this being said, we bump into a conundrum of which came first, the perception or the relationship? Do we arrive at the mythic relationship by transforming our perception into the eyes of love? Or, is it in extending our emotional being into the world that we are empowered to myth? I would say both, but not so much alternatively as indivisibly and simultaneously. The two sides of mything progress jointly, though either side can be enhanced by acknowledgement and practice. The main point in practice is the realization that *mything involves imaginative transmission of our emotional selves into the world,* the very thing objectivity fears and is disposed to prevent. Within the jurisdiction of science this dedication is altogether commendable. But for the sake of meaning, value, belonging, and our psychological well-being, a boundary exists, beyond which objectivity must not go, if the heart desires to have eyes to see and ears to hear. That is the realm of the mythic, the "land of love and beauty."

A series of metaphors comes marching forth, in the attempt to understand what is going on, as we project imaginative affection upon the world. In order they come, *layers, lacquer, glossing, lamination, weaving.* And leave no doubt, as to what is being applied, the heart's affection. In mything we are in the process of transferring our emotional selves to the world. In doing so the world becomes compatible and hospitable, a "place" we are compelled to treat as a lover. Though we ought not bump into trees or drive off cliffs, reality is more than something to watch out for. Rather, the world is the canvas upon which we create our life's work of art. Intuition is the artist's eye; the brush is the deft stroke of imagination; the rich oils are of sentiment. Lo, and behold, after long years in life's natural studio, we discover we have created our very own personal myth.

Reality remains, but in the mything we have arrived at a super-reality. In so doing, we have lifted ourselves up into a transcendental realm, to encounter the core of our being. Others may not know of or understand this mythic extension of our self; still, it is our delight therein to dwell. The traditional myth of our upbringing may not approve of our personalized version, but no priest has the right to exorcise by the Name of God the myth of our own birthing. Once the personal myth comes into being, it is inseparable from the one who created it. To condemn my myth, you have violated me.

To show the painting of the myth in action, should we not start the camera? Lights of imagination, please! To the unsentimental eye, a rose is a rose is a rose. So, also, with a tree, a sky, a river, a mountain. But the mythologizing creation sees more, an ever-increasing superimposition of sentimental attachment. The emotional lacquering of objective reality may be an epiphany, implicit in the encounter, and/or a transfer of a "sealer" from an associated experience.

The appliqué need not be conscious of a specific prior emotional evocation, as much as a transfer of the euphoria. Take a tree. Decorate it with sentimental ornamentation, and what do you have? Not so much a botanical specimen, as like unto a sacred cultic object. A tree meets my eye, or should I say I encounter a tree. What transpires? The loveliness overcomes me. And mixed with that moment are many past moments of pleasure. I feel a joining with the lore of the North Woods and am swept away to distant tree encounters in national parks and in alpine meadows. I hear a melody, "On the Trail of the Lonesome Pine," and behold the colors of April green leaves and autumn gold. In this expanded association, the tree stands for the integrity and reliability of nature.

What happens in a mythic encounter with a tree can, and should, be the transforming experience with everything. It is a benediction upon the world, which, reflexively, blesses us. The consciousness emotionally opening to the world, opens wider the mythic lens. Fuller and fuller becomes the myth, until it encompasses all that is cherished. Thereupon comes the multiplication miracle of appreciation. The more we appreciate, the greater the depth and degree of appreciation. To see beauty in a flower is to set into motion an accelerating power to see beauty everywhere. Beauty may be "in the eye of the beholder," but it is a mythic eye that sees the beauty. If you permit your mythic eye to see beauty in anything, you have given yourself permission to behold beauty in everything. Allowing this to become a lifestyle of worship, in a remarkably short time your mythic painting shall draw in the entirety of the world. The frame of narrow perspective will fall aside and the picture will be all encompassing. Prejudice and fear cripple the mythic vision. Love sends it everywhere, on angel wings.

Trusting that I have not short cut the grand elaboration of mything, I rest my case here. I could have "drawn out" the picture further; still, has not the *what* become clearer? In taking up the *how*, the elaboration shall continue. It can be hoped that the *what* and the *how* will be instructive, as you proceed with your own personal myth.

On Entering the Mythic

The purpose of this chapter is to become more conscious of what it means to enter the mythic mode of perception. We might very well speak of this consciousness as a re-entry into the experience behind and beyond the old myths. The benefit in this venture hopefully will be a lessened certainty in having captured the divine, in exchange for *a conscious lived relationship with the mythic.* All people have a myth. I call you into the mythic, the source of all authentic myth. We concentrate on the how.

The entrance to the mythic may not be the "Pearly Gates" of old, but the passageway is as freeing as the view is magnificent. Simply, the magic wand is mythic intuition. The novice must guard against trying too hard, as well as not at all. You cannot stare forthrightly into the mythic realm and set upon a direct course to it. Too sharp a focus of reason perceives only concrete details. In the way of seeking to unlock the mythic, too much is a little as nothing. Only the key of intuition will fit the lock, *a soft, dreamy state of awareness, stretched to the limits of language.* The mythic moment comes out of the mist, from the periphery, just as its potent symbols are accessible only obliquely, through the intuitive reaches of desire. Life's mystery comes in at the fringes of consciousness; one cannot sit and gaze directly at eternity. I speak of a paradox. The core of the universe cannot be entered through the central opening of ordinary concentration. We must refer to special categories and resort to extraordinary perception.

To pass into the mythic, one has to go quite mad, breaking the boundaries of ordinary consciousness. It is thus a *"divine madness,"* upon which we ride into the domain of the mythic. This holy derangement allows consciousness to hear other voices, to see fanciful visions, as pathways into the hidden, secret self. Better that we dream awake, than that we slam the doors to our souls. Intuition induces a dream-like state of awareness and dreaming frees intuition from the limits of the ordinary. Of their own nature, all our prime symbols of worth lie in the vague intimations of the mythic, what we unfortunately call the "semi-conscious" state. The ego, fearing loss of control, dreads the dream-state nearly as much as death, the apparent extinction of the self. Until the ego is let go, the nether world of the mythic cannot be entered safely, where salvation awaits. Not trusting to intuition, the ego seeks to destroy the demons of its own darkness with the edge of the sword's brutality. Ego has no mythic eye of intuition, only projected fears and transference of insecurity. Unless the self is willing to shed the defenses of the ego and to internalize the eternal light of intuition, there is no entrance into the mythic. To the weak eye of concrete vision, the mythic is a land of shadows and danger. When guided by the light of the Spirit, the eye of intuition sees brightly the mythic depth to life. Let us then go mad, so that we can be well. Let us find our way home, through the shades, so that we can rejoin our true selves. The mythic is the path to Universal Union.

Once more, we pick up metaphor and the power of symbol. A sword will not open the gate; only the magic of metaphor will do that. Just as a myth is as good as a smile, so is the power of symbol better than the sharp edge of reason. Metaphor is the magic carpet upon which intuition rides. It is a "free ride," but intuition must not be a passive passenger. There are no priestly coattails upon which to ride into heaven. A "great boat" of indulgences and rote memory will not get you to mythic perception, only to the masses. (Forgive the terrible pun. The "great boat" is in reference to the broader path allowed for the laity in Buddhism.)

In my less charitable moments, I am inclined to say, the greater the number, the lesser the spiritual awareness. Lest I be accused of elitism, I clarify. While I regard all persons possessing, in varying degrees, the power of mythic intuition, because of preoccupation with concrete activity, or insecure compulsion for absolute certainty, a real appreciation of metaphor is quite limited among the general population. A direct correlation seems to pertain, between the need to believe with certainty and the reduction of symbol into hardened revelation. Regrettably, I believe I speak to a minority of religious interest. From my perspective, the real madness is in the treating of metaphor as fact, for in the world of fact there is no spirituality. Claims of absolute truth will shoot down the metaphorical bird of flight, which would lead us into the mythic origin of spiritual consciousness.

The power of metaphor is to be found in its elusive flight, at the boundary of ordinary meaning. More a tease than a messenger, metaphor "tricks" the mind into another mode of perceiving, intuition. (The object is to flip, or snap, the mind, as in Zen Buddhism's Enlightenment, Satori.)

If there is no intuition in place to receive and deliver the metaphor, the literal mind goes blank, becoming blinking eyes of disbelief. If it is true, that the entry into the mythic is at the fringes, in the periphery, then it would seem that holding symbol at the center of denotation would kill it. That is precisely my contention. Is it not also true, building a stairway to heaven from stone steps of literalism is nothing other than a Tower of Babel? Would it be so surprising that, when you arrive in such a paradise, streets of gold and almond-eyed virgins will be awaiting? No, if we are to pass from physical reality to spiritual consciousness, another vehicle must be chosen. The metaphor of oblique language is the ticket. To perform their magic, words must be freed from the hands of literalists, set loose from the stone fortresses of the religious establishment, and allowed to wing intuition to more distant horizons of sight. If we attempt to control metaphor, it will fall and perish through a tortured misuse. What epitaph will stony doctrine place upon its grave?

If not to build a tower of literal stone, how shall we launch the metaphorical flight of intuition into the mythic? Would not the best answer be to observe intuition in action? Let us take to flight, as active participants. To do this, I shall speak of *"springboards"* (ah, another metaphor). These are the propitious places and spaces for flight, Kitty Hawks of more far-reaching perception. (Well, parallel universes of infinite dimension, one of the body, the other of the soul.) These are the stories of epiphanies, revelations made possible by the power of intuition. Forgive me, if the accounts are not highly metaphorical, heavily symbolic. So, let us go on rides, giving testimonial to what happens when we trip into the mythic. This is an excursion into the heart of primordial religious experience.

Oh, the springboards, the launching pads, the jumping-off platforms to the mythic—I think I have been upon at least a thousand and one! Each day presents me with several. The opportunity is not the question. The determining factor is my disposition and response, whether I allow myself the time and freedom to activate my intuitive powers. Though my intuitive powers come naturally, anxiety and preoccupation short-circuit their operation. But, then, when the time is right and the place is auspicious, the space takes on sacredness. Without an intuitive spirit, there is no sacredness.

So many are the departure stations into the mythic that I feel a remorse in turning aside from any. In this writing I seek to pay tribute to them all. To do this, I condense a lifetime into simple narration and reduce the thousand and one to three: Cemeteries, *The Unity of History;* Cathedrals, *The Serenity of Spirit;* Castles, *The Joy of Living.* In disposition they represent "Being at One with Humanity," "Being at Peace with the Self," and "Being at Home with Life," respectively.

Cemeteries have always held for me an enormous presence. In this sacred place of repose I could imaginatively enter into past living. I was not among the dead, for I had resurrected the departed and walked among them. The skin was not decaying from their bones and their continence was not hideous. These progenitors were vibrant and vigorous, in an idealized existence, admittedly, yet very much alive. I remember, when old enough to ride my bicycle through the streets of our town, riding to the cemetery where the city founders were buried. As I walked through the rows of memorial stones, I recognized names from buildings on Main Street.

All of a sudden, with the magic of intuition, I felt I knew these dear people. I had really lived with them, gone through the agony and excitement of their times. Going home, through the business district and along the residential areas, I could see them strolling the sidewalks in clothing typical of their own time. Passing the park where my father's elementary school had once stood, I observed children of an earlier time at play, their distinct outlines now interred in the cemetery I had just visited. My childhood was headed for a future, yet always was I possessed by a heritage reaching far into the past.

What can be said of cemeteries is also true of battlefields. When first I came to Pennsylvania, a pilgrimage to Gettysburg was a necessity. The visit still leaves me overwhelmed and numb. The sheer numbers! (Not until I visited the Somme, years later, were the numbers greater.) Not so much in the tragedy of death, as in the horror of the killing. Still, I learned to lay aside moral judgment in pursuit of vicarious identification. Whether or not I could have participated in the killing—although I think not, the benefit of intuition's consciousness was that I did not separate myself from those who suffered and died. "Nothing human is alien to me," I would later affirm. This compunction for identification carried me to Europe, where I slept overnight in my rented car, deep in the Argonne Forest of The Great War's Western Front. The spirits of the dead haunted my sleep and I was one with them. "Poppies grow, row on row … ." All that I had heard of World War I, from the few veterans I knew, now became real. Not long after that communion with the dead I made my way to Vienna, to make another. There, on a gloomy, overcast, late April afternoon, I visited the Zentralfriedhof (Central Cemetery). Within an area not much larger than the foundation of a small church stood stones commemorating the Immortals of Music: Mozart, Schubert, Beethoven, Strauss, Brahms, and others. Forever after for me, their compositions were more than music, for I had experienced a personal encounter with each soul and their gifts came to me by acquaintance. From my hometown to the city of cultural renown, I had made one with the past. Much lay between and beyond, but mythic intuition had filled me beyond measure.

May I allow the category of **Cathedral** to connote many names— including among others, *church, shrine, temple, chapel, cloister?* For I desire a preeminent term to stand in for all the sacred places intuition has ushered me into. Ironically, "cathedral" literally means "seat of the bishop," a symbol of religion's authority to govern the entranceways into the mythic, having made absolute the epiphany experience of the ancient myth. Nevertheless, the word shall serve the generic purpose of designating a unique springboard experience for us today. "Cathedral" shall represent *The Serenity of the Spirit.* Cathedrals are filled with soul-inspiring stillness, bounded by security from outside anxieties, providing "the Peace of God." Their spatial loftiness is only a hint at the unbounded peace, to which the intuitive spirit can transport the self. I experienced this peace at an early age, on a rainy day beneath lace curtains in a corner of my parents' dining room. All seemed secure and right, each part of me in harmony with the whole.

In subsequent years I would re-visit this serenity, now and again, in the sanctuary of the Lutheran church my family attended. Although Lutherans did well in inducing a sense of guilt, the peacefulness had, in my case, little to do with forgiveness of sin. As I gazed up at the stained-glass representation of the Good Shepherd above the altar, the spires of heaven and the flowing stream of living waters brilliant in their colors, a glowing sense of indwelling divinity took over my awareness, opening all imaginary realms to my yearning. Call it "The Pearl of Great Price," "the peace passing all human understanding," or "God's grace of salvation," I was a confirmed believer in its worth. And of this I am now convinced. Without the agency of intuition's mythic flight, this being "at one" with my soul would not be possible. Having found it, I no longer needed to seek it. Throughout life, in the midst of toil and travail, angst and anguish, disappointment and heartbreak, I have striven to keep faith with the inner touchstone of serenity, by regular attendance, scheduled and serendipitous, at the numerous cathedrals along the way. I have sought out the magnificently constructed chambers of medieval aspiration, Salisbury and York, in England, Notre Dame and Chartes, in France, and Cologne and Saint Elizabeth, in Germany, to elevate my spirit's imperturbability. I have chanced upon scores and scores of obscure chapels and crumbling churches throughout Europe, stumbled upon Neolithic stone circles and monastery ruins in Ireland, halted at pilgrim shrines in the Alps. At each, I reverently paid respects to the divine peace dwelling in me.

Cathedrals are by their nature solitaire. **Castles** are built for love and conviviality. (This to presume a difference from those used as a fortress.) If sanctity of pure spirit is to be found in a cathedral, royalty of loving spirits awaits in the castle. I cannot recall the first glimpse of a castle in my youthful imagination, but the image had an early claim upon my sense of the symbolic. The symbol must have arisen out of a rather rich assortment of fairy tales, of which I drank without reserve. In midlife I was to visit the nineteenth century castle of Walt Disney's dreamland, Neuschwanstein Schloss, in the German Alps, but its appearance in the last scene of "Snow White" aroused a desire for love and happiness pulsating endlessly ever onward. It mattered little that not every boy and girl could be a prince or a princess. My heart, that of a stalwart knight, would search for true love. And, thereby, my love would be a princess. In the majesty of our castle we would live "happily ever after." I was at a very young age blessed, or cursed, with an undying romanticism. So, I sought out castles in the lands of their tale's origin. Oh, how I delighted in the sight of each and every one, more than a hundred, I am sure, were I to count. Much in contrast to, if not in defiance of, my imagined symbol of love and happiness, castles were constructed as fortifications against the lawlessness of knights errant and rival claims of authority.

The foundation of a real fortress is anxiety and the keep rises to meet a height of false security. But my castle was of far different material, an "air castle" of its own. Mine was closer to a heaven dreamed of, than the failure of a desire denied. My castle is a prime symbol, *The Joy of Living*. To dwell therein is to be "at home with life." Upon all castles actual I superimposed the dream of the ideal, fully aware, as my adult mind was, that I chose to indulge in historical fantasy. Cemeteries connected me to the past; the hope of a castle gave me a passion for living! No landscape in my travels has been more filled with castles than the Rhine River in a thirty mile stretch between Rudesheim and Kolblenz, as it narrows in passage through the Hunsruck Mountains. Perched upon the steep walls of this chasm are no less than eighteen castles, plus two situated in the river. About half are in ruins, but all replete with legend. I have hiked at least twenty of the miles zu Fuss ("by foot"), as the Germans would put it, making acquaintance with over a half of these monuments to grandeur, tramping through ancient vineyards. The footsteps of this vagabond were entirely romantic. With fancy free and ardor flying I beheld visions of courtly pageantry and renaissance merriment. I was outside of time, yet fully in tune with the age. A childhood yearning was realized, all made available through a springboard into mythic intuition. From one castle to the next, I reenacted romantic tales of youth. I knew then, and am ever so more certain now, what came to me in my travels was out of precious intuition. No travel agency could have guaranteed it for me; no one can deprive me of its inspiration.

Through the powers of intuition we have sprung loose into mythic transportation. We have entered the mythic and returned, all the more in place for it. In time orientation, we have gathered in the past, the present, and the future. But all time is swallowed up in the eternal mythic. We are ready for a genuine religious experience.

Scraps, Snatches, and Tidbits
(2004)

In sequel to "Aphorism, Pithy Regards," I continue the work of brevity, what may be called "Wisdom in a Nutshell." Typical of my teaching, I attempt to capture the beginning of thought in a condensed version.

To keep up the practice of succinctness, I proceed to a next edition. Rather than adding II. to the original title, I choose to advance the cause of brevity further by adding the notion of snippets. Not fragmentary in the sense of incomplete thought. Rather, in regard to the stand-by-themselves assortment. Each piece is an extraction from a larger cloud of thought, pleading presuppositions and begging implications. Please realize, these thoughts have not been delivered to me in brief, from "out of the blue." In most cases the quotations are but stand-ins for a whole body of sustained reflection. You might think of each as the title to an essay. Since I will not supply the full text, I leave it to you to fill out the mental picture. I trust you to that, giving my full blessing and best regards. Give further life to my words.

Of Living

Each day lived qualifies all the rest of life.

A vision creates the way to its own reality.

Gratitude rests upon the good we have,
not the wishes of expectation.

The sweetness of remembrance is greater
than the pleasure of the moment.

The mystery comes in at the fringes.
One cannot directly gaze at eternity.

Today is the future of our youth.

Reality is the canvas upon which memory draws its picture.

Passion is the animating force of living.

Living is the experiment by which we gain lasting meaning.

Of Meaning

Truth cannot be assembled like pieces of an erector set.

Circumspection is not given to easy meaning;
impulsiveness bypasses wisdom.

Wisdom stands on its own two feet;
scholarship relies on footnotes.

Meaning cannot be bought, borrowed, or stolen.

Meaning is not found in the word,
rather in the awareness beyond words.

The most profound meaning is the least communicable;
faith is the living out of that meaning's truth.

Give me meaning, or my freedom is empty.

From honest thought comes personal meaning;
out of personal meaning we live rightly.

On Forever

To speak too much of eternal tomorrow
blinds the soul to the eternal moment.

I cannot comprehend eternity;
yet, I sense that the good endures beyond me.

Like the stars in the endless heavens of night,
a light of pure spirit goes forth from our souls forever.

What appears momentary to the eye of eternity
may be the abiding truth of life.

If that which must die cannot go on forever,
then, we ought to leave to life the essence of our living.

My life has been lived in the consciousness of eternity.

This mortal heart died longing for eternity.

To bless life is the most reverent entrance to forever.

From Eulogy to Elegy: A Loving Song of Life

(2005)

Music has been the song of my soul. Accordingly, the story of my longing can be encompassed in this eulogy to life. The poetry of the lyrical combines with the passion of the heart, to sing love songs to life.

An Introduction in Explanation of a Perspective

A combination of curiosity and concern has led me to this writing. Tracing as far back as a college psychology class, I have long been intrigued by the great differences in human personality. Limitless have seemed the possibilities. With further attempts at making sense out of the puzzle, I found certain patterns clearly emerging. Here is the point at which concern entered in. With an equally long commitment to peace, I asked, "Cannot a deeper understanding of human personality be used to promote peace?"

My interest was not only in establishing what **is** the case. I also sought an explanation to empower the altering of the human condition. Merely passively to know is not worthy of us. I was motivated by a more affirmative, pragmatic concern: How can we resolve diversity into harmonious community? I was convinced the problem is not in the diversity. Rather, the problem lies in the manner of viewing it. If there be a flaw, it must not be imbedded in human nature, for that is much too pessimistic. My incorrigible optimism insists, "For every ailment, there is a cure."

After a lifetime of observing the frailties of humanity, I am persuaded a more adequate means of repair does exist. In no way suggesting a social panacea, I do believe a more effective approach to laying out the problem is possible. To a large extent this reformulation requires a redefinition of the problem, the application of an alternative paradigm. The predicament is not due either to difference or conflict of interest. The "rub" traces to how those differences are regarded. *All differences are an interpretation of reality, each interpretation predetermining the course of the subsequent relationship.* Some interpretations are counterproductive, some redemptive. Peace, therefore, is dependent not so much upon agreement, as on how we view

125

our disagreements. Certain perceptions cancel out agreement. These I shall call adversarial. In contrast, a more affirmative perception allows for the enduring relationships upon which agreement is based. Out of affirmative perception agreement grows; adversarial perception cannot long sustain agreement, having a more contentious notion of agreement to begin with. Peace relies upon moving perception from the adversarial to the affirmative.

My concern has frequently intensified to consternation, then to dismay. As I study disputes, from the personal to the political, I am simply perplexed by the extent of animosity. The longing for the good is so easily taken captive by the blindness of malice. Under this impulse, grievances are exaggerated and accusations rise to a flood of rhetorical hate. So many times have I observed disagreement degenerate into a tragic impasse. *In the tragedy of the part is revealed the malady of the whole.* Reflexively, what we see as dysfunctional in the larger political order discloses the distortion at the personal level. The personal and the political are no more separated than abuse is from war. The adversarial relationship carries through in both. The principle stands: As go personal relations, so go the political ones.

This booklet is dedicated to "a way out." Neither necessary nor inevitable is the adversarial, in which two sides are diametrically opposed to each other. In reality, the two competing adversaries are not functionally that different. In their worlds of good and evil, each is committed to the abolition of the other. Taking sides in adversity is actually a "no choice." Neither gains as much as it loses, in spite of compensatory rationalizations. The real choice is between ideological entrapment and a holistic perspective of humanity. These are qualitatively different moral perspectives, the traditional dualistic one and the one I propose. We are not required to be enslaved to each other's hostile perceptions, but reconciliation necessitates a breaking free. For this were the Gospels written.

Tripping Merrily as We Go . . . on the light fantastic toe

I am not an accomplished poet, but I prefer the poetic embellishment of life to prosaic humdrum, dull and tedious. To state the case emphatically, I would rather have the commonplace praised in poetry, than the profound expressed prosaically, though I prefer profound poetry. When it comes to love, beauty, and all the fine things of life, worthy articulation depends upon the poetic vein and a sentimental heartbeat. Would I say it is better to remain silent on these matters, if not in a poetic voice? No, I do not wish to take away common speech's contribution to sincere expression, limited as it may be. Instead, my emphasis is upon the poetic graces endowed by the sacred muses. Especially if the medium is inseparable from the message, why bottle life's effulgence in inferior containers?

The poetic ought to be defined, not so much as to meter and verse, but as in regards to a touch of refinement. The jump from ordinary speech to the poetic involves a qualitative intensification of valuing. Thus, the poetic impulse implies a rise in moral awareness, a shift from the practical arts to the fine. In our desire to be poetic we are seeking to elevate life, through eloquence and elegance. Eloquence is the power of aptness and fluidity, words well chosen, and following in increasing waves of intensity. But it is elegance in representation that poetic language strives for, the opening of an eye pleased by the graceful and luxurious. The hackneyed, matter-of-fact perception of the world will deride the poetic as superfluous, a needless, even illusory, exercise in vanity. My remorseful reply is that in the refusal to permit a heightening of expression is the very emptiness of meaning from which I seek escape. Through the poetic we create paradise, or, at least, its lovely foyer. Heaven is not available to the commonplace. Hell is the no exit from inarticulation's dumb dungeon of deafness. Might there be seven levels to each? Degrees of desire to sing and stages of stubborn refusal to wax poetic?

How can there be song without poetry? What is a song, if it is not cradled in the poetic urge? Yes, there are many genres of song, from cadences for work to tempos for wayfarers. Beautiful songs, plaintive songs of heart and soul, such as Delta Blues or Mahler's *"Das Lied von der Erde"* (The Song of the Earth). But I am in quest for the finest song of all, the greatest song ever written. A Loving Song to Life! For this to be possible, I must open myself wholly to the calling of my higher muses. From them will come the gifts of eulogy and elegy. I still believe in them, have trust in their faithfulness. From the Poetic Bible I read, "If with all your heart you truly seek the gift of poetry, surely you shall receive the Song of Life." Song is indivisible from poetry. We are first made poets, that we might be fulfilled in song. For why do we exist? Are we not creatures born to praise creation, to sing our song to life?

Dirges have their rightful time and lamentation is proper response to the grief of loss. But redemption comes through the Song of Life. Speaking of the miraculous, as well as the serendipitous, in a double helix of blessing, as we elevate life through the poetic, the song of our hearts trips merrily along. I will refrain from saying that poetic song is the cure for all ills, physical and psychological, yet I know of eulogy's therapeutic benefits. As we lift up life, we are lifted up. Praise is best couched poetically, but what is praise other than elevation of the spirit? Praise is neither obeisance to a vengeful god nor a ritual of contrition. Without gladness praise sinks into the numbness of unworthiness. Pessimism damns itself, for it refuses, or is unable, to sing praises to life. The principle of doubled power also applies in reverse. The downward fall of the spirit only increases in velocity; nothing falls faster or harder than negativity, times squared. Even in death, cannot a song be sung to life?

This brings us to the second half of the chapter title, "… on the light fantastic toe." Fantastic lightness of being is endemic to the path leading to the land of song. Fantasy is not so much the result of song, as in the very poetic making of song. In the song I sing fantasy and the poetic are correlative, coterminous, and reciprocal. Yet, in a marvelous peculiarity, the one is the antecedent of the other. Then, in a merry-go-around circularity, the other precedes the first. To enter the poetic dimension a fairer world of fantasy is created, which only impels the poetic urges further. To eulogize we call upon the poetry of fantasy. Enlarging, intensifying, heightening with every turn of the poetic phrase, we arrive at the "somewhere, over the rainbow." That "somewhere" is not an "elsewhere," entirely separated from the "here." Neither an escape nor an alternate reality, the song, borne on the wings of fantasy, is none other than the *merry melody of the heart*. By its magical powers ordinary eyes are opened to the beauty all around. From the fairer world of the poetic streams radiance upon this world.

Singing from the Soul

To sing from the soul, the soul must be filled with passion; however, it must be remembered that passion is not all that it has been maligned to be and that much that is assigned to passion is misleading. Passion does not begin where reason leaves off and passion is not necessarily the appointed gate to rage. Raging anger is better understood as the misappropriation of passion, a self-destruction, for rage only tears at the heart's delicate fibers. Passion is the energy of the soul and the song is the vehicle of its therapeutic grace. In singing from the soul we become both the Container of the Divine Passion and the Blessing of Wellbeing.

Rather than thinking of passion as excessive emotion, may we begin by awarding this great gift the highest distinction. *Passion is the Cosmic Energy resident in the soul*—the élan vital, the Life Force, the lifeblood of our being. This vital energy sustains physical life, but in its singing supplies the implicit meaning of living. Conversely, negativity comes not so much from evil intent or inherent wickedness, as from the soul's emotional starvation. Once set into motion, negativity's deprivation of passion becomes an accelerating downward spiral into barrenness, even in the midst of intellectual cleverness. Such a stark juxtaposition only drives the soul into madness, inviting spiritual suicide. Unless the negative momentum is broken, the Fates will utter their shadowy oracles. There is no darker soul than the crippled heart that cannot sing. Imprisoned in despair, the soul is devoured by its own damnation. What could be more tragic, other than a soul that has lost the capacity to sing? The soul that cannot sing has no salvation. It falls into the perdition of having no song.

In the soul's journey through life are many tempests and much turbulence, cataracts of angst, and depths of despair. Poets will write of *Sturm und Drang* (Storm and Stress) and wail in the torment of unrequited love. And that is all right, for it is included in the full taste of life. But always is there to be a guiding angel in the sky of our life portrait. Many will be the dark clouds of perceived misfortune and fierce will be the rapids tearing from us the dearest of hopes. Yet, not even fate can submerge the spirit, as long as the soul is open to angelic light. Angels are thought to be messengers from celestial realms. But I know them as none other than the promise that,

"Within us is a light, no matter how faint, an inner light shining." It is this Divine Light, which enables passion to express itself in song, even in the grip of anguish. Turn it around and you have, "Music is really the angels singing." Attribute to angels wings, harps, and halos, if you will, for the majesty of their portrayal. But reserve their role as a reminder, that song has close proximity to the purest of human aspiration.

By some strange quirk of morality, confession is said to be good for the soul. But I would prefer song to contrition. Here we are considering song's therapeutic properties. While confession may serve the purposes of honesty and justice, song heals the soul, from the "slings of outrageous fortune" and lesser ills. The soul is in continual need of healing, for the bumps of life's brutal contours are constantly impacting the most delicate of our sensitivities. There is, however, no hurt for which song does not have a melody of solace and cure. Of all the rhythms of life's pulse, none is so powerful as Sorrow and Joy, the alternating beat of our emotions. A song of the soul conveys both reflexes. We are told, "Cry with those who cry and rejoice with those who rejoice." I do not believe this admonition is so much a moral law as a clue to spiritual wellbeing. And, singing from the soul to express the sorrow and joy is the practice of good health. Like some great life diastole and systole, emotionally we take in and we give out. In the authentic ownership of grief is to be found the exaltation. Out of the lament of sorrow arises the Ode to Joy. In the inflexion of sadness appears the reflection of our soul's song.

Life invites us into its flow and we respond with song, the inhale and exhale of passion's vitalizing energy. Strangely, the very spirit we breathe in is the very source of the energy we give off. We discover the song we sang in the passion of the soul circulates throughout the universe, drawing all into one symphony of concord. What else could be the "harmony of the spheres?"

Food is for the body; song is for the soul. Good health relies upon good food and passionate song. Sing for the health of the soul and the peace of the world.

Top of the voice does not guarantee depth of the soul.
Out of the depth of the soul comes the richest resonance of song.

Sometime Thoughts on Religion

(2005)

A built-up collection of bits and pieces on religion. Though previously I had written much on religion, there emerges more clearly than before the duality and tension between what is believed and what is experienced. This theme has persisted since.

The Great Religious Divide: REVELATION versus EXPERIENCE

Does one begin with truth and then conform experience to it? Or, is truth the expression, the venerable testimony of the soul having been dipped into the stream of life. The answers lie with the biography of the self, its affairs, and the sum total relations with life.

The arrogance of revelation is that it demands truth outside of experience, not just valid for the path of the believer, but truth to the furthest reaches of the universe and beyond. The purchase price of this truth is inauthentic existence, a self not located within its own consciousness. It sells its birthright to authority figures and the power of suggestion. The God to whom the self submits is vested with all power and, for the fundamentalist, society is properly run from top down, in a concordat of religion and state. Therein the soul is in subjection to the external powers that be, on earth as it is in heaven. Forever. Amen.

The dispute between Revelation and Experience is not over who trusts to God, for the Divine is within as well as without. It is a matter of self-assurance and self-trust. The grasper after revelation is most often plagued with guilt and low self-image. The Imago Dei has been so lost, so erased from this human visage, that the continence is cast up from the depths of self-loathing to whatever "divinely ordained" power figure stands above, with outstretched hands offering miraculous revelation.

So battered by the vicissitudes of life, so insecure about its own worth, the lost soul is unable to look within, to the tradition of the muses and mystics: Song, poetry, symbol, metaphor, the moon of the spiritual eye. For the worthless soul, truth must be absolutely certain, bound, boxed, graspable, able to be placed under the arm, in the cognitive mind, on an altar. The greater the anxiety over salvation, the greater the certainty of revelation's claim. However, in consequence, the spiritual intuition is blinded by the searing light of the high god's absolute truth. Thus, the pathetic irony: Revelation in its compulsion to attain eternal life in the spiritual dimension beyond the physical is left with a spiritually hollow physical form. With nowhere else to go, the self so addicted is possessed by a revelation without an earthly spirit. The light within has been extinguished. A God outside reigns down power, but there is no divine within, except for occupation by a controlling belief, to which the soul has surrendered.

At bottom, what drives the obsession with definitive truth is the fear of death. Anxiety craves an outside truth with such power as to snatch the trembling self from the jaws of death. Yet, with this artificial escape comes not only the denial of mortality, but a hatred for the sensual and a dismissal of all wisdom deriving from acceptance of our physicality, including the spiritual meaning of sexuality. Again, the cost is astonishingly high: Inauthenticity and bad faith. Revelation based upon a fear of death condemns anyone who thinks otherwise to be burned as a pagan, a nature-loving witch, a child of the Devil. The power of the spirit is subjugated to the terror of insecurity. Under its jurisdiction, life is uprooted from the soil of Mother's nurturing. For spiritual purity sake, mother unnaturally is made into a Virgin, the antithesis of the sexually potent Mother Goddess. The soul is commanded to serve the arbitrary will of the Father's omnipotence.

Introspective Afterthoughts

It is inconceivable, at least to me, that one could shift through years of serious thought about religion, without becoming more aware of how one stands in reference to religion. In looking back at what I have written, most of which, admittedly, comes from recent years, some significant realizations have been reinforced. Laying aside the many lesser personal insights, I focus upon the three most salient features to my religious journey. By these predilections I am defined. I own them wholeheartedly.

Religion has been a constant preoccupation. I chose religious study as a major and a life profession for a reason. I am at soul a most serious and religious person. When I think, I think religiously; when I write, I write religiously. My political side ever draws upon my spiritual awareness. Even my poetry is a vessel for the conveyance of my sense of the Divine. The torture has come with seeking the finest grade of spirituality possible, in the midst of pervasive low grade.

My insistent intellect has whittled down my axiomatic belief. This is not an ordinary skepticism turned cynical. My approach to religion is ever grounded upon a higher motif, the cauterizing benefit of scathing critique. All intellectual property, every article of belief, must be immersed in the scalding bath of its own critique, to burn out the impurities. And there is much impurity in religion. A higher spirit intercedes to guide the intellect, in the name of the Sacred. The principle is no better represented than by this: *"Spirituality necessarily requires intellectual struggle."* I utterly refuse to put forward an unexamined assertion for belief. Whether a doctrine of the religious establishment or a thought of my own, I insist upon close intellectual scrutiny. The result has been to arrive at a drastically revised regard for "belief." What was once religious belief must now be of humbler stature, more metaphorical language than tangible fact. The intellect peeled off the superfluous and cut to the bone, in search of quintessential spirituality. I have cut away the dead flesh, in order to give new life to the spirit. In the name of religion, I excoriate religion.

I am a champion of a purer spirituality. Very apparent must it be that I am a most severe critic of religion. Throughout the writings, especially in the extended pieces, to my words a very sharp edge is honed. Please do not think me merciless, though I admit to much holy anger. I simply have seen far too much counterfeit religion, particularly in its hypocritical camouflaging of ignoble, unspiritual motives. Without malice or arrogance I declare that much of traditional religion is beneath my dignity. In place of piety I demand honesty. Rationalizations of injustice and insincere justifications of cruelty offend my spiritual sensitivities. Shallowness and superficiality have always offended me. Fairly, or unfairly, I associate these personal characteristics with insincerity. Sadly I observe that common religiosity is replete with lower spirituality, a crassness in awareness. Accuse me of condescension, if you wish, but grant me the respect of having striven for a higher plane of spirituality.

Through writing and reflection I have come to greater spiritual awareness and, thereby, greater inner peace. In many respects, spiritual introspection is like unto "the dark night of the soul," witnessed to by mystics throughout the ages. Conventional religion offers the comfort of unquestioned security, preordained and neatly laid out. For the self unaware, and momentarily even for youthful spiritual awareness, this may be sufficient. But it is a borrowed, external religion, not born within the soul's holy chamber. For those brave enough, searching for the inner light is the path to true spirituality. For me, it is not a matter of bravery or choice. I can accept nothing less than the Divine Within.

A Knapsack of Moral Reflections

(2005)

A somewhat playful tease of conventional morality. Metaphors abound and analogies run wild in the imagination. Not recommended for literalists!

Tips On Traveling Bags

A knapsack promptly implies traveling. If travel is adopted as a metaphor for life, then it would seem proper to think of morality as involving accoutrements for journey. But this analogue is at striking odds with the conventional morality of my upbringing, which was far more staid and forbidding. Rather than empowerment, the moral establishment provided an anchor of certainty and a short chain tether against wonderment. My youthful spirit has long preferred permission to prohibition. My zest has been for exploration and the tasting of life's many delicious flavors.

Thus, I am proposing a moral plan many traditionalists would regard as misguided, if not entirely wayward. In turn, I view their moral axioms much too directed toward the heavenly skies of the hereafter. In consequence, I choose a more prudential guide for life's journey, trusting that, for now, eternity will be able to take care of itself. *I simply do not care for a morality in constant strife with the journey,* making of life a "vale of tears" and experience an interminable temptation for the soul. Thereby, I would find it unavoidable to conclude morality is anti-life. But I know better. That is not all there is of morality, no matter what the pious guardians of morality may think.

I like the imagery to the phrase, "carrying too much moral baggage." I can fancifully visualize a person, sweating and panting, dragging great compendia of moral prejudice behind, on life's grand path. Eventually the toil becomes too exhausting, the toll too great. To the side of the road is at that spot erected a temple of certainty, in which to repose veritable idols of rectitude. How can one really know the rich variety of experience in the countryside, if all attention and trust is given to the immovable crates of morality? At that point the journey is given up and life is put under the judgment of immutability.

In actual travel to far-away places by air, I have followed this rule: Take no more weight than can be borne by the body's own strength—that would be, by shoulder strap! This leaves out massive trunks from the Grand Tours of old. I consider them not only imposing, but also preposterous. They are signets, not so much of royalty, as of aristocratic superficiality. Choose wisely your luggage. Too small will bring back little wisdom; too large will hinder the journey. A toiletry case provides for the barest of necessities, leaving little room for polished stones of reflections. A fashionable suitcase may exceed the space needed for durable observations. In the broad span of available travel bags, somewhere between the pocket and the satchel, the pouch and the American Traveler, on that great conveyor belt of moral receptacles, appears the practicable knapsack.

The German has a rucksack, the Brit, a kit and caboodle. I shall press all their virtues into my use of a knapsack, divisions and side pockets provided. Now, there is a usable notion for you, "provisions." The contents are to provide for the journey, not for the benefit of an ancient authority figure's iron-weighted divine will. A few prepared choice bits of prudence are allowed, but at the start the sack will be relatively empty and amply available for acquisition. Much more will be laid aside than absorbed. What does not bear the weight of time, the test of experience, through careful evidentiary hearing, will be known as "fool's gold," out of which many idolatrous calves have been forged.

For acquisition and retention, I adopt "Rules for Contents:"

1. Do not retain what is not usable.

2. No pious ornamentation allowed, not even ID patches of religiosity.

3. Hold on to can openers, to break open moral context.

4. Never give away the Swiss Army Knife of multiple paradigms.

5. Permit only an emergency cell phone; chatter is best left to unengaged by-standers.

Ah, yes, before departure, burn—in a fire at least hot enough to melt clanging cymbals—the Pilgrim's heavy burden of guilt, put upon us eons ago by angry patriarchs. (While you are at it, also toss in your winter garments of repentance.) All of this is to be discarded, so that wisdom be gained. What goes into the knapsack is a mixture of souvenirs and tools, only those beneficial to the growth of the soul. The souvenirs are gems of insights, the tools sharpened to extract awareness from the strata of experience. At journey's end we will realize, the knapsack turned inside out is all that we truly have to our name. Along with the knapsack, take in hand the staff to Life's Steady Course, self-esteem. From its faithful support shall come love for all taken in by intimate knowing.

As a child, I was intrigued by the "crooked man, who walked a crooked mile." I still find him preferable to those who take the "straight and narrow path." Why, oh why, I wonder, why do they have such nasty suspicions about this life? Have they not yet found the herb of healing in the deep forest of experience?

Sorting Out the Golden Nuggets, While Standing On Moral High Ground

I have lost most of the morality I grew up with, for I have abandoned the questionable theological ground upon which it necessarily rests. The letting go was not done in spite or malice. Quite the contrary. It was not in defiance so much as in quest for the Good. If any blame is to be assigned, I would have to confess, the cause is in the journey through the wonders of life and the practice of putting interesting souvenirs (reflections) in my traveling knapsack. There is more of boyish innocence, than conniving rebellion, in my life story.

This writing has been a worthy journey down reflection's lane. From the glitter of keen observation's golden nuggets come shafts of incisive illumination. Reflection leads to illumination; illumination casts question upon dark places. Oddly, it is unacknowledged doubt, which conceals from consciousness those shadowy negative assumptions. Only by traveling the highways and by-ways of life, the level plains of ordinariness and the steep inclines of urgency, are we enabled to perceive the contours of our suppressed moral presuppositions. Not a detachment or disowning. *We observe in order to reflect; we reflect because we want a purer morality.* Unquestioning attachment is blind to impurity, the moral toxins of our common life. It is in the good will of humane reflection I have placed my faith. Without this gift from the angels of conscience, I know of no high moral ground.

I am an advocate for human morality, free from entangling negativity, one that does not cast paralyzing insinuations and does not hinder the natural yearnings for goodness. I have lived through too much moral negativity, to turn back toward the darkness of unexamined belief. The light comes from ahead, in the courage to face the possible misperceptions of the past. From the beacon light of scrutiny shines the promise of an unfettered endeavor to realize our humanity. The journey is inseparable from the undertaking. The knapsack is the mental acumen holding in unity the gems of wisdom.

I have used journey and the knapsack as a metaphor for my style of being moral. Not a set of assumptions so much as a style defines my morality. Admittedly, in the observation has been a strong thread of disapproval. Like with anything of beauty, the degrading of morality is very objectionable. While I have attempted to develop throughout the writing an appreciation for morality's beneficial role, I suppose a reader could exclaim, "You protest too much!" I would defend myself by saying, "Wisdom's vision comes in the aftermath of recognizing what is unacceptable to conscience." Whether in religion or politics, teaching or love, my mode of discovery has been to arrive at *a beholding* beyond the rubble of what is decidedly wrong with the practice thereof. I take that to be the nature of human enlightenment. We arrive at what is of worth, by observing what is not. But this is not merely a way of negation. *A dawning* gradually takes place. I have had visions of goodness and beauty, but they rarely occur in isolation from the experience of vileness and ugliness. Thus, the act of observation and reflection upon what is not acceptable serves as a disclosure of what can receive my sincere approval. In every generation there must be a rebellion against the past, in order to rediscover the Good. That is where unquestioning loyalty and tenacious certitude fail. They know not of what they believe. Their morality is no more than stones for ballast, not compasses for direction into the future.

I must trust that a glint of what I hold as acceptable in morality has come through these pages. But I also assume some responsibility to put it all in order, here in the conclusion of my reflections. So, I offer "An Artist's Sketch of Worthy Morality," with expedition and conciseness.

♦ Authentic morality requires more *Courage* than obedience.

♦ Morality should appeal to the *Best in Us*, not dwell on the worst.

♦ Morality is to serve *Human Wellbeing*, not set notions of right.

♦ Morality may have *First Steps*, but not final conclusions.

♦ Morality begins with *Inquiry* and ceases with presumption.

♦ *Empathetic Identification* is a greater virtue than righteousness.

♦ Morality is not aware if it is not *Awake to Function*.

♦ Morality is more interested in *Healing* than punishment.

♦ The Wheel of Moral Reflection must never cease to turn.

♦ Our Moral Salvation comes through *Honest Love*.

A Tale of Paradigm: Out of Mind and into Sight

(2006)

Contending that all conceptualization is a human product, in this excursus I plead for modesty in truth claims. Behind each claim are assumptions demanding examination. We cannot think without concepts, yet all are relative to the user, necessitating carefully qualified statements as to validity.

Putting Forth a Bone of Contention

With straightforwardness I put forth my contention: A mind which limits itself to only one paradigm does not understand or appreciate other paradigms. The problem is that far too many persons regard exclusive loyalty to only one paradigm as the epitome of faithfulness. If not perfidious, other paradigms are considered to be grounded on pure nonsense. The holder of an exclusive mind-set does not use the word paradigm to make the counter-claim, preferring to seal the case with such glittering moral justifications as, "the absolute will of God" or "true patriotism." In fact, these mono-paradigmists are the living, fire-breathing examples of my contention.

Most persons are unaware of the paradigms they depend upon for the statements they make. They simply assume the correctness of their thought. Yet, once you acknowledge the role of paradigm in thought and knowledge, all assertions are necessarily qualified. Arrogance, of the absolutist sort, is possible only if the subjective character of our dependence upon paradigms is denied. Presupposing a paradigm is unavoidable, but honesty (or, shall we say sophistication) knows the relativity of all knowledge and handles truth with a humane modesty. At the point of honest acknowledgement of paradigm's role in thought, a quantum shift in awareness occurs. But, in that very moment, something very beautiful and liberating happens. To explore this "enlightenment" is a part of my discursive intention. Let us paraphrase our philosophical progenitor, Socrates, and say, "*Unexamined paradigms are unworthy of us.*"

Whether from a constitutional aversion to arbitrariness or the logical training of my philosophical studies, I have had a life-long distrust of unwarranted and unexamined assumptions. Even as a child, I pondered, "Hum, why this and not that?" I was never one merely to accept what was given, in obedience and in absence of wonder. When it came to "curiosity killed the cat," I felt partiality toward the feline. Later I learned of Pushkin's line, "If we are to be bovine, why were we not born with bells around our necks." (paraphrased). In my mind it followed, "Why put bands of restriction around human thought?" With no apologies to cultural conservatives, I was born a "free thinker." Emphatically I claim deliberative thought as a birthright, dangerous as that may seem to conventionality. I do not take well to the authoritative injunction, "Well, that's just the way it is done!" My study of history reinforces the conviction that constricted and controlled thinking has too often been the tool of tyranny, in this case a mental bondage. In this writing I am simply extending a lifetime virtue to the presupposition of paradigm. Our most fundamental instruments of perception must not beg divine dispensation.

I somewhat understand the compunction against questioning the "fundamentals" upon which society supposedly rests, psychologically, not philosophically. *A need for certainty and the resulting compulsion for security are the principal psychological forces driving the mind into a static condition of unquestioning credulity.* In such a state of empirical isolation presuppositions will not be examined and consciousness will constrict itself to fit into a hard-shelled paradigm. Consequences count for nothing and defense of the primary paradigm accounts for everything, no matter the costs. Ensconced in an incubator of falsely contrived security, so is the malicious child of absolutism conceived.

Absolutism is the presumption that the operating paradigm is omniscient, admitting to no fallibility of judgment. And, the greater the claim of certainty, the tighter the paradigm must be constructed, until a schism between thought and reality widens into a delusion. This is the making of *false consciousness.* In "playing god" the fluidity of life suffers at the hands of clumsy ironclad axioms and inordinate, arrogant certainty. Questioning and security run head-on into each other, whenever free thought is set into motion, because the inquiry exposes the increasing dysfunction of an empirically detached paradigm. And, tenacious is the defense of the "homeland." More will be spent on perpetuating the established order than educating inquiring minds. We tend to absolutize the paradigm we know best, then cling to this tradition as a security system. The irony, and rightful outcome, of claiming certainty and security absolutely is that we end up with neither. Instead, we lapse into a make-believe reality, much to the detriment of thinking and responsible politics.

In neglecting awareness of the paradigms we operate under, too easily does presumption enter into our thinking. Conversely, an exploration of the nature of paradigm can liberate thinking from self-imposed limitations. Naiveté restricts perception to one primary paradigm, whether out of simplicity or denial, thereby sacrificing the broader, more inclusive viewing of life. Allow me to propose the Paradox of Paradigm. A paradigm enables us to see, yet possesses built-in blind spots. All paradigms are a qualification of reality, each concealing in the effort to disclose. However, that aspect of reality to which one paradigm is blind may be elucidated by a quite differently constructed paradigm. From this we might rightly conclude, no one paradigm is totally adequate and many are preferable to one alone. Somewhat like the blind men and the elephant, it seems better to lay aside the imperial designs of a self-certain paradigm in favor of collaboration with multiple. Humbly we need to acknowledge that no perfect "unified field theory" exists, or ever will, to which the human mind has access. Honesty leads us to disavow pretensions to occupancy upon the divine throne of absolute truth. The truth of the matter is, any paradigm's claim to all-inclusive adequacy is already far down the road of reductionism. A presumptive arrogance infests all mono-paradigms.

At this juncture my bone of contention transforms into a plea for toleration. Enough with monotheism; let poly-paradigmism return to reign over our fields of common labor! Out with the domination of mind by a paradigm living in the "Big House" (quite the literal meaning of a "pharaoh"). If temples are to be built, may they be dedicated to the Sacred Spirit of Enlightenment. And may the inscription read. *"I have sworn upon the altars of truth eternal vigilance against a single paradigm's tyranny over the human mind."* There is something contradictory about smashing the golden calf of medieval orthodoxy and, then, idolatrously erecting a new paradigm in its place.

In consistency, we should not replace one paradigm's demand for exclusive loyalty with another's. The gods are really none other than paradigms behaving as cosmic rulers. When so elevated, religious wars among the peoples are inevitable. So, my injunction includes: May all absolute paradigms be taken from their thrones, in order that our genuine humanity come through the gates of intellectual independence. The gods of certainty must die, in behalf of our need for tolerance. Our desire for peace shall supersede the urge to control, so that liberty of thought abides. If gods there be, may they be many in the generosity of polytheism. Useful knowledge and the acquiring of understanding do not necessitate the subsuming of all under the dictates of a single paradigm. Something of a devil is in a Summa written under the hand of one paradigm, more than in the details. Monotheism, by its very nature, is intolerant. To the extent a paradigm will breech no rivals and presumes to have an answer for everything, in that manner is it a jealous, tribal God Almighty. "Thou shalt have no other paradigms before me!" No decent human is entitled to utter such presumption nor is even the lowliest among us deserving of such coercion.

After a lifetime of witnessing paradigmatic bullying I cast my lot with a faith in multi-paradigmism, believing it better to trade presumed certainty for reasoned relativity than sacrifice intellectual vitality to one tightly constructed viewpoint. Along with the bane of narrow-mindedness walks the monotony of banality. For, in the mundane amphitheater of popular opinion, if it is not muscular paradigmatic imperialism, in a milder form, the exploring mind is forced to suffer the sing-song of "Johnny-One-Note," the malady of mono-paradigmism. With no flexibility in tonality or agility in imagination, no matter the subject or field of reference, Johnny-One-Note sings the same song over and again, insisting upon playing the same game. Extremely dull and unchallenging, the conversation always comes back to the same point, until exasperation sets in and the mind secretly sets off on its own self-directed excursion. Only at a distance from smugness does a sense of free air return. Curiosity requires new paradigms; the persistence of a single paradigm stultifies with its circularity.

A contention in favor of poly-paradigmism is not, however, to say all paradigms are equal in their power of illumination. Quite the contrary, there do exist instances of inadequacy and outright delusion. This raises the issue of paradigm evaluation. While an infallible verification system is not available, much can be said in behalf of practicality and cogency. Somewhat like the coin of commercial transaction, a paradigm need be struck upon the bar of reality to hear whether it "rings true." An authentic paradigm must be able to speak clearly to life. First of all, the use of a paradigm should undergo an internal inquiry, to assess motive and self-serving interests. A paradigm can very readily and quite deceitfully serve the purposes of hypocrisy, bearing no more charm than the most egregious of rationalization. In due course, these malpractices and pretenses will be illustrated and properly exposed.

With this bone bravely tossed into the ring of contention, the tale of paradigm shall move further on toward its denouement. The path of inquiry leads on, into the ramifications and implications growing out of my central thesis. Let us continue on our appointed way, more fully drawing out the picture.

A paradigm set at anchor
can bar entrance onto the great open intellectual sea.

Afterthought: Where Do We Go From Here?

The first direction we do not go is half-cocked with the weapon of a new paradigm in hand. What I have said about paradigms in general can be applied to the construct of this booklet. I do not seek for my thought to become normative for all future thought. I remain steadfast. Free thought is a verb, not a noun. When used as a noun, thought becomes simply another constricting paradigm.

This whole philosophical enterprise has been a mild exercise in hyperbole, all to the end of a greater appreciation of how we presume upon what we say and propose. Rather than seeking converts to a new persuasion, this writing has been more in the way of an alert and a caution. I can ask no more than that a few persons become a bit more aware of the relativity of the perspective giving authorship to our ultimate claims. I live on in the hope that this awareness increases and spreads as a current of toleration and modesty. What I do not want to happen is that paradigm become the centerpiece of all future conversation. This booklet has used the word often enough, to the point of weakening the semantic legs upon which it stands. Only an absolutistic mono-paradigm would take it further.

With this disclaimer aside, we go on to some suggestions, as to how we may take the contention of this booklet seriously. More important than anything, we would best move beyond the false security of a single paradigm and bravely *learn to live in a universe of multiple paradigms.* This side of mythological paradise, there is no permanent security in mono-paradigm certainty. Somewhat like intellectual jugglers, we need to develop the agility to handle multiple paradigms simultaneously. This requires a detachment of our ideas (beliefs) from our identity (being). Self-acceptance and worth can still be maintained at a distance from creeds of certainty.

Security in a tenaciously held paradigm is artificial; insecurity is the quickest flight from responsibility. Who we are is not the same as what we think, although if you think you are your certain beliefs, like Malvolio of "Twelfth Night" fame, you are too stiff to bend down and touch the pulsating life impulse. A fundamental confusion in paradigm's function has been made, whenever we mistake our thought for life. In the name of decency and human liberty, from this confusion we must be set free.

In the tradition of the "trickster god" we find the art of *shape-shifting.* What this suggests is that we ought to dance with our ideas, not absolutize them. An apt mind can keep more than one paradigm in the air at the same time, without coveting any single one. Then, with a bit of mental trickery, consciousness is able to slip from one paradigm to another, enthralled by the different interpretations allowed. In this artful dance we ought to be light-hearted, particularly about the application of our assortment of analytic paradigms. Rather than being entombed in the darkness of a controlling paradigm, we should rejoice in the fresh air of elusive paradigm shape-shifting. Of some traveling assistance is a sense of self-directed humor. So as to avoid the pitfalls/pratfalls of a grim, clumsy dictatorial paradigm, our discourse will be delivered impishly, with "tongue in cheek." We are to take what we think and say seriously, sincerely, yet in the realization of its relativity. Humor is for disarmament of absolutism, liberation from self-fashioned mental prisons. A god with no sense of humor is dangerous. Or, should we say, beware of true believers with the gift of a mono-paradigm? Especially if they shun parody and satire. What appears to be generosity may be a trap to enslave your mind. A lean and hungry look with little sense of life's comedy is a devil to be avoided. To laugh at our gods is to free ourselves from idols. Better excoriation of idols, than hatred of others. Know your paradigms, and to thyself be true!

Go forth on the wings of a new paradigm,
but fly not too near the burning heat of presumption.

Luminous Moments: An Autobiography

(2006)

Being the mystic that I am, along with intellectual honesty goes recognition of the subjective experiences. I choose to be the reflection of ecstatic moments, the creation of a spiritual awareness.

Forward: "On With the Writing!"

Everything we say bears an autobiographical trace element. Certainly this is true with me. Beyond that, at various times, and in occasional writings, I have gathered together autobiographical material for self-reflection. Still, I have yet to write my autobiography. It is about time, and the time seems right.

An autobiography begun too soon is not an effort wasted, for each stroke at composition of life's memoir is part of the reflexive disposition required for the eventual writing. However, autobiographies more properly belong to late stages of life, after much earnest living. Not just because a few latter chapters have yet to be added, but for the more pertinent reason that the light of the ages has not fully come to bear meaning upon life's journey. Having lived all but a few years of my life portion and with the afore said, I feel I am ready to go forward with the writing, in wondrous retrospect.

In the early years of life, when youth so thirstily drinks in the newness of existence and is so enthralled by the zest for adventure, focus is immediate, upon the joy of being alive. In the beginning only a vague sense of ultimate meaning attaches to the passing of the days. Life is sufficient unto itself. Yet, in anticipation of a larger frame for life's portrait, gradually a value is placed upon "the doing," even while in the present pursuit. The title to life's movie only slowly, by some time-lapse of progression, emerges from the depths of emerging consciousness. Not so much by a changing of wording, as through a layering of meaning. The light of time grows in brilliance as life's value is absorbed into the soul. To put it alternatively, the further I move toward the end, the greater the valuing of the past. What was once memory

149

of ordinary days transforms into the gleam of extraordinary meaning. By this intensification is illumination achieved. Wisdom and worship are the acquired powers.

By these words, I dedicate this autobiography: *As the physical eyes of aging dim, the sight of memory grows more luminous.* It is as though physical sight is exchanged for spiritual understanding. What greater comfort can there be, in experiencing life and growing old? Purposeful living triumphs, even over death. What greater purpose can there be, if not to see life as spiritually meaningful? That is the meaning of "luminous," the shining upon life's contours of a higher light. What is not immediately obvious, in time can transcend to ultimate meaning. This is the function of "heaven," not to take us out of the natural world of human experience, but to cast radiance upon what we have treasured. Heaven comes from within, in the awakening of the spiritual eye. Awakening does not come complete in one moment. The transformation extends over a lifetime. When awake, the spiritual eye fills each moment with heavenly light. Even before the end, it is possible for the last years to be glorious. From glory comes peace to the soul and kindliness of spirit.

One of the wondrous benefits of old age is that you can sit through almost the entirety of your Life Movie, with all editorial rights reserved.

In the loveliness of youthful measure
Appear gems of later treasure.
In the golden glow of aging leisure
The Spiritual Eye takes pleasure.

What's in a Life Story?

All that we say is to some extent autobiographical. The writing of a story, even purported objective narration, is both selective and interpretive. While biographies may strive for accuracy and factuality, autobiographies ought to be subjective, for they are an "inside story." Chronicles of your life had best be left to others, the view from outside, for they are not bothered by what it has meant to be you. Only you can write of the inner realities. Who, better than you, can speak of the experiential currents within, the agony and ecstasy of having lived?

The selection of material for one's life story is not impartial or indiscriminate. No attention should be made to what others may expect or think. In telling your life story, authenticity is far more to be desired than respectability. The writing of your story is really a conversation with your soul, having listened to its quiet murmurings. Not to be honest in the telling is an offense against the Holy Muse and a misrepresentation to the world. In what we unabashedly select is to be found the communication of how we value life, the moral imperative of our being. To leave this wondrous life, without an honest confession of its worth, is an omission too remiss to contemplate. The telling of our story for posterity's sake ought to be a condition of our residency on earth. For that task to be completed, selection out of untrammeled honesty is required.

Writing from inside can be scary, especially when few, if any, visitations have been made to that mysterious land. But alongside the moments in which guilt has burned holes are to be found the glistening gems of who you are and of life's miraculous gift of meaning. The Inner Chamber can either be a tomb of remorse or a resurrection into higher light. Courage gains entrance; love affirms the good that has encompassed us. Secrets seal the door. What is hidden from the world is likely obscure to the self. Writing one's own story is first an act of self-discovery and then a gesture of disclosure. Disclosure is prudently discrete, yet too much concealment is in service to self-deceit. *Writing one's own story is a process by which the best of the self is shared.* For self-understanding, we need to be transparent to our self. We are the substance of our life story.

Concern over what has been left out is an anxiety to be avoided, at the least, a distraction from affirming life's goodness. Far greater in importance is the quality of what is selected. It is possible to get all the details included, but to miss the desired intonation. Of supreme importance is the light we project onto our lives. The act of telling, in reality, is a rite of self-affirmation. At the favorable degree of self-expression the story approximates a song, the recital elevating the spirit in a Hymn of Joy. It would be a very sad life story without joy. But rather than deliberate joy, the story should be written out of joyousness. Then, joy shall be the overflowing.

Yes, our story is necessarily subjective because it is first our story. But in a second significant respect we are engaged in an unavoidably subjective undertaking. I have found the means of selection vary, person-to-person. Not only can you alone know what has illuminated your life's path, but also the very measure by which luminous moments are selected, nay, created, is peculiar to each person. What one person regards as luminous may be quite dull in appearance to another. We remember the moments we most value, but value is subjective. One friend may value novelty, another discovery. What lights up the moments of life may not be same; still we are bound together in the stories we tell of life. The common element in our stories is the irreducible subjectivity. We ought to revel in that.

I add another factor to the story's writing. As we age, a shift in valuing occurs. Old Age represents a drastic altering of what is important, thus the late story of life contrasts to the song of youth. Possibly we should say, the two contrasting stories are not so much in disagreement as different editions. Even better, the shift is in intensification, not a change of heart. It is good fortune that leads a life on an ascending path. Capricious and erratic may be the circumstances of life, but constancy of soul is most to be desired. I am not concerned by radical disjuncture, only that the illumination grows in brilliance as I age.

Not to avoid the obvious, you are what is in your life story. And, the story is your interpretation of life. No one else can do it for you; no one should be permitted to take it from you. Through our story we are defined. I choose to define my life on the basis of luminous moments. Through the question, "What's in a Life Story?" I found my own instrument of selectivity. Throughout the remainder of this writing the central theme shall be luminous moments. In turn, this forces the question, "What is in a Luminous Moment?"

A Final Portrait: How I Wish to Be Remembered

This autobiography has been an examination in life evaluation. I believe I have passed the test. In ready acknowledgement, I am neither perfect, nor have I fulfilled the uttermost reach of my good intentions. I have lived generously and faithfully, gradually giving back in measure for what I have gratefully received. However, for more than that do I wish to be remembered.

Were I to sketch a personal portrait, and I shall, the highlights should be upon the soul substance, not simply the external features. Whatever my accomplishments, may they recede into the margins of my autobiography. Far more do I wish to be remembered for the dearly held qualities within. Partly by natural endowment, then by the consequence of sincere choice, I have been the artist of my portrait. Life is earnest, life is real, because each day we are engaged in the composition of our soul. In turn, our soul is the author of our autobiography. And, what else is an autobiography than a self-portrait?

For anyone interested in knowing me, the one beneath all the outward forms, the pulsating me of endless passion, I provide a profile. I was the one among you, *who thrived on intensity, thirsted for ecstasy, and was transformed by luminosity.* I have experienced the life force as intensity, the animating principle of my being. Having little to do with danger or risk, intensity is the guarantee of what is real. The thriving is none other than the reaching forth of desire to become human in the fullest. Drawn to intensity, I am at the fountainhead of spiritual energy. Then, in extraordinary moments, the thirst for oneness bursts all bounds and I am defined by a heightening and a unifying. These are moments of super-consciousness. All things are in that splintering of time made one. By the empowerment of this expanded, inclusive awareness, I am transformed through the luminosity I behold in the world surrounding me. This is how I desire to be remembered.

As a strong undercurrent to my life, a striving for meaning has been most prominent. I have endeavored to translate awareness into meaning, the commonplace into the extraordinary. I have suspected throughout, "Not everything is as it seems" and "life is more than meets the eye." Ever with a full heart and a sincere intent, I searched to raise consciousness from unquestioned acceptance to enthralled wonderment. Scarce wonder that I became a teacher. I have not found set answers so fascinating as the pursuit of inquiry. I have been far more inclined toward reflection than conclusion. Absoluteness appears to be more of an obstructing barrier in life's path, a shutting down of awareness, than a right we are entitled to. To say the least, certainty is not what it wishes to appear to be. Ever true, I have been convinced that modest uncertainty is the best course and the finest lesson.

Please remember me for this: *I lived, overwhelmed by a wonder passing all understanding, authenticated by Beauty, Music, and Love.* Often have I been brought to tears, swept over by a wave of loving life unreservedly. I am my Luminous Moments. May they be my memorial. And may an unending, enormous gratitude be the garland of my eulogy.

> *All the dreams for which we long*
> *Spring forth from the heart in song.*
> *May melodies without delay*
> *Sweetly fill the hours of each day.*

Synopsis By Ten Insights

Though by most standards of expository writing, this booklet is already on the short side for the purpose of further brevity I summarize the more salient insights through these ten concise thoughts.

▶ *As the physical eyes of aging dim, the sight of memory grows more luminous.*

▶ *The Light of time grows in brilliance as life's value is absorbed into the soul.*

▶ *Writing one's own story is, first, an act of self-discovery, then, a gesture of disclosure.*

▶ *You are your life story; the story is your interpretation of life.*

▶ *The light of meaning comes not in a flash, but in the quiet meditation upon all that is past.*

▶ *The luminosity we attach to a past moment becomes a hallmark of the good life.*

▶ *Each luminous moment is a composite of the many; from the many has been taken the luminosity of the one.*

▶ *Religion can guide you, but is not the Light.*

▶ *We confirm our spirituality through the illumination we cast upon life.*

▶ *Luminous moments are revelation of my multiplicity, yet I am One with the Light.*

Worship: At Last and Forever More

(2007)

Inclined toward reverence by disposition, but not submission, & reconsider what might be left of worship. Based more upon actual experiencing than creedal belief, this booklet celebrates the goodness of life.

Telling Tales Outside of Church: An Opening

A word can conceal as much as it reveals. The more it is stretched, the more it conceals. Some words have more history of stretching, than précising. "Worship" is such a word. The purpose of this writing is to sort through the conventional uses of the past and from the residue to fashion a meaning which will graciously grant serenity at the end of life.

Simultaneous to searching out the beauty of worship, its highest aspiration, I shall lay out, in just another version, my spiritual autobiography. A significant part of that story is the departure from conventionality, en route to appreciating its staying power. Paradoxically, it was not until I found my way outside the religious establishment that I was prepared to see the strength of its durability. Though I was spiritually born in the church, only by going outside was I able to grow up. There among the disenchanted I heard woeful tales, hair-raising accounts of religious blindness and cruelty. Convinced of their rational validity, I entered into a stage of spiritual development I will call Reason's Advocate, proceeding to tell my own well-thought out tales. I became a disciple of the Enlightenment.

From inside the traditional religious walls my newfound faith may have appeared as apostasy. I ventured forth, somewhat furtively, realizing how close to heresy my critical eye to them might appear. The further I permitted my thought to extend, however, the more persuaded I became. Slowly, any sense of guilt I suffered was assuaged by a growing realization. My journey into new spiritual territory was none other than what was necessitated by the Holy Spirit of religious awareness. I was "once-born" spiritually in the church; the "new-birth" occurred outside its confines. Put otherwise, my path to religious authenticity led over terrains incomprehensible to its beginnings. The fact that the spiritual awakening came outside the church made my journey all the more ironic. I do not offer this tale as a formula for all who would seek religious understanding. But I testify to my own search. I had to go outside to see in. Not before I exited the limitations of formal religion could I go beyond. What is written in this booklet should be read in light of that presumption.

Subsequent to my departing the authority of the religious establishment, in what might be termed a Declaration of Religious Independence, I experienced a mixture of exhilaration and loneliness. I could not go back to the old, yet I was cautious over how far the new would take me. Still, on I went, driven by pure, unremitting honesty. In looking back over those middle years, I detect an abiding graciousness. Years of disdain gradually dissolved into a kinder view toward my religious upbringing. More comfortably do I enter the "within;" less disturbed am I by the forms of the old. Having come to a resolve and a peace with myself, I can see an abiding blessedness in the tradition's endurance.

The Tale of Two Houses of Worship

The two poles of religion's continuum have been set off, in the interest of a clearer perspective. (I speak of the two as "poles," because the tension between them generates most of the "electricity" in the modern world's religious debate.) For the sake of comparison, aided by curiosity, we step into their respective sanctuaries for a visitation. For you, the reader, this may constitute a "try-it-on-for-size" exercise. I hope I have not made the choice too easy. That is, may I be fair to those who still dwell in the holy shrine of a highly theistic god. Yet, I nonetheless insist, like an expensive piece of clothing, religion ought be comfortable to the spiritual awareness of the wearer. In the service of a higher evolved spirituality honesty tells us much more about the fit than the look. At a certain point the expanding spirit bursts old wine skins, finding them inexcusably confining and, if forced upon the finer sensitivities, an incitement to revulsion.

Yes, I have found the shrines of coercive religion repulsive, thus requiring an exodus. However, I do not choose to make an outright condemnation of all traditional shrines. My argument is not so much with the idea of a shrine, as in the status of the god dwelling therein. It is, therefore, a question of what accoutrements can be transferred from the old to the new. In time, and with the course of the booklet, we will see.

The shrines of old have well-defined house rules. Call them codes, creeds, or cultus, you have rules. Every aspect of human thought, behavior, and volition is rigidly circumscribed. The more objectified the deity becomes, the greater the legislation of rules. Give God the appellation of "Almighty," place him on a heavenly throne, then wonder why the law books grow so voluminous. Legalism is none other than an exaggerated version of God's Will, taken to its extreme logical conclusion and presented as a form of worship. The fear of this Lord is touted to be the beginning of wisdom. No allowance is granted to question whether this image is the true God, for that is a sin, the initial fall from grace. "Free thought" is in certain league with the Devil, for he dared to question the will of the Almighty. It is only a short jump from the fear of the Lord to the Terror of God.

Within the gloomy, anxiety-laden walls of Almighty God's sanctuary all is regimented under the house rules. HE is a stern and forbidding face of the Sacred. Even when the physical representation of the deity is removed, the Holy of Holies rules remain in residence, awesome and inviolate. We are commanded to approach in the spirit of contrition and praise, warned of the consequence of impropriety. Priests are present to guide the worshiper through precise ceremony, so as not to incur the wrath of a petulant deity. Through the course of a sacramental procedure the penitent soul is permitted to plead upon the mercy of the Omnipotent One. At this point in the dealings, depending upon the whim of the god, intercession before the Cosmic Power System is inaugurated. By appeasing the wrath of the deity with a sacrifice, the supernatural reservoir opens to divine grace—good health, prosperous crops, victory in battle, and forgiveness. "Prayer" (early known as conjuring) serves as the currency of transaction, a facilitation of a covenant of "chosenness."

A turning point in religion came with the craving for immortality, attended by the alternatives of Divine Approval or Damnation. Eternal bargaining, with this novel surge of expectancy, was not merely over "earthly goods." Now we are engaged in the worth of human nature. When offense against God became ontological through the doctrine of Original Sin, humans were "sinners" fated to eternal damnation. The adjective to describe human behavior, "sin," assumed the status of a noun, a substance, and all hell opened to swallow the defilement. The human offense of rebellion was so enormous and complete that nothing of this world could adequately propitiate the unwavering divine demand for justice. The sacrifice necessarily must come from the supernatural world. A supreme deal was negotiated among the Godhead.

Thus it came to be, a Holy Child was born, when grown to teach the way of truth, thereupon to be offered in satisfaction to the Father God's Righteousness. Nothing less than the actual Son of God would do. This House of Worship has extended its longevity into the present world, its endowments still well established and its mission enhanced by high technology. In varying degrees modern perspectives have penetrated this archaic mode of thinking, yet the presuppositions of its house rules remain intact.

When God is released from religion's control, amazing epiphanies follow. Rules of the House relax in favor of perceptiveness; authority internalizes as individualized priesthood. Irrespective of what official doctrine may assert, the freed self sees what it sees, in the full range of undeniable experience. Expanded awareness goes out into the world with broadened receptivity, prepared to receive the blessing of spiritual renewal. The exclusivity of the religious establishment must give way to more inclusive revelation. One odd revelation is a restatement of the truth that God is "other" than our preconceived notions. Odd, because to go beyond the religious authority is to be stigmatized as an "infidel." Questioning the old containers of God and risking the ambiguity of doubt are forbidden fruit in the garden of security. The traditional House of Worship equates doubt with apostasy, not appreciating its didactic value in leading awareness higher. Doubt is a venture into the unknown, yet, very possibly, a re-encountering of the Divine. Through doubt the rubbish of accumulated misconceptions and the history of religion's abuse is cleared out. Before religion can be renewed, certainty must be relinquished. On the other side of doubt, not prior to it, awaits the True God. Without a doubt, religion degenerates. God must be reborn in every generation.

Going beyond the orthodox religious tradition into the vast territory of spiritual liberty brings awareness not previously realized. Simultaneous to inclusiveness of experience is a heightening of comprehension. Deeper into the Sacred Presence goes inspiration. Isolated facets of experience weave together in a web of divinity. At the center of our humanity awareness of the Sacred is born. Then, all is indistinguishably fused into One. Between the individual breath and the Divine no final separating distinction can be drawn. In all earthly things can be perceived a heavenly radiance. For a soul aware of the Sacred Present there is no hell. Nevertheless, for this enlarged awareness the matter of membership is problematic. No ready transfer to an appropriate House of Worship is available. Certainly, clusters of new awareness do exist, but by their own nature the organization is looser and the worship less regular. The privilege of spiritual freedom is purchased at the price of marginality. The freedom is genuine, yet at some loss of formal worship.

Strictly speaking, no "rules" pertain to the Expanded House of Worship, other than an obligation for personal integrity. Being most idiosyncratic in regards to revelation, scripture is no more inspired or authoritative than the light it shines within the individual life. Uniformity is more in the spirit of love than in professed belief. Where there is love, differences in understanding only enrich the conversation producing corporate unity. Worship consists in bringing together the collected and shared moments of reverence. Religious independence does not cease to worship, only to seek new forms. The practice of religion is the form, but only the content of feeling can grant the reality of spirituality.

Just as the Divine is in the Spiritual Eye of the beholder, so is the New House of Worship everywhere it chooses to look. If God is that Spirit Presence whose center is everywhere and whose circumference is nowhere, is there a space where a soul cannot worship? The Enlightened Soul can worship anywhere, at the will of sincerity and in the spirit of reverence. Not even the gates of Hell can shut out the grace of sincere longing of the heart for the Divine. With compassion abounding the worshipper of the Everywhere

Sacred can even enter the House of Old and transform the ancient symbols into higher consciousness. Though, I confess, if the accoutrements are too rank with vestiges of an Almighty God's Will Power, then my spirit reviles.

The chapter began with two poles, when in actuality there is a continuum of "houses," representing a gradual evolution from the old patriarchal god to the more expansive, inclusive awareness at worship. The traditions and denominations can be strung out along this spectrum, while at the same time within a specific tradition striking gradients can exist. If a New House cannot be found, one nearest to the soul's enlightenment should be sought, even if it be at a distance. What the soul does not need are dross elements undermining aspiration. Spiritual nurture can only take place where there is soul affinity. For myself, that has well been the cathedral of Nature. Once the Almighty's anger toward all things natural has been replaced by reverence for all life, the partition separating the Sacred and the Natural World is removed and all becomes holy again. In the solitude of Nature I find a sublime worship.

In sum, worship is a disposition, rather than an assumed position. The practice of observing religious form does not guarantee spiritual content. The spiritual content of the form is in a disposition of feeling inseparably at One with the Sacred, permeating and running through all being. Whatever is conducive to this awareness is in the employment of worship, be it the sacrament of communion or the focused beauty of a day. The feeling of reverence is the purest content of worship; an unqualified love of Being is its greatest expression.

Expanded spiritual consciousness is born
in the House of Worship.

Once on its feet the Spiritual Eye
can go anywhere and worship anytime.

Transformation in Ascension

We have observed the ascension of spirit as it worships. Now we shall reflect upon the personal transformation occurring in the Inner Sanctuary. In doing so, a return will be made to autobiographical testimony, yet with an even more circumspect focus. This is the story of how consciousness expands in spiritual ascent and how this greater inclusiveness elevates worship. The subtitle of this chapter could well be, "The Eye altering, alters all."

Consciousness can ascend no higher than the actualizing of the spirit within. Worship directly correlates with the transformation. The further the transformation, the more awareness in worship. We may speak of spiritual ascent in a number of ways, yet ever figuratively, for the Sacred is not to be objectified, not even our relationship to the Divine Thou. I do, however, borrow a term, "God consciousness." By this I mean the internalizing of an awareness of life's divine nature. With *God consciousness* all things are made new in a progression of intensified valuing. I also like to use **Spiritual Eye** to refer to the same inner transformation. As though peering beyond what meets our physical sight, the Spiritual Eye connects our soul with the depth of existence. The edges of worldly forms radiate a luminescence and their centers become fountains of beauty. Into consideration again comes the highest refinement of worship, unqualified reverence, the recognition of the spiritual worth in all things.

The word worship implies the residence of extraordinary worthiness. Not the pragmatic value of that which can be manipulated for physical benefit, rather the presence of a value granting spiritual meaning. For that to be possible, the eye must behold something more than an object. When I revere the radiance of morning sun upon new fallen snow, something wondrous transpires within me. The world is revered and I further realize my spiritual being. The Spiritual Eye is that much more brought into perception and I experience elation. This supernatural encounter with life is our genuine confirmation class in spirituality. Once achieved, with the spiritual eye it is proper to speak of the Kingdom of God Within realized.

The degree of ascent, and thereby the inner transformation, has great implication for morality. The refinement of morality's life-serving potentiality depends upon the ascent and inner transformation. Lower levels of consciousness are only aware of the external doing, not the inner effect. Literalism, and its variant sub-species of Legalism and Dogmatism, reads moral situations very poorly, quite superficially. Rote memorization and mechanical carrying out of rules is the crudest of morality, often destructive of human wellbeing. Rules can be no more life enhancing than the spiritual awareness guiding them. The same can be said of scripture, no more revealing than the eye reading. The reason that the Pharisees could tithe mint and anise, but ignore the weightier matters of the Law, was due to their spiritual blindness. That is to say, they had no depth of spiritual perception. Preoccupation with particulars external to the heart of our humanity is a sure indicator of a soul that has not ascended. This stage of morality is useable for social control, but has little to do with spirituality. And, without spirituality (God consciousness) there can be no judicious wisdom. An absolute, rigid morality devoid of perceptiveness is unworthy of our spiritual inheritance.

At beginning stages of self-actualization "sensitivity" is associated with ego defenses. That is what is meant by taking something said "personally." Ascension reverses the relationship of sensitivity. Just as worship in ascension is ever more encompassing, always more absorbing, so is spiritual realization a widening and deepening of sensitivity. Awareness is upon the other and the altogether, not merely upon the isolated self and its defenses. An even better way to think of sensitivity is: *The beholding of the divinity at the core of existence.* This substratum is inclusive of both the subject and the object, the self and all others. A morality based upon anything less is dichotomous, fated to fall into the abyss of an eternal war between Good and Evil. Having come this far, I conscientiously refuse to go into retrograde, worshipping gods beneath my dignity. My dignity is bound with the intensification in sensitivity I have experienced over a lifetime. Nothing in my life story is more gratifying than that, a binding together of God consciousness and Divine sensitivity. It is not sufficient merely to be alive. I must live sensitively aware of the Divine Presence. There is far too much sacredness to life, to miss any of the days given me. An added blessing is this realization: Our greatest security is in being at one with the ever present Sacred. The higher the ascension, the greater the security.

Awareness of Divine Oneness necessitates a reconsideration of God, which moves us to a new chapter. Yet, this chapter and the next are integrally linked. Without the ascent in spiritual awareness, the gods remain unchanged, relics of lower stages of human evolution. Thus, may we hurry on our way.

The Last of Worship: A Closure

Having achieved a revised version of worship, I am more at peace with myself, relatively comfortable with some old-fashioned forms of religion. Through the writing of this booklet, more clearly do I see why I experience such ill ease in traditional orthodox sanctuaries. Far too many relics of an anthropomorphic god still remain. At times it seems as if I am trapped in a musty museum of out-dated misconceptions of the Sacred. Still, I do not want to leave this life, without a sense of worship. Though I have passed beyond most all of the word's associations from youthful gullibility, a need to hold a worshipful attitude remains imprinted in my heart. It is not the disposition which has changed, rather the manner of speaking about the reality to which it is directed. Here at the last of life, nothing seems more important than to sustain that reverence, within and toward the furthest reaches of the universe. My purpose for living has not been completed, yet I am at peace.

My concerns have come through sufficient pages of thought. Now, I bring closure by drawing together the many into a statement of one. Conciseness has the virtue of pointedness. May the point of the following abbreviated profession of worship be in tribute to worship's blessing.

> *The practice of reverence is perfected in worship. As reverence takes on regularity in our relationships with life, the way is prepared for intense expressions of spirituality, worship. Reverence is an assumed pervasive disposition; worship is a more soulfully conscious act. Through worship the soul becomes one with what is cherished. With the transcendental value of life our soul seeks union. Through the tree, the sky, or whatever be the "face" of the Divine, the soul encounters mystical depth and is made one with All. In worship, through intense concentration upon a sacred focal point, we unite with the spiritual ground of the world and of our being.*

In transforming consciousness into an eye for the spiritual we are supplied with what the soul most needs for wholeness, positive energy. Much of life, as such and somewhat of our own doing, is fragmented and conflicting. In order not to become victim to this negativity, we seek out places for worship. Quite necessarily, these will be settings of beauty, grace, and serenity, whether conventional sanctuaries or natural. In states of inner tranquility, immersed in loveliness of sight and sound, we ward off the internalizing of negativity's darkness. With worship we are made into creatures of light, resplendent and shining. It is with the positive power instilled in us by worship that we re-create the world into a place of love and justice, the Kingdom of God. Those who worship in beauty and truth are the first blessed, the seed of a new creation.

Worship is the art of providing forms for the spiritual.

Living My Conscience: A Political Testament
(2007)

Conscience brought me to politics, not a social proclivity. Once there, I further discovered the liberal inclination of my conscience. This booklet is the most extensive account of my political involvement in troubled times.

A Title Unfurled: A PRELUDE

Various are the ways to track a lifetime. Each will tell its own story, seemingly of a different character. In my writings I have traced the development of many strands to my collective persona. However, I have not written of my political lifeline. Yes, bits and fragments here and there, yet not the composite account. Thus, I bring forth my Political Testament. I owe this to myself for retrospection and to my descendants for future reference.

The title, "Living My Conscience," is inseparable from understanding my political orientation. On its own, I find politics dreary and somewhat alienating. Never have I desired high political office, far too introverted. Still, I have been very political for most of my life. Though the story does not start out that way, I became political. Thus, the tale is one of unfolding, disclosing a series of awakenings. I developed into what could be regarded as a fairly trenchant political critic, through joining movements of protest and writing thought-provoking letters to editors. But all of this was merely in an attempt to be relevant to the times. I did not become political out of some penchant for controversy. I beg that my political history be seen as necessitated by conscience, in a most humane response to indecencies. I am by nature one who avoids conflict and prefers serenity. Along the way I have frequently said to friends, *I would much rather spend my life peaceably as a poet, than perturb my spirit through politics.* Birth endowed me with a strong loyalty to conscience, imbued as I have been with a fierce sense of fairness. Rather than enjoying politics, I endure the responsibility out of an aversion to self-contempt. To do nothing, to remain quiet in the presence of injustice is to wound the soul. Times are gloomy, if not evil, precisely because of silence. Conscience requires that the political word be spoken.

In tracing out my political journey a curiosity precedes me: What about me and the path I followed, leading conscience so far leftward, beyond liberal to meta-ethical? With difficulty would I simply assign this to discontent or disdain, though there has been aplenty of that. More accurately, response to a series of events led me on to new awareness and alternate paradigms. I acknowledge the relativity of this political metamorphosis. Still, I feel a fulfillment in the process. I can live with that, assured that I have been true to the light given me. Political will power has gradually waned, leaving me less actively engaged, but I remain steadfast in my convictions. Dire times will not steal conscience from me.

To make testimony to gloomy times is not a cheery thought. I could choose much more favorable topics to write about. That, however, would not be honest to my life story or true to my testimony. I cannot avoid the times, any more than I can pretend that my life has been free from disappointment. I have been disillusioned, recoiling repeatedly from the slow progress of political enlightenment and honest perception. In disappointment I have asked myself, "Was your conscience born before its opportune time?" With such pangs of anguish I have struggled, preferring suffering with my people to cynical condescension. Nevertheless, through most of my life I have been beset by consternation, astonished at the retarded political thinking in the land of my birth. The sad state of political affairs is made all the more gloomy by the near tribal level of unquestioned conformity. Prejudice, fear, and violence take precedence over clear perception, wise judgment, and constructive measures, leaving the world worse off for all the effort. Without enlightened conscience, politics makes the worse appear to be the better cause.

I could quip, following Will Rogers' lead, "I am not a member of any organized party. I am a Democrat." But conscience transcends all partisanship. Paraphrasing Bertrand Russell, I could entitle the book, "One Hundred Reasons Why I Am Not a Republican!" But I choose, to the extent possible, to be affirmative. In the end, all of the strands making up the life of an individual are best woven together into one cloth. Holistic health recommends it. But for now, with less ambition I simply draw the outline to my political profile, acknowledging in passing that an attempt at synthesis is a venture in the direction of eventual integration.

A Confession and Plea: This writing does not pose to be anything other than a very personal political accounting of my times. Pretense to comprehensiveness and objectivity are laid aside. However, I do claim the presumption of having seen the times with discernment of reason and in the light of a higher loyalty. Please forgive me for any excesses and misrepresentation contained in my story. Where there is anger and rage—and much is beneath the surface—do realize how troubled my soul has been throughout most of my political life. I do not wish to regard even my political adversaries as less than human. This underlies all that I say, consistent with the liberalism I profess. I will, however, insist that anger can accompany clarity of conscience, just as well as clouded perception. Conscience awakened cannot remain silent.

Synopsis of A Synthesis: A TRANSPARTISAN POLITIC

Once upon a time, many years ago, I could have calmly, somewhat patiently, listened to the inane thesis: "Partisan politics are just two different sides of the same issue, that a vital democracy needs a conservative and a liberal side of the aisle, to balance viewpoints, that each person is entitled to his own political opinion, with due respect." A cruder and more insipid version, if that is possible, is: "Each political opinion is equal to another. Every view deserves to be heard. All political positions bear the same validity. Truth lies somewhere in between." If ever I had such bland tolerance, it is entirely gone by now. I dismiss any such indiscriminate nonsense summarily. I have the resurgence of a religious political conservatism to thank for that, though I contend I have good reasons to go far beyond this revulsion

Yes, I know, freedom of speech must not, for the good of the open society, be abrogated and I really do have a dislike of puritanical censorship. Yet, blabbermouths, hate-mongers, and demagogues will have their say, on the same mixed airways as sane, prudential, generous-hearted citizens. While some tortured and torturing souls deserve to be assigned to loony bins—certainly hells of their own making, they will freely walk the Main Streets of our towns and undeterred spew their malice. But just because they are protected under the right of free speech does not mean I shall automatically accord respectability to what they say. Some words invite reproach and twisted, sick souls deserve to be exposed, especially when they are on a political platform. Sometimes solemn scorn and satirical ridicule are the only appropriate moral responses to malicious blowhards. Hypocritical, self-righteousness is a theatrical act waiting to happen when hatred roams about. But theater is not to entertain our self-delusions, rather to shatter our pretensions to rectitude, in the wake of denied foul deeds.

The open society is a permissive society, so that it not devolve into the caldron of internecine war. The difference between a totalitarian society (theocratic or monarchical) and a state of limited, balanced power is this: One faction makes its personal moral commitment normative for all others; consensus and collective good will is the foundation of the latter. However, open, progressive societies are prone, by virtue of a deeply implanted desire to avoid conflict, to confuse advocacy of free speech with legitimacy. This vulnerability makes it all the easier for totalitarian, absolutistic moral factions to take over control, wherein private norms ascend to primacy in the public realm. Tolerance can be the open door for the onward march of intolerance.

In their eagerness to accommodate differences. would-be promoters of the liberal ideal will often close an eye to malice masquerading as respectability. The higher one goes into mannerly accommodation the more appears a tacit oath of politeness: "Let us not fight over our differences!" This do-good intention can function to legitimize the malice, a pretense that certain persons involved in the public discourse are not addicted to vile speech. It would seem courteous to entertain all office-holders as decent human beings, to smile and shake their hand, to offer them a cocktail of accolades. However, the Republican Party appears, to me, to be a "Society of Mutual Cynical Self-Interest." All of this could pass for gentility, if not so deep into willful denial. No amount of politeness can negate addiction to alcohol or to political callousness. No affectation of civility, intellectual, or mannerly, will grant moral redemption to mean spirited conservatism.

Once again I challenge the assumption that because the two-party system is our preferred process of decision-making, everything going on within the two parties is "in bounds." Admittedly, an erosion of this glib, gullible presumption has taken place. Hate and raw self-interest, even in excess of the Republican Party, has broken off to the extreme right.

Still, I consider the point to stand. If you belong to one of the two time-recognized parties, presumably you have built-in respectability. However, from this platform can come some of the most hateful pronouncements, the darkest shades of racism, the meanest legislation, coded as they may be, all wrapped in the bunting of party legitimacy. The presumption of respectability is too dangerous for societal good. It is possible for one or the other of the two parties to gain such controlling power that animosity spills over into everything. Little comfort can be had in being told, "It will all work out in the long run." Pathology must be confronted and be made accountable. The voice of the social critic is ever needed. If it is legitimate to write of anti-intellectualism and the paranoid style in American political life (Richard Hofstadter), why should the meanness factor be out of question? Partisanship may mean malice.

Characteristic of traditional conservatism in general, and of recent Republicanism specifically, is an excessive preoccupation with individual behavior, to the near exclusion of attention to structural defects. It prefers to blame individuals in favor of the traditional "values." Otherwise stated, conservatism has lacked an authentic social ethic, confusing accountability of the individual for social critique. As traditionalists, conservatives sanctify the structures, assigning any dysfunction to the moral failure of individuals. For analytical purposes, I term this stance Personal Morality. Rather than holding the social structures ethically accountable, blame is transferred to the individual, usually in the form of a moral indictment. This is what "family values" and the cultural war is all about! In this respect, conservatism can be regarded as a willed false consciousness, denying the impact of collective effects. The ensuing proposals for social improvement are necessarily unrealistic, based mainly on eulogies of personal virtues and a psychology of self-help decked out in patriotic costume. Beginning with reproach, this false consciousness of individualism ends with a split between exemplars and failures, a type of sanctimonious moral elitism. To say the least, this is cruel preachment for those caught in disadvantageous political and economic positioning. One does not need to speak of "the opiate of the people" to recognize the manipulation of morality by the powerful. Along with challenging the viability of social structures, Social Ethics asks the question, "For whom and what does traditional morality function?"

Another egregious conservative presumption I utterly reject—shall we call it a "faith-based value?"—is the false dichotomy between private interest and governmental undertakings, between "free enterprise" and "big government." In large part this division is allowed by an exaggerated emphasis upon individualism, to the detriment of collective well-being. Holding a negative view of government and a glorified regard for the "private" sector, in a near Manichaean moral dualism, conservatism rules out a positive role for political structures, a priori. A negative view of the state is implicit in Reagan's famous line, "Government is not the solution; it is the problem." To me, this contention is essentially dishonest, a self-righteous pretext for narrow self-interest. Republicanism does not include in its analysis of power the negative effects of unregulated "big business," having exempted it by virtue of ideological bias (laissez-faire economic theory).

The dichotomy is false because individual interest and public interest must not be set in diametrical, exclusive opposition. In a synthesis of the two legitimate interests government has a positive role. Indeed, in many historical instances of individual well-being's denial, mainly due to disproportionate distribution of power, the government has unjustly served private interest. This possibility is ruled out of consideration by conservatism's definition of government as a usurper of individual rights. The line between conservatism and the isolation of libertarianism is very faint and quite unreliable. Of course, again, the ulterior motive is self-interest and a low trust level. Preferring a "republic," conservatives have had discomfort with the opening line of the Constitution, "We, the people," always parsing it in individual interest terms. In stark contrast, I have found synthesis in this definition: *Government is the people working in concert to promote the social well-being.* Needless to say, democratic principles are the instrument by which this collective good is accomplished. Anything else is to leave the field to the devil of uncivil interests and the plight of the powerless to imaginary heavens.

Given my life immersion in political discourse, ever the child of the Enlightenment and constitutionally an egalitarian, I believe I shall die an incorrigible advocate of democratic principles. *If I am a partisan, it is in devotion to democracy.* With this established I will still insist there never has been nor will there ever be a perfect instance of the principles. With all sincerity, without cynicism, I concur with the quip, "Democracy is the most inefficient form of government, but is preferable to all others." In practice democracy is not a structure, though in inauguration it rests upon a "constitution." Like all compacts of human relationship, democracy is a process, an agreement as to how we proceed to make decisions affecting the society we live in, not a static formulation. Yet, necessary precepts pertain, perpetually subject to emendation and re-vision, as fitting the emergence of new realities. The following listing is not exhaustive, rather a foundational beginning. The abolition of any diminishes the effectiveness of them all.

What Democracy Cannot Do Without: Basic Precepts

1. Sovereignty lies in the will of the people.

2. Those given the power of office are accountable.

3. The powers of government must be offsetting.

4. The rights of the minority must not be abrogated.

5. The collective wellbeing supersedes individual aggrandizement.

The Principles of Democracy deserve commentary, to guarantee their preservation and to guard against their usurpation by tyranny. Popular sovereignty does not mean merely the right to vote, the periodic selection of those in decision-making responsibilities—government officials, that is. An equal basic freedom of citizenship is the right to know. How can the "consent of the governed" be real if the people are not well informed? And what mechanism exists by which the citizens can know, other than inquiry and oversight? The Fourth Estate, an independent news media, certainly is essential to governmental accountability, especially when its agencies become captive to executive control. However, under our arrangement for the division of powers, the branch nearest to the people, the House of Representatives, bears constitutional responsibility for keeping government open to view. Oversight hearings should be the normal course of business, not the exceptional, as a parallel role to that of enacting law. The "balance of powers" arrangement required by the Constitution is most in danger when one political bloc is in control of two or more branches. Too readily can the obligation of oversight turn into a "Star Chamber" of partisanship. Then is when self-interest rules and oversight falters. That is the time for popular sovereignty to reassert itself and public discourse to force the issue of accountability. Power must not be permitted to ensconce itself in closed chambers and take unto itself exclusive privilege. Over against such eventuality must inviolably stand a Bill of Rights and the collective well-being. That is the inspiration of equality.

Democracy is a wonderfully freeing concept. But not all that calls itself democracy is democratic. Not all that dresses in glittering rhetoric of freedom is democracy. Many who tout "Founding Fathers" are really charlatans in disguise, monarchists in modern costume. By its own nature, privilege resists power-sharing, concocting all varieties of hypocritical rationalizations to defend its monopolizing of power. Since the presidency is a single-headed consolidation of power, no branch of government is more tempted toward monarchy than it. Historically it has been the executive branch that has most overreached its constitutional powers, particularly in the course of executing war. In consequence the mechanisms of democracy are obviated. "Presidential prerogative" substitutes for divine right and "executive privilege" is a cover for old-fashioned "state secrets" of monarchy. In principle, democracy knows of no executive privilege. The canard, that the executive needs secrecy for candid advice is just that, the creation of sinister power. Tyranny dressed in the rectitude of executive privilege is still tyranny. All of government under democracy must be transparent. Every claim to the contrary is suspect.

Which brings us back to conscience, the only true recourse against tyranny. However, conscience is poorly understood by most persons. They confuse it with obedience to moral code. In my intellectual evolution I have come to honor conscience as far more, even consider it quite differently. I lay down the prerequisites for conscience.

    1. An **empathetic disposition** toward life.

    2. The **courage** to stand on one's own truth.

    3. Unrelenting **honesty** in the face of altering reality.

Empathy opens us to life; courage enables us to be honest. The greatest courage is in the willingness to remove all distortions in one's perception of reality. Perception is never perfect or ever entirely complete. *Conscience is the on-going process of clearing perception of aberrations, a receiving of life in a higher light*. From earliest socialization and in the course of abrasive interaction we accumulate unreliable presumptions, leading to inaccurate reading of reality. These fall under the category of bias and prejudice.

Presumption generally serves the function of a defense mechanism, when not challenged producing a system of denial. If the greatest lie is the one we tell ourselves, surely the greatest act of conscience is in giving up distorted perception, no matter the dictates of tradition or the codes of society. Most often acts of conscience involve disconcerting encounters with life situations, cognitive dissonance in how life was previously perceived. Experience and perception are at odds. Critical thinking, indispensable to conscience, is the power of courage in the pursuit of clearer perception. To that employment belongs our loyalty. Anything less is not honesty. Conformity is not conscience and obedience is not loyalty to conscience. And, in the end we are saved by the measure of empathy in our honesty.

The nemeses of conscience are many—rationalization, hypocrisy, and delusion being the most insidious. Rather than clarify our relationship to reality, they obfuscate. When persisted in, these enemies of conscience become structured false consciousness. The most devious trait to false consciousness is that it becomes inured to its own falsity, unaware of the incongruity between what it thinks and reality. Under its misleading, shall we say dishonesty, consciousness becomes its own enemy. When the disparity grows to extreme proportions, the denial approximates the disabling of psychosis. Just as false consciousness is the adversary of conscience, so is conscience the cure to the malady. Not simply a onetime battle and a quick remedy, conscience is the ongoing work of keeping the waters of awareness clean. In the most evil of times, conscience is both most called upon and most under duress. Then must conscience and courage join to serve the wellbeing of life. Conscience is not for the fainthearted or the simpleminded.

Synopsis suggests conciseness and brevity. I confess, up to this point, the chapter has not been condensed. So, permit me to conclude with a synthesis of the previously written, all digressions and excursuses drawn into a confessional synopsis. Synthesis implies a fusion of counterbalancing considerations. I believe the overarching synthesis of my political, philosophical, and religious journey has involved the best of tradition emendated by the undeniable truth of experience, *a blend of the enduring with the empirical.* Most of the time I have found these two, thesis and antithesis, are in dynamic tension. Not choosing to sacrifice one in preference for the other, I have sought reconciliation and harmony. What I have most endeavored to filter out in the process is all that traces to the negativity built into our morality by fear and prejudice. I have fought consistently against lapses of faith in our better humanity, violations against our inherent worth. The spirit in which a person enters politics predetermines its outcome. A positive common spirit transcends all differences, ethnic and cultural, uniting our humanity. A distrusting negative spirit divides, no matter what its purported justification. These are my basic political convictions.

Now, in as few words as possible, I state **My Political Testament.** Politics is indispensable to loving life and caring for the neighbor. This obligation rests upon an affirmative disposition. With dedication to distributive justice politics must take seriously structure and power. Democracy and its resident guide, conscience, are the procedural rulers. The prudent political act is not in destroying the existing fabric of societal life. Yet, *under the scrutiny of conscience's critical eye each degradation of humanity, individual and structural, must be incisively confronted with one's whole personhood.* Anything less lacks equation between the forever and the here-and-now. A religion which does not affirm this incumbency has lost its saltiness, likely concealing dishonest complicity or hypocritical sanctimony. In my native country I have found far too much religious irrelevancy leading to political irresponsibility. Being "saved" for eternity does not make up for a failure of political will. Cowardice can be more easily forgiven, than abdication in the face of social injustice, for that is usually accomplished through denial of complicity. Willful naiveté is no excuse for not knowing. Citizenship imposes an obligation to know, not simply the "state of the Union" but the wellbeing of the people. Politics has to do with people. So be it!

All in conclusion, my survey of the political landscape has left me more than ever persuaded that the choice is not between two parties, one less desirable than the other. Yet, I find it extremely difficult to extend respectability to conservative politics. To the recent rash of conservatism I recoil in dismay, feeling morally offended and intellectually insulted. John Kenneth Galbraith put it well, "They are too wrapped up in themselves."

If forced to give explanation, I would be tempted to say, current Republicanism lacks an essential humane element, representing a hideous character flaw. Adjectives cluster together: *Selfish, suspicious,* and *sanctimonious; distrusting, disingenuous,* and *disparaging.* Therein you have the soul of a conservative. I simply do not see reactionary Republicanism as a viable option in political discourse. Its main "contribution" has been nay saying and obfuscation, channeling great underground streams of subliminal ill will and suspicion into public life. My assessment of contemporary Republicanism may be a bit too sharp for bipartisan purposes. But these comments are my true, measured regards. I will allow, what I have written prefers to error on the side of "Father, forgive them, for they know not what they do." It is the nature of my liberalism to assign obdurate conservatism to dysfunctional modes of thinking, instead of villainy, delusion rather than meanness.

A liberal spirit, in contrast, arises out of *trust, courage, openness,* and *generosity.* So, rather than dwelling upon the cringe factor in my regards, I choose to elevate to a higher, more circumspect terrain. This I shall call a **Transpartisan Politic,** the underwritten theme of this chapter. Neither a joiner nor a true believer, I shall prize my independence of thought to the end. And permit the pieces to fall where they may. Please include in that as much compassion as I can manage.

How to Survive Dark Times: A POSTLUDE

Even though I am too incorrigibly an optimist to despair of the future, due to my stubborn desire to believe in the essential goodness and purposefulness of life, I echo Bertolt Brecht (in 1939 calling out against Nazism and anticipating war) and confess, "Indeed, I live in gloomy times." I simply acknowledge my people have lagged far behind my idealistic hopes for wisdom's guidance. The world at large has stumbled, sometimes fitfully, through the darkness of a self-made cultural lag toward the light. But I had expected exceedingly more from my country. Rather than taking the challenge of modernity, I sadly judge that my people have regressed into a fearful rearguard defense of their privileges. Indeed, I live in gloomy times.

I was greatly inspired by the outburst of idealism during the Kennedy years, then radicalized by the incisive critical thought of the Sixties. Is it traceable to the ebullience of that period of my political evolution I remain in disbelief over the dismal, regressive state of contemporary politics? At that time I would not have allowed myself even to contemplate to what low level the current political discourse has since fallen. My erroneous assumption was that once higher awareness is achieved, it could not be revoked. To be sure, pockets of progressive thought still exist. And, a widespread residual generosity along with an apolitical good will, continues to bless the land.

American people do have caring hearts. It is their thoughtless, reflexive fallback upon obsolete notions of virtue that gets them into trouble. That a reactionary Republicanism, with all its pretensions to goodness, should have such a strong hold over such a large segment of the population is a travesty upon all the glorious idealism purportedly guiding the Republic. With all of its mindless rhetoric and smug cultural war self-righteousness, this most recent version of conservatism is a throwback to its nineteenth century ancestor, the Know-Nothing Party. Not identical in platform, yet one in the spirit of reactionary, regressive solutions to social ills, the two stand together, years apart, to further the cause of nativism, pure culture at home and supremacy abroad. How good-willed people, especially when they attach to themselves the name "Christian," can hold such uncritical, parochial values is a riddle beyond answer. I cannot easily forgive, much less accept, such betrayal of the universal human spirit. Indeed, I live in gloomy times!

What does one person do, when his/her upward elevation of consciousness exceeds the political perception of the many? I do see the vast majority of the world's population, the fellow citizens of my country included, walking in the darkness of antiquated shibboleths and anachronistic values, no longer viable for confronting the problems of the present, much less comprehending the challenges extending into an uncertain future. Sir Francis Bacon's "idols of the tribe and marketplace" persist to the perplexity of a New Age groaning to be born. Once I had what now appears to have been a naive faith in the power of cogent rational discourse to advance the grand vision of enlightenment. Now I realize the crux of the human predicament lies not in the intellect, rather in the inordinate fear of change and an animal instinct for self-preservation. But a revolution in technology and the resulting concentration of power render traditional values no longer workable. The dysfunction of our values lies in how we think and the consequent economic manner whereby we live. Worst of all, a fixed consciousness prevents us from even framing our problems realistically. Rashly and vindictively we would prefer to victimize others by refusing to face our need to change. Easier to blame than to change, others are sacrificed so that we may clutch to our false idols.

Civilization stands at another brink; a formidable challenge of our own making awaits a life-saving response. *Peace will come from a willingness to give up old ways of thinking and a re-birth of intelligent love.* History invites us into the cusp of a New Age. If we refuse to enter this strange new world, we default in our moral responsibility, choosing death of the spirit in preference to renewal. Renewal demands unprecedented response, not the reaffirmation of the old. Conservatism holds to values of the past; trust in life opens us to new understanding. In that latter respect, I regard myself as a progressive liberal.

The curse of those in dark times who grow to be too aware is that they see too deeply into the social malady and cannot pretend to know otherwise. What to others seems nothing more than popular news is perceived by the socially awake as grotesque. Without alarm, yet with unremitting seriousness, the social prophet is compelled to witness to the time, in the name of humanity. Not out of rancor have I spoken in critique of my world. Always in love of people should the prophet speak. By all means, the social critic would best avoid sharp-biting jeremiads, for mournful complaints and pessimistic lamentations deflate the vital spirit of any age. Unredeemed anger sends forth a wave of vengeful violence, rather than life-affirming currents.

To the end I will strive to keep my words directed toward the light, longing for a new and more glorious enlightenment, a Golden Dawn. It is my wish that the course of history will bring a generation ashamed of the religious and political conservatism, which has pulled this country into a dark age of self-righteous indifference. I do not expect to live so long. But I can anticipate in my dreams the return of a more humane spirit to guide the country I have loved since birth.

Shafts of Light Toward the End of the Spirit's Journey: Revelations of Religion's Redemption

(2008)

A tender reaching out late in life to embrace the mystic religious sentiment that has resided in me from the beginning. Though much on the surface has fallen aside, a center of spirituality has remained, to comfort and to complete the yearning.

Words to Begin

The journey has been long and the soul has grown weary of unending search. Much of what was sought has not been found and what is left is less than had been hoped for. Still, earnestness has been a constant companion and sincerity has never left my heart. More of an assurance than a vision, the truth I have gained soothes the restlessness once impelling my pace. Most of all, an inner peace welcomes each and all sights of beauty.

Shafts of light illuminating understanding have guided me along the way. But now, in approaching the end, a brighter luminescence envelopes the worthiness of life's venture. What I know, with much forgotten, coalesces into an epiphany of goodness. Many coats have I worn, only to be cast aside; various excursus into curiosity broadened the path, only to be left behind. But, in sum, the collective light of consciousness blesses me with euphoric wellbeing. What was rejected in religion as unacceptable has been replaced by a contentment beyond all ordinary understanding. However, I have not lost my spirituality. Religion has been revealed in a higher light. In its redemption I find completion to my spirit's journey.

Never have I wanted to rebel for rebellion's sake. What may appear to the traditionally religious as skepticism has really been my desire for authenticity. My thrusts into orthodoxy by critical thinking have not been in the intent to destroy; rather they are in response to the shining of a higher light upon unquestioned assumptions. If anything has been destroyed it is the thoughtless stumbling through life's challenges, the dishonesty of pretending that unexamined conviction is sufficient for wisdom. My critical mind has been the surgical tool by which the dead weight of unwarranted presumption is cut away, guided as much as possible by a holy light from above. And now, in the twilight of life, I am convinced that without the faithful critique of religion all along the way, I would not have the gift of a much higher revelation.

The journey has not been for naught. The portions and times fit together as a holistic revelation: My life has been encompassed by meaning and purpose. Therefore, any regrets have to do with the quantity, not the quality. How I have chosen to use time recedes in importance in face of the existentially verifiable way in which I have valued life. Maybe not the typical "good and faithful servant," I shall go to my peace in deep reverence for life.

These scraps, bits and pieces, shreds of thought and streaks of insight represent some of my final revelations, yes, *ultimate shafts of light*. Their profundity lies not in a compendious inclusiveness, rather in their seasoned measure. The wisdom therein contained is of a decidedly different kind, to that of youthful intimations. However, lest I mislead the reader, this journal of revelations does not comprise comprehensive utterances so much as commentary on perennial religious questions from a more extended journey's view. No more than a rather random collection of inspired moments, still the point-of-view is more mature and seasoned, than it was earlier. Not the complete word, yet have I ever spoken of life from such a wealth of experience? May the pieces fall in new alignment of thought, beneath a more comprehending light.

Reader:

Once upon a time

my life's work was

to consolidate my understanding

into a tight bundle of consistent thought.

Now, as I approach the end of the road,

the connecting threads are coming apart

and the distinctions are dissolving,

leaving a lifetime of knowledge as a thick matrix

upon which to cast these last shafts of illumination.

A transcendental glow of resplendent goodness

emanates from the merging of light and understanding.

Tranquility supplants consistency.

I have been made one with my being.

THE TREE OF
ILLUMINATION

Religion, Once Redeemed, Reborn

How does religion enter the Stations of the Cross by which to be redeemed from its own defilement? Certainly not through piety of muttered ancient incantations, for they may be a part of the contamination. Equally, new life will not come by the power of an otherworldly cheap grace baptism. Its waters may be just as polluted. Critical thinking will be a tool in the reconstruction, but alone cannot bring deliverance, only biting cynicism.

Prophets spoke of hardness of heart. I prefer to speak of fearful mind-set. Paul had scales removed from his eyes. I emphasize empathetic perceiving. Anxiety and the fear born of insecurity have a way of clinging thoughtlessly to old shibboleths, lapsing into what can be termed moral inertia. When religion loses the moral "salt" of critical evaluation it languishes in blindness, spending inordinate time mouthing moralistic precepts in place of moral perceptiveness. Breaking forth from this fixation is extremely difficult, for the mind and heart have in the course of rote recitation ossified into a rigid orthodoxy, predetermining thought and behavior. In its lexicon "faithfulness" is defined by the degree to which the self obediently remains within the structured mode of believing. The world in crisis pleads for a new word of deliverance. With built-in prejudices established religion is left with reiterating the old word. Out of desire to be true to the heritage, the religion becomes irrelevant.

But wait, there will come children who see visions and the walls of settled thought cannot stand forever, especially when the times they are a-changin'. When moral circumstances become tight, the transcendental vision comes through at thin places. Moral perception advances ahead of conventional morality and all hell breaks loose. Defenders of traditional religion stone the unbelievers with charges of secularism. Fresh waters of spiritual awareness are relegated to the cesspool of infidelity. Therefore, epiphanies must be preserved with courage. Unnamable sensitivity will be cherished without doctrinal certification. New revelations of how life's goodness can be embraced must take precedence over fearful conformity to old moral codes. Without knowing what to call oneself, for even language has been made new, one's voice is rendered dumb in the presence of spiritual quickening. With revelation's new clarity the way is forward. Once called, the soul cannot turn back. The risk of orthodoxy's rejection is accepted, even while love of the ancestry is preserved. Willingly conscience chooses the path leading away from the crowd, while realizing its deviation will be confused with those who fall beneath conventional morality. Society crucifies its moral rebels on the same Golgotha as its outlaws.

At this point in religion's redemption the truth of paradox becomes real: In weakness is abiding strength. As the entrenched institutional power of the inherited religious tradition is relinquished, a greater power is given. The self has been empowered by the visitation of higher moral awareness. Rather than submission to institutional religious authority—as embodied by priest, guru, or prophet—the liberating act is in acknowledging the inner revelation, the transforming experience of the transcendental vision. This is the Mount of Transfiguration, after which transpires the Baptism of Cleansing. (The reverse of the sequel implied by the controlling notion of sin.) A double cleansing is performed by the fresh waters of enlarged awareness. Simultaneous to washing away religion's defilement by decades of moral dullness, the self is no longer plagued by those same poisons. Hope springs fresh from eternity's viewpoint. Faith in living is renewed; belief is measured by conscientiousness.

The power of religion redeemed is that in the moment of enlightenment the limitations of parochial vested interest fall aside. The shackles of servitude are broken. Religion is freed from serving as an ultimate legitimization of cultural provincialism. The irony is that the traditionalists that charge the fresh moral vision with being "secularism" are far more bound to the values of the culturally embedded religion. In the place of this cultural captivity redeemed religion is empowered to critique all cultural equivocation and compromise. The moral vision flowing from transcendental detachment is marked by circumspection and universality. Yet it is precisely by this disengagement that religion is able to thrust itself into the immediacy of this world with nonpartisan perspective. **Religion serves culture best when detached from partisan entanglement.** But that is only possible if religion is periodically cleansed. In religion's redemption is found its power. Unless willing to be reborn, religion dies. In repeated rebirth religion is redeemed.

Now I Better Understand "Going Home"

Home has always had an honored place in my emotional chambers. In youth I was yearning to experience the world, but I never wanted to abandon the strong tie to where I came from. Now, after these many years, I have come to understand what "home" so profoundly represents. As a mythological metaphor, *home is the ground and return of our being.*

I have traveled far from home during my lifetime, gaining all the riches of experiences and transmuting them into the treasure of wisdom. I found and absorbed much goodness, love, and beauty. Thus I am forever grateful and feel enormously full. But here I am, toward the end of the path. I hear a clear calling home. As the years turn into repetition and my energies go into decline, weariness overcomes this traveler. Homeward bound I am, toward the completion beyond all travel. A realm of rest and peace calls me.

Most of life is outward bound, compiling the substance of what it means to have existed. Nothing has been entirely lost; not much more is needed. It is not necessary to remember everything, for with the good fortune of age the mind becomes porous and the memories grow too numerous. Sufficient is it to know you have been granted a full measure of humanity. At the end of the journey into existence the self is inward bound, seeking culmination. How filled with anguish must be a returning soul, who finds home empty. The inwardness of going home can be no more than the residue of the genuineness of life lived. How tragic it must be to go home and find nobody there. Insincerity has no homecoming.

As a mythological construct, *home* has more to do with a state of being, than a location of the body. This emotional place evokes feelings of being cared for, security, and love. Secure in an awareness of acceptance, uncomplicated by demands of responsibility and pangs of anxiety, at its best childhood is a study in simplicity. Neither remote political concerns nor abstract metaphysical ruminations intrude into the blithe innocence of protected youth. The daily gifts of life are taken in readily, not perplexed by thought of how to put it all together in one intelligible whole. The desire for experience is greedy; only with time does reflection trouble itself.

In maturity, once the necessities of existence are satisfied, life is rendered complex by a quest for meaning. Yet, from this comes the wisdom of the ages, the treasury and enhancement of the arts. To the implicit melody of life are added the grace notes of enduring value. At a second level, superimposed upon the immediacy of taking in life is a sense of purpose not available to youth. The meaning of life grows in depth and richness. We glory in that awakening.

Toward the end of the life cycle comes what some would call a "second childhood," often referred to as the last act in the "stages of life." This finale, in preparation for the drawing of the curtain, is brought on by the dimming of awareness and a weakening of the body. One should be grateful for having lived so long, but not ashamed of the inexorable move toward seniority. The reversion toward a second childhood should not be understood as merely a loss of inhibition and a decreased sense of propriety. Under the appearance of "I don't give a damn any more" might be found a more profound truth about human existence. The real message could just be, please take away all the unnecessary life complications and leave me to the ultimate task of going home. For myself, I hope to remain cordial and gracious in confronting the reality of my death, for I believe there is a correlation between honesty in dealing with the inevitable and the kindness I wish to preserve. Far too many tortured souls fight others, as they wrestle with death. However, it is important to know, the reversion is not to childishness, rather to the state of desire represented by "home."

Recently I listened to Dvorak's *New World Symphony*. Once again the plaintive strains of the "Largo" movement, serenely performed by an oboe, overwhelmed me in sweet sadness. "Why for that," I asked myself. "Why is the effect always so melancholic?" Even in the prime of life the mood was the same. It almost always brings me near to tears, if not over into deep sadness. What other than a meditation on life's finality could it be? Is the call not to the culmination of all yearning, condensed into the anticipation of cessation? Blended inextricably into the sadness is the beauty of an unlimited life urge. In hearing the maudlin tinged lines of Stephen Foster's song, *Ah, May the Red Rose Live Alway*, we may ask, "Why should the beautiful ever weep? Why should the beautiful die?" In reply, do we weep for the death of life's beauty?

I do not know when the words, "Going Home," were added to Dvorak's tune, but I hear the words every time I hear the melody and a poignancy pricks my heart. Acutely I realize how much goodness has been bestowed upon my life and those I have loved. But in the same moment I am aware that it will come to an end. In the days toward the end I am certain that I will desire to be left in the pure simplicity of uncompromised reverence. Busyness will pass away and concerns will not hold me hostage. Responsibilities will recede in importance and the untrammeled joy of childhood shall return. My obituary will not include, "He went home to be with the Lord." Still, how fitting will be the expression, *"He heard his call to go home and followed."* Home is not an imagined heaven of theological postulation. It is a mythological construct to grant the blessing of lasting peace. Yes, I am blessed by the words, "Rest in peace."

In the simplicity of "home" is the plentitude of spirit. In an end is the entirety of life. It is not that life passes too quickly, but that it contains so much and must end. In the consciousness of home lies the completion of life, more in substance of soul than detail of experience. The wellbeing of soul transcends the loss of memory. Two images come to mind, of a *lovely maiden*, reclining upon a rolling Nebraska hill, and a *shy lad* miles away, lovingly looking out upon the world so fair, both bathed in the hopeful sun of youth. Now we, she and I, have grown old together. The first picture symbolizes all that life was to be for her and him. Our picture of age represents all that life has been. Going home will not erase the imprint of those images. Yet, a grief shall inhabit their passing. The haunting strains of the song anticipate that moment, with a heavy melancholy. Oh, life, thou hast been too much.

On this exquisite April day, when all of nature reaches out with desire for life, when new growth appears everywhere, abundant beauty is able to assuage the thought of going home. Spring is the affirmation of life, its beauty a birthplace for a love of life. Wrapped in one day is a lifetime of love. A spring day is the epitome of life. But eventually, maybe in autumn, the call to come home will take over my being. And I shall follow, simply, peaceably.

In writing this I have found peace beyond pathos, gratitude triumphing over grief. It is finished. I have done the work of redeeming life from death. I can go.

Words to Conclude

So to bring to conclusion shafts of light upon fragments of writing. Through these pages I have enlarged religion, so that I might once again fit into its company. Ever have I regarded myself as religious.

In retrospect, I see how strenuously I still strive for purity in religion. Not for the purpose of righteousness, but in order to have something to embrace and esteem. This has been my life's work, though it will remain unfinished. Not in the least, I possess the sense of having been true to my calling. Some have been called to preach, a vocation I have eschewed. I believe I was called to teach and this writing is another form of teaching. My profession may have involved some measure of imparting wisdom, but that not in the mere delivery of information. Just as meaning comes in at the edges and at "thin places," my encountering of wisdom has come more in the wake of questioning.

Questioning is as indispensable to learning as memory. Memory is the substance of the past; questioning is the path to the future. Without question the pool of knowing becomes stagnant. With the agent of questioning we grow and retain vitality. To finally conclude is to bring all to a close. So, I am left with more questions than answers, more subtle flashes of awareness than well-formed theses. In this I am not disappointed, for it is in the nature of an honest, seeking mind to remain open ended. What would disappoint me, dear reader, is that you did not see the thrill of inquisitiveness written over all of these pages.

Let not my thought be finalized. Grant what I have written only the dignity of being cast upon the universal ocean of human consciousness. If my thought should open fountains of thought in you, may they flow in streams free and fresh. Do not take from my words truth. Instead, receive them as threads in weaving the fabric of your own meaning. Nothing more than this should I want for my legacy as a thinker and a teacher.

Seek ye first the light of your own spirit!

By Metaphor Saved, By Mysticism Made One

(2009)

Possibly the most advanced version of my religious regards. Mysticism remains as the preservation of spirituality and metaphor serves as the mode of speaking about it. In effect, love is adopted as the Cosmic Christ.

The Inception of a Destiny

May we begin with this paradox: What will be, already is. Only in the faintness of intuition is the truth of this apparent contradiction perceived. Not until an advanced stage in the journey is the meaning realized. As the riddle is dissolved, consciousness enters the mystical.

Jesus said, "The Kingdom is coming; the Kingdom is already here." In following his teachings we live in the intersection between the now and forever. The contradiction is only logical. Truth is in the passing beyond. While time waits for no one, the wisdom of truth comes from a process of patient waiting in the stream of experience. Time flows, yet completion comes in its own good time. To the mystic all is double-entendre.

A central strand to my life story has been the living out of this paradox. In retrospect I see my emotional and intellectual growth has come in couplets: *Desire — Realization; Awareness — Completion; Inception — Destiny.* The merging of the two active elements has provided the dynamic for movement and creativity. The energy generated has been the vital motive power in my self-actualization.

What does this have to do with mysticism? Without the mystical temperament I would not have been enabled to make movement toward completion. Reflexively, the progression brought into play greater mystical awareness. It can be said mysticism succeeds under its own power, for it doubles back on itself. The more we mystically absorb, the further we can go into mysticism. Yet, all along I have kept companionship with my critical powers of reason, to refine and articulate the mystical awareness. In the mystical moment reason and intuition unite, to usher in a greater consciousness.

191

The mystical path is hidden from the ordinary eye, the gate sealed and the course obscure. However, the path is made easier by initial awareness of where one is going. Thus, I provide a schema of the booklet's direction, the sequence written into the chapters.

INCEPTION	*Thirst for Experience*
DEPARTURE	*Beyond Conventionality*
MERGER	*Transcending Particularity*
UNITY	*Mythologizing Universality*
DESTINY	*One With Love*

All this goes to say, *the ending is implicit in the beginning*. Our destiny is forecast in the seed of our inception. Life is emergent, not fixed. I thank my lucky stars that I was set on my path with a proclivity toward mysticism. My destiny has been to dissolve the Many into One, the One into the All, to become one undifferentiated being.

Not without cognizance of implication did I compose the title of this booklet. The lead parts are played by Metaphor and Mysticism. However, in spite of the sequence, the headliner is Mysticism, with the supporting role of Metaphor in the way of an opener. As to salvation, that shall remain a relative property. The salvation I promote is not liberation from sin into eternal life. Quite otherwise, Metaphor has spared me from the very salvation that its literalism would condemn me by. Indeed, the "by" is entirely instrumental and free from entangling theology. Finally, to speak of One is the same as to follow Mysticism, and vice versa. Each is implied by the other.

Thematic Threads of Thought Tying This Treatise Together

❧ *To speak of the spiritual, language need undergo a transformation.*

❧ *Metaphor is the appropriate means of expressing mysticism.*

❧ *Myth is the vehicle for unity of value.*

❧ *The physical is redeemed by the incarnation of Cosmic Love.*

❧ *Wrapped within the Peace of Oneness the soul is fulfilled.*

The Physical and the Metaphorical

Language originates in the physical. Some would say, "That is all there is to reality." Then, on the basis of reason and inference these empiricists construct the enterprise of science. With that I have no quarrel. The physical realities rightly belong to the jurisdiction of science, including human wellbeing and the preservation of nature. Let us be clear, religion is way out of its field when it poses to usurp the jurisdiction of science. If there is any legitimacy for religion, the claim will rest on other grounds. Religion's inception flows from a different wellspring. Logos and Mythos shall remain peculiar to their origin, *sui generis.*

If science is all there is to intellectual legitimacy, then religion and poetry are fated to a paltry existence, if not outright nonexistence. These fine arts would rightly be relegated to the inferno of pernicious superstition. However, if only science is to reign, where shall emotion and sentiment go, other than into servitude as a second class citizen? Is it not enough that science be dominant in space and time? Why should science also take over the intimations of Inwardness? To talk only of material particulars, as interpreted through relevant theoretical constructs, is to deprive life of its deeper and larger meaning. If sentiment is permitted to come in, the entrance is made surreptitiously under the laboratory door. Or, if formally recognized, sentiment is reduced to scientific modes of explanation. Why cannot science acknowledge that it is unable to satisfy the human need for emotional connectedness to the universe in a manner other than its own language? Science may allow that we are made of stardust, but not that we are metaphorically destined for the stars. For the pulsating, yearning heart science alone is too barren a landscape. In allocating our monies, may we grant allowance for both science and the arts? As the proverb goes, "If you possess two coins, use one to buy bread, the other for a book of verses." The first is science, the second the arts. Accordingly, we press on to linguistic coinage for the mystical.

I begin anew, with the premise that emotions are the lifeblood of our lives. In order to accommodate this life-affirming impulse, we devise a language, by which to own and communicate our deepest sentiments. As previously stated, language originates in the physical. The way by which it is enabled to serve as a vehicle for Inwardness is through radical transformation, almost unto equivocation. (I use "Inwardness" like I understand "soul," to designate all subjective, relational awareness.) The appropriation of literal language for the purpose of Inwardness is nearly subversive in its evasion. Yet such transformation is necessary if we are to avoid misunderstanding and false claims. When we speak of the spiritual and the arts, we need to be aware that we are using language differently and for a different purpose. The use is for inner effect and not physical attribution. Those who do not make the linguistic switch deceive themselves into believing physicality pertains to the spiritual. The language of Inwardness relies upon approximation and analogy, a tweaking of ordinary meaning, and must never be taken literally. Decency requires some notification of this altered use of language, an implicit admission that empirical verification is not possible. Religion and poetry share the same epistemological predicament. With their utterances on tenuous grounds they cannot challenge science on its. On the other hand, without the metaphorical, our lives are left emotionally bereft. It is better to fess up than to be misunderstood.

Metaphorical language depends upon the power of suggestion for its expressiveness, even to the point of tricking the reason. In its equivocation, metaphor denies as much as it permits. Hilarity ensues, when the two are switched, for then the metaphor falls on its own face. The content of metaphor is connotative, of feeling awareness, more than denotative. With "spiritual language" nothing of the outer physical world is implied, only the inner experience of relatedness. That is what makes correct metaphorical language so religiously effective. In religion's interest we ought to make the linguistic switch consciously clear. For materialistic minds that is extremely difficult, nearly impossible. For their benefit might it be advisable to flag metaphorical use? But of what gain is color marking, if spiritual denseness persists in seeing only the surface meaning? A certain degree of intellectual sophistication is required to appreciate the subtlety of metaphorical meaning. Figuratively speaking, it is like shutting one eye and opening another side of the brain. Something is borrowed and something is new. Literal language conveys particularity, while religious language is best in reference to universality. Literalism imprisons the spirit in the limitations of the physical.

In way of an exercise into the nature of metaphor I appeal to a nursery rhyme, "Jack be nimble, Jack be quick; Jack jump over the candlestick." Here we have a metaphor for how to be metaphoric. To understand, use, and appreciate metaphors the mind must be agile and quick. Sort of like dancing in the air, twisting and turning on the slightest hint. Metaphorically the candlestick is the physical given; jumping is the lightness of metaphor. Clumsy minds cannot get beyond the literal. By contrast, metaphor teases, coaxes, and seduces us into new appreciation.

We turn to the Historical Jesus—Cosmic Christ typology. What did Paul see on the Damascus Road? Particularity or universality? To fuss over the historical particulars is to distract from potential metaphorical significance. The sum total of details does not add up to a universal metaphor. In selecting a religious metaphor it is necessary to dip into the particular world for one half of the reference, but the meaning exceeds the physical. The other half comes from a subjective source, what we term the "spiritual." Not to acknowledge this is to commit a category mistake. This brings onto the scene the function of "miracle." In a pre-scientific age, to assign a miraculous cause was not to make a scientific ascription. Today, religious literalists aver it as such, but in that claim they deplete the utility of the metaphor. The "tag" is more properly regarded as a cue for the metaphorical universal. The "Risen Christ" remains ambiguous. In traditional orthodox circles the term became the doctrine of literal physical resurrection and immortality. However, for those initiated into the mystery of life, the metaphor can just as well render the Historical Jesus into a Cosmic Christ. The transmission serves the purpose of connecting individual consciousness to an emotional universality. Metaphor is always a statement of subjectivity, not a scientific assertion. Nevertheless, the metaphor serves to hold in place the feeling of having experienced the universal dimension of the spirit. Being translated, the singularity of consciousness is not isolated from totality. Metaphor can be a sacrament for union with what we most value, the Sacred. At that point religion and morality merge.

What can be said of the historical Jesus can be extended to other major elements of Christian affirmation, for example, "original sin," "atonement," and "salvation." Between the physical and the metaphorical there is always ambiguity; with each, meaning can go either way. The physical mind dwells upon external particularity, transferring it literally into the spiritual. This is the metaphysics of medieval Realism. That is, an actual correspondence of physical reality in the spiritual is asserted. Under the influence of Neo-Platonism the pre-existing form (Ideal) in the eternal, immaterial world was more real than the physical. Thus, the Church of Heaven prefigured the historical and was its ontological basis. In reversal, the indulgence of sexuality in this world taints the soul in the eternal. And the actual physical blood of the Christ in atonement for sin suffices to turn the wrath of an anthropomorphic deity into the mercy of divine acceptance. In all of this theologizing does it not appear that negative subjectivity is projected into metaphysical certainty?

Would it not be more charitable to treat the malady psychologically and avoid the ascription to the physical of the illness, as in the fallenness of the natural world? The curative of resorting to the metaphorical is that it transcends metaphysical claims. For salvation, maybe a fuller understanding of the subjective is enough. Metaphorically "sin" can be understood as the inherent alienation attending the solitary state of individual birth, "atonement" the repair of existential fracture through self-acceptance, and "salvation" the eventual reuniting of consciousness's singularity with the All. Why all the metaphysics, when metaphor can heal? Unfortunately, the insecure self craves the assurance of absolute metaphysical truth and unnecessarily transgresses the proper boundary between the material and spiritual. The resulting consequence is that the language of Inwardness is sacrificed to the literalism of material properties. The crass mind cannot resist the temptation to furnish Heaven with the treasures of eternal truth. Metaphor is crucified for the sake of unambiguous certainty. A metaphoric trickster is preferable over a literalistic fool. One is a poet, the other a preacher.

This proviso—that metaphysical claims based upon materialist forms are not conducive to conscious spirituality—brings us to the role of mysticism. But, first, may we further consider the terminology and use of the "spiritual." Already I have spoken of Inwardness and subjectivity. Beyond that, the category of "spirit" allows for values not reducible to space–time continuum. No normative value can be derived from the physical, without the unverifiable insertion of a non-empirical presumption. Science is value neutral. For the lasting good of subjective experience and the preservation of what sentiment values, I reserve the right to use the category of spiritual. To be sure, the preservation of the subjective is not exempt from rigorous critical thought. Indeed, only through the most strenuous criticism is religion rendered redeemable. Still, without the concept of the spiritual, the precious baby of sentimentality would be tossed out with the filthy water of indecent theology. The spiritual—and its individualized repository, spirit— is where we put all of value, none of which can be empirically validated. Even materialists, who deign to use the term, have an equivalent place to put value. What an emotionally barren existence it would be, how very cold our standing before ultimate meaning, without the spiritual. Can we honestly embrace our normative claims, the arts, and the best of culture, without acknowledging the spiritual? Though the spiritual cannot be empirically proven by objective research, the scientist cannot have value and meaning without the subjective. It is just the nature of the case and we ought to be as straightforward about our choices as possible.

In order to avoid confusion and wrongful assumptions, mysticism is the appropriate and most reliable bridge (a metaphor!) between the physical and the spiritual, with metaphor as the ferryboat (to mix metaphors). In illustration, we consider the history of the **icon**. In the eastern tradition of Christianity all three-dimensional representations of the Sacred were smashed in a controversy over idolatry. This protest was ironically called *iconoclasm* (the breaking of icons), but two-dimensional icons were eventually accepted.

Eastern Orthodoxy was spared what it considered to be worship of idols through the practice of the *gaze*. As the natural eye gazes in a contemplative disposition at the pictorial image, awareness goes beyond the physical representation to an inner state of bliss. The physical assumes the function of a sacrament, a vehicle to the desired subjective state. The transportation is related to the destination, yet is not to be identified with it. In this manner is the icon a metaphor; the metaphor is the safeguard against the equation. Since all imagery originates in the physical, necessarily does the metaphorical draw upon the forms of the material world for its texture. But it is the spiritual that is the substance. And who is to say the psychological— sentiment, charity, appreciation—are not worthy of embrace? The problem is not in spirituality, but in the spirit it bears: Malice and negativity or love and life affirmation. Call it the spiritual or regard it as pure subjectivity.

However, do not dismiss its role in the persistence of mysticism. Mysticism is *the requisite consciousness for the intersection of the physical and the spiritual, in order not to confuse the two.* Mysticism is the portal of awareness at which the physical passes/transforms into the spiritual. The mystic knows, but is not able to say in ordinary language. To say is to make unwarranted metaphysical claims. Spirituality does have its own reality, but must not be confused with physical reality. Neither religion nor science should be reduced down to the other, each having its own role and contribution.

All worthwhile theology is metaphor. And doubly so. What we say about the Sacred and what we understand about divine immanence in the material world is to be taken metaphorically. The pure concept of the Sacred is "an enigma wrapped in a cosmic mystery," for even if "real" in a spiritual sense the Sacred lies beyond all language. We speak of divine visitation as an epiphany, even though it is a mere figure of speech. While we may be awed by the intricacies of nature, attributing divine design to the universe is bad science. A Divine Creator is no less a metaphor than the God who shapes humans as a potter throws a clay pot. Poetic metaphor is beautifully evocative, as long as it remains metaphor. Mysticism is what keeps metaphor in its place and spirituality in the stead of idolatry.

In concluding my quarrel with conventional religion, I offer a compromise. Though I may not always revere its religious objects, if used aright I will strive to respect them. In return, of conventionality I ask, put your truth less often on the altar of literalism.

Everything we say spiritually, must be intended metaphorically.

At One With Love

We can truly love
only that to which we belong;
In unity with the whole is the part made strong.

The more a mystical sense of oneness is carried within, the greater the love for everything. Simultaneously, to love is to embrace the world and to affirm the worth of the self. With that starting point, admittedly subjectively asserted and factually evasive, may we examine further the nexus between the unifying myth and the empowerment of love.

Nature, the material world, is morally neutral. From our standpoint, it is indifferent. Some, of a naturalistic orientation, contend that value is implicit in the natural order, in "natural selection" of the species or the wellbeing of human life. But all such claims are arbitrary, for even if evolutionary process is assumed, the choice of whether or not to preserve life is a human intervention. In natural adaptation, who can judge the moral direction? No, value derives from human moral agency, not a foreordained natural law. If there is to be a "good," we are the creators. There is more of humanity in morality, than cosmology. And, without the quality of myth, can there be love?

Myth is a conveyer of morality along with meaning. That value is applied particularly, yet meaningfully, is also universal. We do have higher (intrinsic) and lesser (extrinsic) goods, though for the sake of unity, if not consistency, we hold to oneness of the Good. By virtue of this unity we find our complacency in the world. By this I mean, *a personal place in the universal order.* We come to this decisive commitment either through socialization and/or mystical affirmation, compliance or conscience. The consequences cannot be too heavily stressed or overly estimated. To which I now personally testify.

I was raised a faithful Christian, sincerely accepting its orthodox view of the Sacred, albeit an innocent theism. When it came time to make an earnest commitment, I found that the passages in the Sermon on the Mount emphasizing love struck a responsive chord within. More than divine law, these glowing words answered an inner mystical need. In the passing years the Sermon transformed from an invitation to follow the call of Jesus in

199

discipleship into the icon by which I internalized my highest value. Love was adopted as my Cosmic Christ.

In choosing my unifying myth I do not intend to cancel out the viability of other centralizing myths. After all, each of us is in the unavoidable predicament of selecting the frame which best reflects our own life experience. I am simply professing the gratification I feel in my own myth. The icons of a myth are taken from the symbols of the culture one is most comfortable in. Where else can the ego go, made up as it is largely from that culture? There is no cosmic metaphysical repository for myths, preexisting and sent down from on high. Quite understandable, the icon of value comes from within the context of culture and each culture is entitled to its own peculiar myth, for otherwise the elements would lack emotional power. My only insistence is that the myth not be life denying and abusive; always should myth be under the surveillance of our humane critical powers. So, I go forth, with metaphors drawn from my cultural heritage, to realize my cosmic myth of Love. Yet, let it be clear, while the myth is particular (from the physical), the value is universal (a spiritual creation). To integrate the two is the deftness of intuition and the benefit of wisdom.

What is the meaning of Love? Spiritually, Love derives from the monistic principle of unity. Love is harmony of the parts, *the nurture of each within the inclusion of All.* Love may be kind, forgiving, and absorbent, but it is not indiscriminate. Always affirmative, Love will not participate in the depreciation of any, not willfully and unnecessarily seek the demise of itself or others. Jesus taught us, "Love your enemies." By which I believe he was universalizing Love, for Love universalized knows no enemies. You cannot be at-one with the Universe and kill indifferently. This is the essence of peace. Whether it is thought of as the Cosmic Christ or the Buddha Nature, the wanton harm of another is an injury upon the self's integrity and a fracture of universal belonging. All is one; each is All. If Love is the unifying principle of the Universe, then hatred and enmity are its negation. Love is our reconciliation.

Recently I took an early morning walk in the unmatched beauty of spring, the perennial season for all that is vital. In love with life, I felt inseparable from all that surrounded me—blossom breezes, leafy trees, singing birds. I was ebullient and all this was in me. Then I came upon a wretchedly disfigured opossum lying dead in the gutter, its body mangled by an earlier passing car. The poor fellow creature's entrails were spilling out from within and its facial features contorted. "How very much like my own," I muttered in anguish. I could have dismissed so disconcerting a thought by drawing a qualitative line between animals and the human soul. But with such empathetic identification as I felt, that moral finery was not possible. My unifying myth would not permit the luxury of such superiority. I had to accept that what affects one in the grand scheme of the universe, impinges upon the All in me. Love is not only the unity of All. The ultimate value therein contained is what I depend upon for meaning. *The consummate test of Love is the sensitivity we bear for all that is.* In the physical particular is incarnated the metaphorical spiritual All. This is the mystical consciousness uniting Heaven and Earth.

Each of us is a Christ, a Savior, a Buddha, to dip into particular reality and to draw the parts into concord. While the value is universal, each of us is called to enter into the supreme myth of the Universe. The Christ sets the example, to bring the spiritual reality of Love into the physical dimension. "Go and do likewise," is the admonition of the Savior and the path by which Love is made real. The work of the Christ, of the Buddha, of all teachers of Love is not finished. In deed, each of us is called to be a "savior," the means through which particularity is rescued from chaotic discord. The spiritual journey is from unitive metaphors, to icons of longing gaze, to the Cosmic Love, and back again. May the cycle of redemption be completed in every generation. Love must be reincarnated over and over again, for the physical to be filled with meaning and value.

Love empowers us for life, but it also prepares us for death. Nothing more fulfills the purpose in being than the realization that our choice of ultimate value was worthwhile. We construct a super-physical entity, God, to assure our trembling hearts of our life's lasting significance. In that assurance we find consolation. Within a good life lived well and long is to be found completion. If the self lives the sacred myth, how can death erase the divine imprint?

Eternal life resides in the Oneness of Love.

The End: Late Edition

(2009)

An unabashed confronting of death, as experienced in the declining years of life. These thoughts are in contrast to the braver attitude of early years. Yet, to the end the tone is life affirming. What is past, what has been is not lost.

WARNING:
The Contents May Be Injurious to Your Cheery Outlook ...
Especially If You Are Under Seventy!

While I have been this way before, please do not consider the persistence to be an obsession. What I mean is, I have contemplated the matter of death on earlier occasions—many, many times, probably too many a time, though I have benefitted from each pause for reflection. Generally the result has been a sharp intensification of life appreciation and a renewed determination to "get on with it." So, I shall.

Six years ago, shortly before I turned seventy, I penned a musing, *Meeting Death in Every Vein, At Every Turn.* I even included a last chapter, "Learning to Say Good-Bye." I thought the overall treatment of the subject to be quite good. But having been granted these extra years, I deem it permissible to bring my affair with death up-to-date. Will I plead another such extension of commentary, if I am privileged with six more? I do not consider these to be my "last words," but do allow me another round in my swan song. Whether or not I am able to write yet another is still to be determined. I do know I am drawing nearer to the event every year. So, on with the task at hand. As much a confessional as a duty, I am compelled to submit my report.

In the interlude since the previous booklet on death, the aging process has significantly set in. I am not only old; ever more do I feel the signs of age. Before, the losses were gradual, but now the slope of decline is sharp. Earlier

I courageously accepted the onset of aches and pain. Never a complainer, I merely assumed physical deterioration was in the nature of living. However, here in my eight decade I am beset by that mental weakening, which erodes self-esteem. In place of inconveniences have come those markings toward death, playing upon my trust is life's goodness. Ailments edge toward anxiousness; affliction threatens composure. The road leads ever on. But whither? What will be the challenges of a ninth decade? Life, grant me the serenity to be gracious.

From my vantage point, if you, the reader, are over seventy, and do not smile at what I have written, you are not wholly honest or find the subject too disturbingly dismal. With the latter I have some empathy, for I, too, find the matter dreary. In the former I detect pathos. If you are under seventy and chance upon this booklet, be kind. What does not make sense in your experience may come to visit you in years to come. I neither claim universal validity to my experience nor do I wish to cancel out other strategies for dealing with death. I simply put forward my ruminations, in the hope that they resonate with some other sensitive souls. No commandments, just stretches of the mind. Strangely, in that there is a kind of immortality.

If you resent death,
The older years will be a curse of bitterness;
If you deny mortality,
The older years will escape into illusory waiting;
If you choose the gift of life,
The older years will be blessed with overwhelming compassion.

Pondering What is Left Over

Can it be, all that is left over is the good I have sown? Or, not even that? How much good must be sown, before it endures ever more? Whereupon does one realize that the contribution has been sufficient to register indelibly in the annals of time and the hearts of others? Without vanity I will that something of me endures. My bodily remains will go back to the earth. Is it too much to ask, may my spirit remain in good company?

How can I transfer to lasting form what has taken a lifetime to create? What is the best of my life for the preserving? Certainly it is the life-affirming core of me I most want to pass on. This transmission is of the spirit, more than the tangible, though it is through writing that the tangible and the spirit are combined. Thus I write with an earnestness approaching a mania, as with this writing. Many times throughout my life of writing I have considered the effort to be an embodiment, my words being body to my soul. If this be true, then the latest of the writing preserves the most of my soul.

I desire that all of my writings stand in testimony to my life, the least articulate along with the finest. All have been in gratitude for the gift of life. Each has been in respect of life's great value and high importance. However, it is these late writings which have reached a maximum level of worth. What earlier had been conceptual exposition, expressions of my craving to understand, have now taken the form of a supreme eulogy to life, drawing upon my poetic depth. I believe the two are sequential and interdependent, the eulogy emerging from the reflections. May both the quickness of my mind and the poetry of my heart remain as reverberations. Grateful am I, to have lived life thus.

Death greatly qualifies the worth of life. By its reflection everything is enhanced. In example, I revisit in memory a place and time of deep impression. The gloriousness of the moment returns and restores life in me once again. I bask and glow within its aura, a tremor of desire rippling through me. But the awareness that I shall never be able to visit that long gone place in time heightens the worth of that passed experience. The past magnified by that realization extends itself through me into eternity. The song of the road translates into the Eternal Hymn. Upon the wall of death, the portrait of life is most dramatically displayed.

Throughout life I have diligently sought my voice. Now in the face of death, by some incomprehensible grace, I have received my fullest, deepest, richest voice. I rejoice in the songs I have sung to life, nourishing them until they can go forth on their own. May I believe, though the song is over, the melody of my life lingers on in the world of my associations? What can be more rewarding than for my song to blend with all the love songs of the world?

I believe love endures, that in a mysterious way we are all bound up in one Great Love. For years I have maintained the spiritual inseparability of genuine sincerity. That sincerity was a bond in life. What remains of its positive energy shall continue at death. It shall be my legacy.

We live on in those we touch with our souls.

THE END

How does one trembling soul write of **THE END**, before the moment occurs? In a reversal of life at death we live backwards.

In the great dialogue with life the "I know enough to last the rest of life" eventually translates into "I know all that I need to die." At death's portal I accept the great gaps in many areas of my knowledge, for they no longer bear significance. I am amply supplied with the solace of wisdom. The most profound wisdom consists in knowing how to bless what life has been. Thus, Life, fill me to capacity with the power of blessing.

While I have life I strive furiously, not with body but with soul, to complete my destiny, so that I will be ready for rest. Life has not cheated me. To do less would be to cheat life. More than ever, I owe to life a eulogy. In eulogizing life I embrace all that it has been. I am greatly appreciative for each day left, receiving it without presumption and whole in itself. At its close Life ceases to search for justification.

In The End I feel a loneliness. We all must walk that lonesome valley. But the loneliness is made more acute by the sense that the songs of my heart were understood by so few. However, I realize that the basis of the loneliness is in the longing to be known by others. That knowing, I am assured, has been secured in many and various ways. Friendship and affection have been real. Love has been abundant. I shall not die alone.

A prevailing solemnity has taken over my days; a premonition haunts my hours. The most poignant encounters toward The End are The Last Sights. Places visited and faces greeted may be for the last time. Will I ever pass this way again? In the silence of thought the heart murmurs good-bye. An ache for return penetrates the soul, but all is to be left behind. Sad that life is over, grateful that it has been so enormous. Into the solemnity floods the wonder of a lifetime.

No floral sprays will be needed at a memorial service. Scatter my ashes among the flowers of open-skied meadows, send my spirit to mountains overlooking the ocean, and allow my lingering mirth to mingle with the glee of children. If there be a memorial celebrate what have been the dearest moments of my life, the deepest intimations of my heart, the most transfixing beauty touching my life. Shed a tear, but do so in recognition of a life well lived.

Death is the ultimate union with life, the utmost of our urge for oneness beyond particularity. At death the soul draws into unity all that it desired while dwelling in this bodily world—woman, man, culture, birds, flowers, beauty, mind. The mystery of our sexuality is revealed most fully late in life. Not just with another physical form do we crave union. It is with all of life. All the yearnings of a lifetime are made one love at death.

Maybe the end will be painful and consciousness will be confused, leaving me unable to maintain the high appreciation of life I now possess. Therefore, I commit myself to glorifying the days and years remaining before death.

The Work is done

My last will and testimony has been given.

Now I can go back to living.

Ruminations: Pointed and Far Flung

(2010)

A third venture into succinctness of thought. The emphasis is upon the immediacy of thought and the intuitive composition of meaning.

Catching Up On Random Thought

Here I go into a third edition of what I initially labeled Aphorisms, Pithy Regards, and Other Snapshots of Life. That collection appeared in 2001, to be followed three years later by *Scraps, Snatches, and Tidbits*. Now my incessantly ruminating mind has passed through enough time so as to warrant another drawing together of random thoughts, into a booklet of assorted pigeonholes. All titles need apply.

Typically my writing has been more discursive, carefully structured and inferentially sequenced, adding up to an imposing body of thought. Or, at least, that has been my intention. But, here again I celebrate the virtue of brevity and randomness. Conciseness has a way of clearing the mind of the extraneous. True, in accord with a persistent pattern, the pieces will fall into some degree of logical ordering, with an explanatory introduction and a concluding afterthought. Yet, and this is the primary contention, the more structured the composition, the further the idea is from its inception. Pithiness might well be the distillation of a great volume of thought, arising intuitively out of a vast sea of prolonged synthesis. However, based upon my own experience, significant understanding of the way things are has come in great flashes of insight. Seemingly from out of nowhere? No, out of a lifetime of unceasing endeavor to make sense out of awareness.

Therefore, slightly reversing my previously stated view, these "random thoughts" are to be regarded as surface appearances from a long intellectual history. The worth of these random flashes would not be possible on an empty tank of cognitive fuel. Behind every mole hill of particular observation stands a mountain of diligent mental mining. I resist any insinuation that

I have indulged in mindless, fly-by-night, off-the-top-of-my-biases kind of pronouncement. These are not "cheap thought shots." In being true to logical honesty I have earned my stripes of intellectual respect. Yet, not even if I tried could I reveal all that stands in the wings of my conscious stage of thought, so myriad the moments and so wide the flights of conjecture. Having said that, I leave some of the work of deciphering the larger world of my random thoughts to you, as you weave the particular strands into your own fabric of meaning. I do not claim infallible truth, only sincere rigor. This is a gift, not an intellectual inquisition. Take for what it is worth and leave the rest.

The subtitle of the booklet may have the appearance of being contradictory. How can a thought be both "pointed" and "far flung"? However, quite so can a thought be both directed at specific life situations and extensive in moral implication. It is possible for the point of an arrow to be both penetrating and capable of landing at a greater distance than expected. May truth and wisdom fall where they will. While I may have targeted certain prevailing claims I deplore, considering them to be beneath human dignity, I have done so without malice or rancor. May good will prevail in the chambers of shared thought.

Endearing

The endearing is most enduring,
when generously given.

Time cannot be taken back, but sentiment can preserve.
Love is the mother of emotion's dearest children.
To shame our emotions is to abuse our need for affection.
Love sees more than reason can know.
Love is the moral clarity by which to see another's humanity.
Sweet memory leads to mysterious realms of love.

Romance marries the elegance of art
to the yearnings of the heart.

Loving others adds up to a love of life.
Tears do not approve of joy suppressed.
The soul can speak and hear for the universe.
The soul is the self's refuge; friendship the soul's embrace.

Peace of soul is more desirable than scintillation;
union with life is more fulfilling than distinction.

The body is limited to space,
but the spirit is free to travel the limitless regions of desire.

Glorious intimations of beauty rush in,
where angelic feelings do not fear to enter.

A mystical sense of Divine Presence is the healing before death.

In the end wisdom knows how to reconcile all,
for it has an awareness of wholeness.

While in the end the glass of time may be empty,
the flask of Life's Elixir is full.

Tying Together Witticism and Wisdom

Do I rest my case on the succinctness of random thought? Yes, to some extent, for there is an immediacy to brevity, a personal invitation to an intellectual tea, the tidbits of thought being the crumpets of delight. Again I return to the potential authenticity of randomness. No plot of control, no guile of deceit is involved in these pages. I consider them to be gestures toward the end of sociable encounter.

Whether you regard these ruminations to be a rain shower of mental droplets, free-floating petals on a reflecting pool of thought, or whatever metaphor you prefer, do appreciate the blend of witticism and wisdom. And why for the marriage of the two? First, a dash of humor is good for the intellectual digestion. Yet, secondly and most important, a gentle wit turns aside anger, buffering the sharpness of truth. While I cannot say my attempts rise to the level of classic humor—I have always been a little reluctant to put my thinking in the guise of comedy, I have endeavored to keep a smile on my lips and a twinkle in my eye. Best understood, my kind of humor consists in tweaking the ordinary, reversing the commonplace, to delight the mind in the face of newness. My intent has been to flip the mind, arrest the standard presumptions in their tracks, and expose the inconsistencies of our suppositions. I will have succeeded if one thought brings to the surface a second. Wit, be it satire or parody, clever phrasing or cutting edge, is a humane defense against the tyranny of grim certainty. Remember, the pointedness of thought has a far reach in its merry flinging. Not even the emperor can alter the melody of the songbird.

I believe in the collective power of piecemeal thought. In no way should this be interpreted as license for sloppy, illogical reasoning. I do relish paradox and conundrums, but I renounce lazy, dishonest argumentation. Serious thought and specious debate are contradictions in terms. The object in exchanging thought is intellectual communion, not tag-team wrestling going for the "take-down." If I have offended you at any point, I beg of you, retrace the steps of thought and consider the new horizons, which might have been opened. In the wholeness of even piecemeal thinking, when shared by two as a loaf of soul substance, is to be found integrity and communion. Wisdom is not the property of any one person, always elusive and ever capricious. Yet, if with all your mind and heart you truly seek wisdom, you shall surely not be left in the lurch. Much can be said of wisdom, but consider this: *Wisdom is the particular incarnation of broad understanding, infused by the spirit of generosity.* I trust that these ruminations have served to that end and that some grains of wisdom have trickled through in life's great stream of thought.

In repeat of the second booklet's injunction, *"Sew the patches of your own thought into a usable quilt of meaning. Write your own essay. The pages of the booklet are few. May your thoughts be voluminous. Honor them, each and every one."*

The Great Divide: Ideology Versus Free Thought

(2010)

Provides a template by which to distinguish the rhetoric of closed systems of thought from genuine responsiveness to life. The former leads to antagonistic posturing while the latter offers the tolerance of mutual interest. The implications for both religion and politics are profound.

A GENEALOGY: From Ideology to Empty Rhetoric

As we go further into an examination of the Politics of Antagonism, I state my main premise: Ideology and rhetoric do not create negativity; these devices are merely auxiliaries. Ideology, in opposition to change, is already predisposed to negation. Yet, the flaw is of the spirit, not in the inescapable predicament of using models to interpret reality. The difficulty arises with how we choose to regard these tools of the mind. (Throughout the writing I shall use the lower case, ideology, to indicate the general meaning and the upper case, Ideology, in reference to the form I am undertaking to critique.)

The original meaning of the word ideology had to do with the study of ideas, a fascination with their use and interconnectedness. But time has not been kind to this word, rendering it an object of reproach among minds of scientific inclination. Rather than condemning the practice of formulating ideas to provide a ground for further thinking, I prefer to point out the dangers. As an operating definition consider this: *Ideology consists of absolutized thought disconnected from empirical verification.* A more vivid way of putting it: Ideology is a graveyard for antiquated thinking, a mausoleum of dead ideas, all posing to represent a world now past. In hardening our views of reality we contract arteriosclerosis of our thinking about reality. The conditions of our existence are irreversibly mutating, yet fear of that reality tempts us to hold on to immutable ideas. That is Ideology. The rest is obstinacy.

In the fluctuating waters of life the role of idea formation is to provide a compass for direction. A "bench mark," a set of "first principles" aid in making sense out of existence. This collection of ultimate presuppositions becomes normative, under which all subsequent thought is classified. For the most part, ideology is simply "inherited' through the transmission of tradition. When made absolutely normative, ideology is sacralized as religion. All ideas are thereby swallowed up and thinking becomes little more than mechanical deductive reasoning. This mental fixture is of conglomerate composition, both cultural and idiosyncratic. Francis Bacon, of the sixteenth and seventeenth centuries and often referred to as the "Father of the Scientific Method," spoke of four idols. To his conviction, these false notions must be expunged in order for the mind to be free in pursuit of scientific inquiry, inductive reasoning. Though the momentum leading to an Age of Reason was well underway, Bacon popularized the "New Science" and set into place an ongoing challenge to the old ideologies. Religion, always on the defensive, would take umbrage yet would never be the same. The great divide still lingers into the twenty-first century, to be seen in both religion and politics. One side, conservative, remains fixed in worldview; the other, liberal, more empirically oriented.

As impossible as it is not to make metaphysical assumptions, the danger in ideological construction is its tendency to become cut off from conversation with experience. Interaction with physical reality is the corrective needed to prevent ideology from going mad, that is, succumbing to the worst of its demons. In the great mixture of our inherited ideology along with the "tried and true" are to be found the lingering trace elements of fear and prejudice. Discovery of this malice is prevented by a built-in, self-serving epistemology guaranteeing its own correctness. Cut off and insulated from contrary evidence, absolutized thought hears nothing and fears everything. As stated initially,

> *Ideology is truth by definition.*
> *Ideology needs no proof, for it relies upon no facts.*

When thinking is hardened into absolutism it becomes Ideology and takes on the intolerance of certainty. The other side of certainty is intolerance. At this point in its devolution Ideology becomes imperialistic.

216

Because Ideology unquestioningly accepts its core principles as final, difference gravitates toward a moral dualism. This bifurcation reaches its antagonistic limits when disagreement is identified as the work of Satan or an enemy of the state. When Ideology is left to itself, unaccountable, it trends toward hostility, for it regards inquiry as infidelity and compromise as capitulation. Ideology thereby comes into tension with democracy, wherein process toward consensus is honored over victory. Ideology bears the seed of violence. Therein lies Ideology's greatest threat to human well-being.

When it comes to legislation, Ideology either constructs punitive sanctions out of prejudice (its inherent intolerance of other fixed ideologies) or imposes absolute articles of belief, unproven before the court of factual evidence (its empirical distrust). Call it belief, or prejudice, the subtext of Ideology functions as dogma, unexamined and unquestioned. Faithfulness is defined as accepting its precepts as such. Salvation comes through submission to Ideology's authority. A leading example from current politics is the debate over how to stimulate the economy. In the most smug satisfaction manner imaginable free market conservatives repeat the mantra, "Lower taxes will stimulate the economy and create jobs." They might as well be reciting a rosary, for all that reasonable inquiry counts. It matters little that the axiom has not been proven in the actual world of dynamic economic forces. Impervious to counter evidence, loyal membership in the Church of Ideology consists of pious repetition of doctrine. Irrespective of circumstances, the same formula is repeated, over and over again. Nothing can count against it, for it is based upon belief alone. Truth is a priori grounded. Therefore, not to legislate on the basis of Ideology is to offend God.

I regard this political stance as indiscriminate groping, flying blind in the thin air of prejudice. Legislation based upon the prejudice of antiquated belief is scarcely what the Founding Fathers, children of the Enlightenment, had in mind when they set into motion deliberative bodies for guiding the fortunes and well-being of society. Quite the opposite, democracy was born out of the good intention to free humans from the shackles of Unreason. What did Jefferson mean when he advocated a revolution every twenty years, if not to release politics from acquired entrenched Ideological biases? Ideology is the bane, the scourge of the legislative process, better classified under veneration than responsible politics.

The content of Ideology often includes elements of malice and life negation. These sources of conflict ought in decency's name to be expunged. But there is also another component of its inadequacy, the obsolescence of its value system. From an organic analysis perspective "value" is an intermediate category, an instrument for mediating between the Good and the conditions of existence. When the conditions are altered, as they radically have been by a series of industrial and technological revolutions, values must be modified by redefinition, a responsibility Ideology is ill equipped to assume.

In addition to elements in our presuppositions that should never have been there, conservatism persists in holding on to values which no longer serve the common good. In time what was a value can become dysfunctional. Of such stuff is false consciousness made, i.e., "knowledge no longer adequate to comprehend the actual world." Once false, consciousness will drift off into delusion and cantankerousness, hostile because the world does not behave as one thinks. As Einstein reputedly said, "Insanity is repeating the same mistakes, thinking that the result will be different." The longer Ideology is relied upon, the more resistant it becomes to contrary evidence and the less adaptable it is to emerging realities.

What are the field markings of Ideology and why is it so poor when it comes to corresponding with reality? Taking the "markings" first, here are a few clues. The source of truth is fixed and the answers to questions are predetermined. When you encounter such signs as "infallible scripture" and "strict construction" you know you are on Ideological grounds. "God's Will" and "original intent of Founding Fathers" are signatures of thought frozen in time, most likely the universal projection of that person's will and intent. Any time an argument falls back upon "indubitable truth" you know you have met an Ideologue. There is no real communication with an Ideologue, no dialogue. Parameters are set and possibilities are limited. This brings us to the second question, why is Ideology so clumsy in programming solutions to existential problems? The answer traces to the growing isolation of Ideology from empirical input. Because Ideology's conceptual framework is progressively generalized into vague, imprecise abstractions, the acuity of application diminishes. More and more, judgmental pronouncement replaces program and blame substitutes for analysis. *Negativity is the last resort of Ideology gone to irrelevancy.*

Ideology, in spite of its detachment from reality, can display a degree of internal logic. However, at best the ordering is of categorization and itemization, as in listing the commandments and doctrines. It is more rule-oriented than procedure-directed. While general, Ideology's precepts, being absolute, can be in tension without the believer's acknowledgement. Logical consistency is secondary to tenacity of conviction. Take for example these three propositions, core conservative values: Lower taxes, deficit reduction, and increased defense. These are not merely tactical proposals. They are part and parcel of its value system, traceable to fundamental assumptions about human existence. Yet, upon logistical examination, the three are in practical opposition. Only one can be held, without contradiction by the other two. No two can be held in a compatible relationship. So much of this disconnect between thought and reality characterizes the protest of the Right. The politics of "No" requires no viable program for solution. With malice mixed in, it is making us all sick.

In putting the Politics of Antagonism through the test, I judge it to be Ideological to the hard core. This brings us to the second screening of this political trend, its pejorative use of rhetoric. One salient feature of rhetoric's misuse to be noted is its compounding of Ideology's detachment from reality. Once empty rhetoric takes the place of descriptive language, the mind is defiled with nonsense, all messed up in reference to the real world. Good words are corrupted and nefarious deeds are transformed into honor. Self-interest, fear, and paranoia are rescued from moral indecency by the rhetoric of meaningless words. The military occupation of other countries is deemed in defense of "freedom" and the "free market" justifies the gross inequalities of wealth distribution. Ideology bastardizes the most beautiful of our ideals. *When words are voided of empirical reference, they can do whatever they maliciously please.* As Humpty-Dumpty would say, "The question is which is to be master." Yes, dear Ideology, how so are our words authored, by malice or by our common humanity?

To Hell with the Devil!
An Expurgation and a Confession
(2011)

Having grown up with a theological overdose of the demonic, I seek out what I can conscientiously live with. The pervasiveness and persistence of sin and salvation theology is seen as inimical to peace and understanding. Laying aside the negative presumptions of orthodoxy, the call is for a new awareness of the Sacred. All in the way of a theatrical parody.

The Pervasiveness and Persistence of Sin and Salvation

The overarching theme of this chapter, and of the booklet, is the mythic framework of Sin and Salvation. As to origin, the myth lies in the mists of antiquity. (This construct, which I shall refer to as The Great Myth, represents a large corpus of constituents, some in incompatibility. The term is collective, a composition representing the presupposition of western religion.) The contributors are likely innumerable and the contents have mutated over time into an elaborate fabrication. But this we do know: Sin and Salvation, as a view of reality, has dominated the religious traditions of the West, the so-called Abrahamic faiths. My contention is not that other mythological elements have made no contribution. But that the Sin and Salvation motif is the most determinative. This western myth of Sin and Salvation has spread throughout all institutions of society, coloring our thinking and behaving. It is ubiquitous, an omnipresent state of consciousness, pervasive and persistent.

Think of mythic consciousness as the superstructure from which our assumptions about life are derived. It serves as a platform upon which all else is constructed. It is the context from which all conscious ideas take their meaning, for example, *faith, guilt, law, justice, truth, goodness.* Other imagery helpful in understanding the role of myth in consciousness includes Walls of the Mind, in the midst of which the furniture of thought is placed; Ultimate Presupposition, a prompter in the wings of our existence, giving cues so as to keep us on script; Pond of Unconsciousness, upon whose waters our ideas and values float. The mythic underpinnings of our lives—and our civilization—are not reasoned out, assumed rather than chosen; they lie behind conscious deliberation. We acquire them through inheritance, implanted at an early age by inculcation. Like innocent children we received our membership in community without question. Then, only by the good graces of sustained critical thinking do we become even dimly cognizant of mythological presence. The purpose of this analysis is to become more aware of what we are mythically committed to and to offer alternatives. Traditionally, religion has been very resistant to higher criticism, out of an instinct for self-preservation based upon an impulse for control. Having sanctified the myth, any thought to the contrary is the work of the Devil. In a real sense, to advance religious consciousness the reformer must become irreligious. Be assured, I feel the sting of orthodoxy's stone of "heretic" every step of the way.

We know the scenario of Sin and Salvation by rote, only the details are in variation. The story begins with a separation between the sacred and the human (see Expulsion from the Garden). The sin/disobedience grows into wickedness (see Human Depravity), until all historical calamities are traceable to human agency (see The Flood). To repair this schism a gesture of sacrifice is given (see Atonement and Surrender/Submission) and life becomes a carefully watched path of obedience (see God's Will). In capitulation to God's Omnipotence (His Primacy and Sovereignty) Evil and the World shall be brought to an end, with the faithful divided from the apostate/unbelievers (see Last Judgment). All too well do we know the scheme of how things got the way they are. The particulars can be elaborated, but the outline remains well intact. It may appear that I have contradicted myself, in putting the story so clearly, after having contended that the myth lies in the subliminal. Permit me to clarify. The story is well rehearsed; it is the why and wherefore which is most of the time concealed from our active awareness, the source and the application of its predisposition. The effects are far more than we can imagine. The pervasiveness is so great that even secularists are touched by its outreach. So, let us turn to the far reaches of The Great Myth, remembering that myth is the parent of the age's civilization, the codification of its morality. In the course of our examination we shall consider the connections of the dominant Myth and the larger scope of life, bringing in politics and morality.

First, we pause at the not so humble abode of Saint Augustine, to pick up a major later development of the Myth. Augustine, sometimes referred to as the "Father of Western Theology," had a profound influence in determining religious attitudes toward material existence. He both drew upon the past and advanced the asceticism of the Myth. Being a follower of Manichaeism and Neo-Platonism before conversion to Christianity, his theology was a synthesis of the three. Manichaeism reinforced the split between Good and Evil. Neo-Platonism estranged God and the World, leaving the soul too much in the clutches of the flesh. The result was a strong bias against knowledge based upon the senses and a priority for the divine, the experience of which was the "beatific vision," a direct visual perception of God. God's Sovereignty took precedence over all, more than the pleasures of this world and was the basis of eternal salvation. Nothing disturbed Saint Augustine more or cast greater fear into his hopes for salvation than "concupiscence," abnormal desire, especially of the libido kind. It is of little surprise that he has also been credited with being the father of western monasticism.

Much of his theology was a rearranging of what he inherited, but a few formulations are unique, original sin and creation ex nihilo among them. I will permit the first to speak for itself, except to add it is a condemnation from out of which no one can slip without the mediating grace of the Church. But it is the second, which reaches to the heights of absurdity, playing with words as if anything goes in the spiritual realm. Rejecting Neo-Platonism's emanation theory of the world's creation (the universe emerged out of the Divine and is progressively returning to Oneness), Augustine prevented any confusion between the material world and God by arbitrarily postulating that the world was created out of nothing, ex nihilo. Taken together, this saintly man put an eternal kibosh on all chances for a genuine Humanism. Earlier nature religion could not make the distinction between the sacred and the world, humans included. Now the Myth would permit no conjugal union between the material and the spiritual. Mary would remain a perpetual virgin. At the apex of monotheism the Great Cosmic Divorce was performed.

All this has trickled down into the way we perceive human existence. In this brief synopsis of the Great Myth I do not care to debate origins and the intermingling of influences. That it has persisted for millennia and has pressed its arbitrary morality upon our lives, even down to the present, is incontestable. The presumptions of the Myth color, therefore predetermine, most of our primary moral categories and their application. Again I stress the half-conscious state of our thinking. We operate on the basis of corollaries, not the axioms authoring them. The Myth sits in the back row of our moral decisions, whispering directions, while we concentrate on the specific situation. Whatever is on the stage of that day's play, no matter the title of the melodrama, the Myth has prewritten the outcome of the script.

I do not believe it unfair to say, the mythic framework behind the moral presumptions of American Christianity is medieval, archaic. Although in a concession to modern thinking mainline Protestantism has softened the harshness of the Myth, it still is more in accord with Evangelicalism than with Humanism. Science and technology is accepted at the utility level, but in spite of the internal tension the Myth persists. The "family issues" of current politics are a page right out of Augustine, with enmity toward homosexuality and prohibition toward abortion. Ever so many examples can be given as to how the Myth still taints politics and jurisprudence. To provide just a few: *Suffering* is redemptive; *punishment* is largely punitive; *rights* are God-given. In conditions of conflict the enemy is demonized and *victory* requires the overpowering of the adversary, if not the annihilation. In so doing the Will of God is furthered. Little consideration is given for conciliation. "Either you are for God or for Satan. Every war is a prefiguring of the battle to end all wars, Armageddon, when finally the reign of Satan is ended. Until then, vigilance against the forces of evil, in both the physical and the spiritual realms, is the mark of rectitude. To die in the cause of *righteousness* is the witness of *martyrdom*, the reward of which is eternal Divine favor. Thus spoke the Great Myth of old. With this Ultimate Presupposition the events of the present are interpreted by the *faithful*. Even Easter, that gorgeous pagan festival of Spring's coming, is tainted by deprecation of the physical (Lent) and triumph (victory) over the powers of evil. What a tragedy! How medieval can you get?

In fundamental orientation the Great Myth is negative, at the least dualistic. The whole idea of sin, sacrifice, and atonement is in essence cynical, representing an ontological alienation between the sacred and humanity. It grew out of a period in human evolution when adversarial conditions were the norm and rule. Retaliatory defense of the High God canceled out tolerance of differences and love was a luxury for the obedient. Compassion was mingled in with power struggles and the cult of the warrior. God had mercy upon those who bowed to His omnipotence; the king followed in His stead. Oddly, or maybe significantly, only by violence can the schism between God and humanity be repaired. The greatest flaw with the Great Myth is that history has outrun its feasibility. Technological war—death by millions, social infrastructure destruction by megatons—leaves in its wake the rubble of the Myth's primary assumptions. Not only is the Myth archaic; worse yet, its understanding of power and governance is obsolete. The negativity infests today's politics. The war against abortion traces to medieval ambivalence toward sexuality and the denial of global warming is in league with rejection of evolution. Its providence is not for the Good, rather, it is in league with the Devil. We simply cannot afford the high social cost of paying tribute to the supremacy of the Myth. It is making us violently sick.

It is difficult to carry on a positive conversation regarding strategies for living, when the walls of our minds are plastered with mythological negativity. When sin and salvation are built into the foundations of our consciousness, then all else is dictated by the Myth's prejudices. Because of its a priori absolute epistemological status, no questions are permitted and dissent is anathematized as diabolical. Just how does the honest person get outside, to breathe in some fresh air? Looks like it might be time for a newly-fashioned myth, one collectively we can live with. Might we say, all to the glory of the Sacred?

Cleansing My Soul of Toxic Waste

While the menu of traditional religion contains some trace elements of goodness, its aspersions and negative insinuations against our human nature have been noxious to the general wellbeing. Our religious diet has been feeding us toxins, resulting in a tainting of our lives. The damage has not been merely an impairing of our outreaching limbs, but a poisoning of the entire system. Once in the circulation system these foreign substances permeate everything and seep down into the very psyche of who we are. To think or be otherwise has been hitherto inconceivable. With the tradition I take leave. In the respect of possession, this version of religion is a demon. I must cleanse my soul of it.

Various are the chefs who dish out the tainted negative theology. Under the influence of sexual repression the ancient Austerity School limits intake to only that which will reinforce body loathing. The diet is totally adverse to earthly existence, an essential ingredient for masochism. At the other end of the cafeteria line are those, who in some concession to modern Epicureanism, hawk the wares of Comfort Food. God is all loving and earthly existence is not all bad. The ingestion feels real good, but the residual toxicity leaves you overweight with shallow presumptions about selfhood. To a fatuous head is attached a fat popularity. Still, the underlying negativity is in the residue. Then there is the more discerning culinary school, Higher Criticism Exculpation. Under its tutelage we are instructed on how to pick out the toxic ingredients, while concentrating on the healthy food for our souls. For all its respectable straining at the gnat, the question is forced, "Why eat at this mixed bag diner at all?" Oh, how numerous the recipes and so many the servers in the sanctity of the Great Myth's negative theology!

Sentiment in conjunction with habit and in deference to seasonal rites would have us return, over and again, to a feast of "home cooking." Family solidarity and social loyalty require the pilgrimage. Dressed in religious compliance and civic pride, these re-enactments guarantee the perpetuation of the toxins. Leary-eyed I must decline the invitation, no matter how much I loved my mother. Pleasant as is the remembrance of mom's fried potatoes—one of my working-class family's staples, the lard-laden reality of such a diet does not commend itself to a life-long intake. Heart-felt as the sentiment may be, the mental plaque is not good for the arteries of clear thought circulation. And, as one wise teacher years ago advised me, "If you don't want to get in over your head, don't wade in the water." If you want to cut out the bad, don't mix it with the good. Negativity will always cancel out the positive, just like with bad money driving out the good. There is, you know, an economy of moral reflection.

I began my spiritual journey as an innocent child, almost totally unaware of what was good for me. I ate nearly all food put before me, with the exception of cooked parsnips and creamed elderberries. Blech! (That would be the equivalent of original sin and final judgment.) Partly indiscriminate and wholly grateful, in the beginning whatever was dished out by my elders—parents, pastor, and teachers, society and religion—I swallowed without the slightest chew of discernment. How can you blame the innocent for that? Gradually, not doubt or disobedience, but rather curiosity held me to a higher obligation. I had to investigate the source of the stream and find out the why or the wherefore. Reason drew me to the Fountain of the Enlightenment, until eventually I was left dumbfounded and incredulous. The more I searched, the more foreign to my higher sensitivities became the religious tradition I had trusted in. The guiding light of decency burned so brightly that I despaired of redemption for the old, while uncertain of a new path. Yet, slowly and cautiously I stepped onto its inclined plane toward understanding. I know, was I not told this is the Devil's devious trick, to draw me into his clutches? But I dismissed the thought as just another devise for captivity to religious negativity. In honesty's name I had no other choice, unless I wanted to assign my intellect to Hell, based upon the claim of human depravity.

At this juncture in the progress toward authenticity, two options appeared viable. One religionist suggested that I pick and choose, in the manner of a wise patron at a delicatessen. Separate out what is unworthy of belief and reinterpret the rest. That did not appear unreasonable. For many years I followed such a modus operandi. Not altogether honest, yet sparing frowns and avoiding excommunication, I held to a low profile. (I all too clearly realized orthodoxy had already cast me into the outer darkness, though unbeknownst by them of my heresy.) I will not say this is the cowardly way out, for the hidden agenda approach is often due to gentle consideration of others. (You know, do nothing to offend the early growth of a brother believer.) Still, the merit of a "silent treatment" soon wore out. The need to know myself was too powerful, no matter the possible cost to social acceptance. Merely to internalize what is taught is not to know the self. A more thorough cleansing was necessary. Thus opened the door to the second and more systemic option: To do the impossible, to step outside and start anew. I say "impossible," for how can one person, let alone a society, step entirely outside all modes of thought? Are not even the tools of critical thought somewhat tainted by the old assumptions? I needed a clean break, to the extent that is possible.

How does honesty clean out a closet of accumulated religious rubbish, without also pitching the baby? In sorting through the artifacts of the past how does the paleontologist distinguish between the weapons of destruction and the chalices of healing, the inhering contradictions and the positive functioning values? At a certain point in a thoroughgoing inquiry, each component part must be pulled out and examined for its impact upon existence, human and environmental. This requires a moratorium in belief and practice. To continue the food analogy, some components nourish the body politic and some deaden its vitality. Shall we say a little fasting is in order? In the preceding three chapters I analyzed the toxic waste and repudiated it through regurgitation. Now is the time to turn toward the reclamation of my soul, through the careful evaluation of what is to be put into its deepest chambers of consciousness.

In retrospect I am astonished that I could ever have believed the malicious assumptions of my religious upbringing. But, was I not like so many before me and the many to come after me, a wide-eyed child? (What is this thing about, those who would mislead a child, how that it would be better were the false teacher thrown into the sea with a millstone around his neck? Or, is this just another version of a vindictive god of control, a compounding of the violation?) Though I cannot undo the damage, I cleanse my soul in behalf of all children. Unclear as to what shall be lodged therein, I shall go forward with a clear conscience.

Accepting What I Can Live With

So we ask, is there anything left over, which will not taint the health of the new? How do we distinguish between the viable good and the detrimental old, in order to replace what we repudiated? What unit of measurement is to be adopted in evaluating the possible? Do new beginnings always begin with new questions? Well, here we go on an uncertain but necessary ride.

The first step in replacement of the old is getting rid of it, wiping the slate clean, delegitimizing its absolute claim. This I have done by regurgitation. The second step in advancing into new territory is through finding the courage of one's honesty, a commitment not to lie in pursuit of another self-validating perversity. No gain is made in exchanging one preposterous axiom for another. This should have come with the "cleansing of toxins," but alertness must last forever and a day. The real work begins with experience and is built upon wisdom, measured by reason, and modified by good will. That is the third step in genuine acceptance, a thorough and consistent evaluation of the materials in the rebuilding. We need and the times require a redefining of our value terms, the virtues by which we live. Only from systematic rejection can an authentic acceptance come about. No longer the obedience of religious control. Instead, we take on the virtue of discernment. We dump all, in order that we can analyze everything.

Have I faithfully followed the stringency of my own method? Throughout this writing I have drawn upon bits and pieces of the old religious tradition, some even intimating a favorable taste. I do not wish for my repudiation to turn into hostility or my sentiment to blind my discernment. Each step along the way calls for a pause, to reintegrate what one can live with. My method is dialectic as well as complete suspension of belief. We bring to an end, in order to begin again. It truly is "the road less traveled." May we take it?

So the question becomes, "Upon what can I rely for discernment and evaluation in the creation of a more life-serving myth?" Unavoidably that brings us down to experience. And that draws us once again back to indigestion. Before us for consideration are the vomit (expelled belief) and the digestive system (moral sense), the evidence of incompatibility and the underlying testimony of who we are as moral beings. We can choose to dwell on the regurgitation, picking through it, attempting to find some remnant of goodness, something worth keeping no matter how small. But, as noted earlier, the toxins have stained everything.

Methodologically everything must be thrown out, before anything is brought back in! Everything—assumptions, presuppositions, axioms, revelations, scriptures, doctrines, law, folk wisdom, ways of the fathers—all! Only that which can pass through the moral fiber of my intellect shall have any chance to enter into the chambers of my soul. (By "soul" I mean the operating principle of my existence, the integrity of my selfhood.) Given the experience of retching, three options emerge: Deny the vomit, dwell on the discharge, or focus upon what forced the event. Denial is the first step in dishonesty and dwelling on the vomit perpetuates the illness. We shall follow the third.

Moral indigestion is a clue to our selfhood and a way out of the absolutism of arbitrary authority. It is the repeatable story of the great reformers, religious, political, and intellectual. Something was detected in the tradition, which offended a deep part of the moral sense. The sensitive soul, directly informed by the world, does not vomit for the fun of it. Just as the bodily system finds intolerable an overload of poisons, so do our humane instincts of caring and nurturing revile at certain preposterous assertions about others, especially those of judgment and blame. There we have it, the most dependable ground upon which we can build a new myth for the living: an indwelling streak of positive life affirmation. What else do we have to rely upon? I have come to trust my sense of decency more than tradition's pronouncements. Enough of the innocent child remains in me that I still expect the teeth of those who say something grossly untrue to fall out and persons who are especially hateful to go morally blind. Well, I will persist in holding to such convictions (in a figurative manner), for it confirms in me what I consider to be the bedrock of morality, conscience. Anything else ends up in oppression and in the interests of control.

Call it "fellow feeling," a moral sense, a meme, or DNA; depending upon your field of expertise, experience tells us that some integral component exists in us upon which we can rely for wholesome living. I name it Conscience.

In conversation with life this disposition is an empowerment rather than an annoyance. Conscience is the author of prudence and wisdom, the ultimate court of appeal. Over and sometimes against it is Law, the social framework of acceptable external behavior. By democratic process the law is a social compact of collective conscience. But when the two are in disagreement, the individual must honor the preeminence of conscience. Conscience cannot be qualified by law or repealed by authority. The only alternative to the primacy of conscience is to refer belief and behavior to external prerogative. This, as Thoreau asserted, was equivalent to making "wooden men," servile in obedience and mindless in morality. I may empathetically walk in another's moccasins, but I refuse to attire myself in another's moral uniform. I cannot wear someone else's meaning. Therefore, before death parts me from those that I love, I must claim my own moral compass, in all circumspection and in accordance with the peace of my soul. Only by this process can there be something I can live with.

The Great Myth does not accommodate this mandate of my soul. Its presuppositions virtually eliminate the right of conscience. The cynical doctrine of human depravity leaves no room for autonomy, for humans are declared incapable of determining what is true, right, and good. In the place of conscience, religious scripture and priestly intercession are enthroned absolutely. Revelation comes from outside the self and must be enforced. The greater the emphasis upon sin, the more the external authority must take command. If human nature is entirely "fallen," no genuine democracy is possible, only theocracy. To that I refuse to bend my knee. I believe in an immanent divinity, much to the horror of St. Augustine and much to the credit of Quakers. The Inner Light must mean something, other than sitting in silence! Before time silences me I will pay up my account of meaning. What is it that I believe in and how does this define my soul? Little, other than love, is more important to me.

May it be clear; I am not unalterably opposed to myth creation. I see no way around the human predicament of epistemologically falling back upon non-provable presupposed affirmation. Those who deny this quandary dishonestly fool themselves, whether religiously or scientifically. If myth is the stem cell of consciousness, the primary metaphor by which we relate to the world, all persons have a myth. The nature of myth is mythical and must not be taken literally. Yet, it provides meaning. My main insistence is that this primal act of being be done consciously and based upon the most humane instincts we possess. My final chapter consists of what I have found to be worth holding, a replacement for the Great Myth. I do not adopt this preferred life-view either out of obligation or external authority. It is born out of my true self, that which I most honor. Therefore, it is a genuine confession, not a concession. How can there be honesty, if what is confessed traces to what I am not? Not even torture or threat of damnation should be permitted to overturn our true confession.

An Honest Confession at Last

The other side of confessing what you cannot believe is the emergence of what can be honestly confessed. This is not simply an obverse of the Great Myth, for that would be to jump in the fire with the Devil. I distinguish between "nonbeliever" and "unbeliever." I do not believe in the presuppositions of the Great Myth, but I am not thereby an unbeliever. So, let me proceed to a confession, of that which it has taken a lifetime to acquire, piece by piece, revelation by ecstasy. So to speak, I have been on the road all my life. The picture has become clearer and the conviction more sincere. Why has it taken so long? How could it be otherwise, if life is growth? I have arrived at a point of belief without arrogance, possessed by a great love of all. Could I have asked for more?

Although I will not simply flip the Great Myth on its back, in some muscular tour de force, it may be illustrative to take three of its cardinal presuppositions and narrate how that from their repudiation has come the substance of my emerging myth. It is one thing to abandon ship, another to construct a more durable vessel. Otherwise, from the vacuum of meaning arises a sense of emptiness. The three central elements of the Great Myth that I challenge have to do with Fallen Nature, Atonement, and Moral Dualism. Without any respect for them, they shall be known as the "Unholy Trinity." I identify the three as such, for they are intellectually unbelievable and morally pernicious. Holding to these assumptions deprecates our lives;

they do not enhance our living. In mentioning them, in turn, I identify why they are unacceptable and what has come to take their place.

1. *Human depravity requires revelation from outside human consciousness.* For all it intends to say about "freedom in obedience," such an assertion precludes genuine freedom of conscience. Human nature is cursed with defamation and the moral sense is subjugated to external authority. To say we are "born in sin" is a very poor template for understanding humanity, even approaching malevolent distortion. Orthodoxy stubbornly assumes there is only one explanation for human behavior, SIN, fighting off a multitude of other considerations. Seemingly, those locked into the Great Myth cannot even conceive of another explanation. Experience in the world, however, has assured me that good will far outweighs ill will and that love is stronger than malice. In terms of the human condition the need for healing takes precedence over induced guilt. Refusing from the start to assign human existence to damnation, therefore, I confess: **The Sacred is Immanent in All Life.**

2. *Jesus had to die for the sins of humanity.* The assumption is not peculiar to Christianity. All religious systems of the West, from ancient times, have relied upon salvation through sacrifice, propitiation, and redemption. Only the particulars of the narrative vary. The consequence is to hold humanity in bondage to a "blood code," as ceremonially enacted by an officiating priesthood in endless repetition. In behalf of humanity I declare freedom from such negative tyranny. There is to be no ontological alienation between heaven and earth (symbols for the spiritual and physical). Jesus is an example of true humanity, not a Sacrificial Lamb. We, all are incarnations. In realizing this, we become the embodiment of the Sacred. Thus, in reply to atonement I confess, **Compassion is the Divine Presence.**

3. *History is best understood as a war between God and Satan.* In addition to being metaphysical schizophrenia, this moral dualism makes for egotistical pretension, for both individuals and nations, and legitimizes war as "holy." Such a scheme encourages tribalism

(even imperialism) in an age of requisite global cooperation. God versus the Powers of Evil is not the only paradigm available for explaining the tensions within history. And clearly not the most viable, given all that we know about structures of injustice and societal dysfunction. The Devil would steal from us the prudential understanding of what ails us, canceling out all the social sciences. Premillennialism, worse yet, stands by while awaiting the total destruction of the natural world, enemies included. This history has no ecological reverence, in spite of its glorification of the Creator. Underlying it all is contempt for this world, with its alleged plethora of sensual temptations. In the end, Satan will be banished, that is, desire will be limited to the spiritual. The Son of God has no sexual desire. In revulsion against this perversity, I confess: **Peace is the Purpose of Our Morality**.

We are called by a life instinct to bring harmony to the parts, to provide inclusion of our differences and integration of our commonality. Rather than the category of "sin," which carries with it implicit judgment and punishment, we are better equipped to bring wholeness through empathy and identification. Violence in retaliation is not a resolution of the problem, only a compounding of the complexity. "Bad" is best analyzed as "out of alignment." As caring humans we bear the responsibility to draw together community from conflict, "to clothe the naked and feed the hungry." This may be found in scripture, but more fundamentally it is written on our humanity. No extraneous authority is required for its incumbency.

In contrast to the Spirit of Peace, the Unholy Trinity of the Great Myth can be, and has been, utilized as a mechanism for guilt and control. All of its presuppositions emerged at a period of human evolution when struggle for existence was paramount and social organization demanded conformity. But that time has passed and its morality is passé, calling for a new awareness of the Sacred. For me, that includes what I call *a Spiritual, Poetic Aestheticism.* A pleasure in enjoyment, a worship of natural reverence. No longer do I accept the Seven Deadly Sins, for their entire medieval obsession. My virtues remain constant: Compassion, Generosity, Gratitude, Wonder, Awe, Celebration, and Joy. If there be proof in the pudding, then the goodness and mercy which comes from the living of my virtues is evidence beyond what any scripture can give. By this confession shall I live and die.

As can be seen by the above written, though I am not an orthodox Christian, I do retain some wholesome elements from that tradition's testimony to the Sacred. Having repudiated the Angry God of Atonement, I still hold Jesus as a deep-seated and revered example of how I am to treat others. Not an incarnation of a theistic almighty God, but what the Sacred would be like, if human, the closest we can get to theism. The first veers off into the futile God-Man dispute; the latter opens the way to an affirmation of humanism. We are divine incarnations, although incomplete and so often injured by cruelty, marvelous in potential. Into this value system, a new myth, flow the humane qualities of service, empathy, and non-calculating love. Depravity is not an apt description of humanity! More the punitive edict of a peevish superior upon an underling, irritable over some disobedience. Not the expression of a universal loving force. I consider the doctrine of original sin slander against the order of nature.

Again I repeat. If you cannot accept the presupposition beneath the premises, the conclusion is suspect. More convinced than ever am I, we are not defined by belief—be that God, sin, salvation, heaven, and hell, the affirmation or denial thereof. We are defined and saved by the grace of love.

Late Writings on Religion

(2015)

A loose collection of reflections on religion's function in how the world is perceived. As it would seem, a lifetime of devotion to the study of religion ends in fragments and loose threads.

An Owed Explanation

Over a considerable lifetime I have devoted my powers of thought to strict logic and tight organization. At least that was my intended literary ideal. Thought is to follow thought in inferential progression, with the overall product neatly packaged. The implied outcome of intellectual labor is a grand final product, the definitive piece in its field of expertise. Always somewhat reticent to assume the mantle of authority, I certainly do not present the following writings as bearing the mark of being authoritative. Yes, I am the author, but honesty and modesty require that I pose merely as an inveterate thinker. From the tree of my thought has fallen a milliard leaves, each one from the stem of my life. Still, none the totality or the finality. I prefer to tickle thought, rather than command intellectual assent. I would rather open new thought, than close the page on a subject. Please accept the written thoughts of this booklet in that vein.

Significantly I have used the metaphor of tree leaves to refer to my writing. Earlier in life, closer to my philosophy studies, the writing would be in carefully defined categories, organized into cogent and compelling conceptualizations. Still honoring those years of diligence, largely because I see preparatory vigor in such intellectual exercise, I look kindly upon the keenness of younger colleagues. However, I have found that toward the end of life I am left more with tokens of insights and less with unassailable conclusions. I no longer work in the mental factory of packaging and sealing boxes of manufactured intellectual goods. Now thought is a stream of reflections more than its product a rock of solidified knowledge. I live on in the belief that this provides wisdom not available earlier. "Late" in the title does not denigrate the enterprise; so much as emphasize the character change in the thinking. Increasingly I turn to the majesty of metaphor to express the wisdom, for discrete categories alone will not do.

Once upon a time, in the olden days of my intellectual training, I assumed that cognition belonged exclusively to the domain of discursive reasoning, perception piling upon conception until reason triumphed. The more exacting the categories the more the precision. For science this is axiomatic; in the realm of relational sensitivity the precision may block out the awareness. Thus, I use the "soft" reference of metaphor. For it is out of the cradle of indirect language that the humanities are born. And the arts and humanities are the conveyers of wisdom's meaning. Metaphor is not ostensible reference—you cannot just point at the meaning. Metaphoric meaning is implied. Unlike the tangible minded self, wisdom seeks to see beyond the obvious to the subjective layer of value. If cognition constitutes a perception, can there be a kind of cognition active in the awareness of what is valued? No matter how peculiar to an individual that may be, could this be a form of empirical meaning? Not known by reason is the connection to life provided by intuition?

Therefore, do not be offended by the heavy dosage of metaphor and symbol in these writings, for my words may only be opened by the subtlety of suggestion and the obliqueness of language. I trust you will join me in the fun of it all as well as the seriousness of the search for wisdom. There will be the rough road of analytical thinking and the weary tedium of terminology exactitude. I cannot give up my penchant for reasonability entirely. But my hoped for outcome is to open further the wells of wisdom, for does not the sweetest wine await therein?

Little of orthodox religion will be found in these pages. But does that negate the religious content? I prefer to think of this undertaking as an ongoing spiritual journey toward a higher level of humanity. For that reason I can be very severe, sometimes seemingly rejecting. However, I do not so much condemn, as call for greater decency in mind and spirit. At times please stop to read that between the lines.

The Path of Life I Follow

So often have I drawn on the metaphor of journey to guide my footsteps upon the path of life. Underlying the imagery is a belief that existence is for the experience. Therefore, the path is one of engagement, not avoidance. Early did I know the path I was not to follow: "the straight and narrow." A distant voice called, beckoning me to follow "the road less traveled." Mist conceals the destination in the distance of time. Thus, confidence and a bit of innocence are requisite for the venture. Dangers there may be and uncertainty will accompany each new encounter. But to hide in the safety of certainty's illusion is to betray the conditions of one's birth. Selfhood is in the becoming.

A life rigidly planned diminishes possibilities. Like a stream, life is to flow, following the terrain of its own gravity. The more restrained, the greater the stagnation. While intended to be an ever-widening terrain, the journey is no broader than the receptivity of empathy's vision. It is not enough merely to see with the eyes. One must perceive with the heart. Otherwise, the eyes will only see the limiting images of its narrow path, household idols. The journey of the free spirit is like to that of a lover seeking embrace. Without intimacy only the appearance is believed. At depth love is the passageway to the essence of goodness. Wisdom is the fruit of love's journey through a magnificent creation.

Just as fruit, wisdom cannot be held into perpetuity. If canned, wisdom loses its living authenticity. It is nourishment for guidance along the journey, plucked from interactive experiences along the broadening path. Ancestors can pass on the gift of their vision, the conviction of their hearts, but we, each one of us, are called to make our own journey. Simply to borrow and imitate the detailed plan of another is to cut the self off from what constitutes life. A scripture can be revered, but must not be an obstacle to experiencing. Without the instruction of experience, prudence, scripture is a blinder to love's eye.

Rather than looking outside of experience I have relied upon the inner guide: *Know thyself* and *to thyself be true.* The line between authenticity and artificiality is not always clear, yet is crucial for the self's actualization. It does no good on this account to defer the matter to such artificial constructs as, "the nature of man" or "the Will of God." To live a prescribed programmatic existence is not to live in the empirical world at all. The movements are wooden and the reasons contrived. Worst of all, the accompanying morality is more an encumbrance than an empowerment. In contrast to the path of imitation, genuine selfhood calls for "the courage to be." The actualizing self does not know the destination ahead of its arrival. Therefore, implicit faith in life's goodness is required, otherwise intention becomes inactivity and longing leads to a search for escape. The strength of the emerging self is found in acceptance and purpose—that being to taste the full measure.

Authentic existence embraces all that incarnation involves which is the entire range of emotions and predicaments, vicariously, if not in first person. Those who seek heaven without the Via Delarosa have not tasted of life's plentitude. For agony or ecstasy, the way of wisdom is through the valleys and promontories of the world we were born into. To curse the world as evil hinders all steps toward understanding. The righteous, who walk the "straight and narrow," can neither understand the great breadth of human experience nor cry with the stranger who weeps. All that righteousness knows is the barrenness of its own narrow path.

The journey, you see, is toward our fuller humanity.

A Needed Afterthought

After all the pieces have settled down, what might be left of religion? Have I gone too far, so as to leave very little trace of my religious upbringing? Can you scrub the face of religion, without altering its heart and core? Is the ugliness of its past merely superficial, or a part of its nature? Looking back at my intellectual life I see a constant theme: *Redeeming religious sentiment from the prejudiced particularity of culture.* Especially does this apply to what I have come to identify as the marking of tribalism. Yes, religion wears the garments of culture. But, unless reality is morally dualistic, divided between good and evil, supremacy of a particular culture's religion is not consonant with omnipresence of the sacred. This duality I have long ago set aside in preference for an inclusive principle of the divine. Apocalypticism is antithetical to Universalism; Monotheism should transcend Particularity. How shall religion be cleansed of all the blood its sanction of warfare has spilled! Does peace require that the traditional gods die?

I have found that excoriation alone leaves little space upon which to rest the case for spirituality. Honesty clears the deck of accumulated excesses, but provides no replacement for the extraneous. Worse yet, it leaves a bitter taste in the religious sentiment. A positive reconstruction can scarcely be built on skeptical grounds. Still, the peeling away is necessary, required by undeniable experience and the decency of civility. But what is left after all the gods die? What can replace the assurance they grant? What allows us to go forth in confidence? Shall we become the gods? Should we not press on to a new understanding of the Sacred? Without question, humanity has further to go to realize its oneness within the demands of sustainability. In this magnificent undertaking will we be the heroes of our future myth?

As we refashion the myth what shall happen to tradition and the beloved rites, which sustained religious sentiment in the past? Tradition is the container for sentiment. But when the container is empty it becomes a hollow imposter, the author of hypocrisy. Morally loathsome as that insincerity may be, the alternative is not the opposite, sentiment without a "preserving jar." Without the container of tradition the religious moments come and go and do not accumulate as affirmation. Some would say such transitoriness is enough. For me, however, experience has shown that remembering the moment by sheathing it in a repeatable "rite" enhances awareness of the Sacred. With the repetition comes an intensification of sentiment, a compounding of its extraordinariness.

So turns the question, from the benefit of tradition to what fills the container. Most important, first things first! Orthodoxy puts tradition first, out of which the sentiment is to come. For me, less and less does the meaningful religious moment follow from "correct belief." Much of the spurious can lodge therein. Belief becomes obsessed with the form over the essence. The deceit of set tradition is that it substitutes itself for the Sacred. Therefore, I claim the right to reform my "practice" of being spiritual, putting the sentiment first. I take the religious moment and fashion new tradition to empower it. Wonderfully, the more I return to the moment through remembrance, the larger it becomes. Repetition preserves the spiritual; the practice makes more perfect the moment.

What, might you ask, are the religious moments to fill new containers? That is, what is the essence of religion? Authentic religion is derived from moments we value, when we say, "Yes!" The moments are varied and peculiar to our disposition, but the two strongest sentiments are *appreciation* and *empathy*, by other names, *awe* and *love*. They are the "exceptional encounters" which bless time. The setting initially is quite mundane, no more than the ordinary. But, then, by the power of sentiment the ordinary transmutes into the extraordinary. Over a lifetime, existence itself becomes an ecstasy. Spirituality, then, is the perpetual awareness of life's value. We create religion to preserve the overwhelming good we experience every day!

The Sacred emerges out of the mystical mists of consciousness,

when we give up the need for certainty of belief.

In Memoriam to Life:
Lasting Thoughts and Final Words

A Final Extended Epigram

Throughout and at the end we are brought to the Pearl of Great Price, the meaning of human existence. Looking back at the long and broad landscape of my life, I can say, the meaning of life has more to do with the fine arts than either theology or metaphysics. The meaning of life is in the appreciation of it. Not merely in the valuing of each day, but in the glorying of being at all. The meaningful life is an artistic act, a conscious art form.

As I contemplate the meaning of my life, a cluster of abstractions coalesces into symbolic design: TRUTH – BEAUTY – LOVE. To be sure, these transcendental ideals are no more than universal nouns from my native language. Yet, they are my Holy Trinity of Meaning, serving like all good symbols do as stand-ins for the treasured essence of my living. The content of these abstractions can only be communicated through shared awareness, and that by virtue of intuition's finest perceiving.

Meaning at the most profound level will always remain in the vagueness of an irreducible mysticism. However, I draw the veil slightly aside, as I behold the countenance emerging from behind each form and face in the experiential substratum of my being.

In final recitative, may I say: TRUTH is the unending search of the mind, not its product. The awareness within, at any moment, is truth enough. In the act of consciousness knowing is an exhilaration unmatched by all thoughtless doing. BEAUTY is all encompassing, in whatever the spiritual eye beholds. Like Truth and Love, Beauty grants instant implicit meaning. I need not reason Beauty; Beauty has its own reason for being. LOVE binds the whole together. In the divine quality of Love we are made full. Having sought Truth, drunk deeply of Beauty, and honored Love soulfully, I have lived meaningfully.

Life is in the living; meaning is in the valuing. My greatest memories are of the living I have most valued. In those memories lies the greatest meaning. As in the ancient parable, the Pearl of Meaning has been with me all the while.

May these words speak to my loved ones beyond my death. Through them they will know me, as I desire to be known — body, heart, mind, and spirit. Forget me not and forget not my words, for therein resides the meaning of my having lived.

In this I have believed. Of this I have sung.

Oh welcomed edge of day
    carry me on your way
        beyond where grief I lay
To the twilight of dreams.

In the pure clarity
    of your serenity
        from dark mortality
Your life my soul redeems.

Upon the world so fair
    bathed in luminous air
        now a heavenward stair
Leads to infinity.

Light from above does shine
    leaving on earth sublime
        an indelible sign
Of near divinity.

When last I do breathe
    free my soul to unsheathe
        to life I shall bequeath
The Spirit's mystery.

Upward shall I take flight
    from all that darkens light
        to behold with delight
Fantasy's victory.

To Seal An Anthology

To seal is to bless. To conclude this anthology I bless my writing. To bless my writing is to honor myself.

I contend that my writing is conspicuously autobiographical. If it were not, I would be less insistent over its self-disclosure. With deliberate intent I put forward this book of select pieces as representative of the person in life I have been. The pieces are none other than parts of me as they came to be in the course of earnest searching. Thus, in blessing the anthology I am giving myself the peace of repose.

Composing the anthology brought forth a clearer profile of who I am, with all the features and details of my uniqueness in bolder relief. More than owning the portrait, I take great delight in the reviewing. In the re-reading I was reminded of some of life's most intense moments, those that most define who I am. Revisiting life and reflecting upon its landscape make us larger. With some reservation and only a little embarrassment, I look at my life story with great satisfaction. I have lived true to the integrity residing in me at birth. I would do the same, were I to relive life. By this anthology I celebrate my life. Like unto an encore, I am assured that I have sung my song of life with full voice and rich resonance.

At memorial services a display of life's photos is frequently to be seen. I, too, have an extensive photo album, to attest to time's etching of appearance. Set in the scenery of places memorable and people embraceable, photos of the visible are icons of existence. This anthology, however, is of a more inward experience, that of consciousness. As I rewrote the pieces, reawakened to mental chambers past, I felt as though I was sorting through intellectual photos of my existence. Indeed, that is what I offer you, the reader, an inner portrait. I own and cherish both the visible and the thoughtful of my life, but of the two it is my consciousness I most want to pass on. Decrepitude will take the form; the lasting is in the substance. I much prefer to be known for what I thought, than for my appearance. Remember me as the one who drew pictures of thought with words, an artist of the mind.

We live in the flux of an ever-changing world, the effect including subtle modification of our personality. If it were not so, of what purpose

would be experience? Along with the world I have mutated and evolved, all for the better I choose to believe. Otherwise, what would be the tension in the story line? Nevertheless, re-reading my writings provides the benefit of highlighting the constancy of certain themes in my personhood. By nature and inclination, while intellectually possessed by a rigorous sense of logic, I am at the center a poetic mystic. I rely on reason to assess the situation, then, give authority to a higher intuition for the sake of loving relationship. In turn, what does not bear the light of basic decency incurs the wrath of my sharp-edged rhetoric, what I like to call my social conscience. Even children know what is terribly wrong. It is in behalf of the divine child in us all, that I call out.

The Anthology began with words and I shall conclude with words. Words are to the spirit as the body is to the soul, a container of something more. Though I use "spirit" and "soul" metaphorically, without some such reference what is life but a shell of emptiness. Over the years I have formed my spirit into the shape of words. Now they bear testimony to who I am, expressing the slightest quiver of life. Some day, when my physical form dissolves into dust, the words will continue to be the repository of my spirit. I shall live on in word, unto posterity. The words expressing my soul in life will contain my spirit in death. May it be said: a true poet's heart lies within. In reading my words I again fall in love with my soul.

Anthology, I bless thee! Of all my writings, you are my most definitive expression. You are sealed for eternity.

In writing I transpose the spirit of my body into the body of words.

Sealed with much affection for my life companion, Vada Hostetler;

My treasured children, David, John and Kristina;

My beloved grandchildren, Lorelei and Samuel G.,

Samuel C., Meredith, and Amelia,

Alec and Mitchell

At the end, for serenity to be gained, all of life must meld into the indissoluble. Each moment of awareness and every touch of love in the complete measure of yearning is absorbed by a divine transformation into Wholeness. Transcended through transfiguration are the Crucifixions of Duality: Light — Darkness; Good — Evil; Feminine — Masculine; Longing — Incompletion; Joy — Sorrow. Every encounter that gave form to the soul is cherished in the embrace of memory. Graceful and quiet as the shades of evening the Beloved Hidden Self withdraws from the world of forms, to dwell in the peace and tranquility of Holy Oneness. Understanding emerges from Forgiveness; Grief gives way to Gratitude; Love encompasses All Being. Particularity becomes Universality.

Time merges into Eternity.

www.ingramcontent.com/pod-product-compliance
Lightning Source LLC
Chambersburg PA
CBHW030757150426
42813CB00068B/3195/J